D0464112

Curfewed Night

One Kashmiri Journalist's
Frontline Account of Life, Love,
and War in His Homeland

BASHARAT PEER

Scribner
New York London Toronto Sydney

Scribner
A Division of Simon & Schuster, Inc.
1230 Avenue of the Americas
New York, NY 10020

The names and characteristics of some individuals have been changed.

Portions of this memoir first appeared in slightly different forms as essays
in *N+1* and *The Guardian*.

First Scribner hardcover edition February 2010

SCRIBNER and design are registered trademarks of The Gale Group, Inc.,
used under license by Simon & Schuster, Inc., the publisher
of this work.

For information about special discounts for bulk purchases, please
contact Simon & Schuster Special Sales at 1-866-506-1949 or
business@simonandschuster.com.

The Simon & Schuster Speakers Bureau can bring authors to your
live event. For more information or to book an event, contact
the Simon & Schuster Speakers Bureau at 1-866-248-3049
or visit our website at www.simonspeakers.com.

Book design by Ellen R. Sasahara

Manufactured in the United States of America

10 9 8 7 6 5 4 3 2 1

Library of Congress Control Number: 2009040416

ISBN 978-1-4391-0910-6
ISBN 978-1-4391-2352-2 (ebook)

In the memory of the boys who couldn't return home

For Baba and for my parents, Hameeda Parveen and G. A. Peer

⌒ Contents

People are trapped in history and history is trapped in people.

　　—*Notes of a Native Son*, James Baldwin

The city from where no news can come
is now so visible in its curfewed night
that the worst is precise:
　　　　　　　From Zero Bridge
a shadow chased by searchlights is running
away to find its body.

　　—*The Country Without a Post Office*, Agha Shahid Ali

Part One   Memory ➤

1 ⮑ Fragile Fairyland

I was born in winter in Kashmir. My village in the southern district of Anantnag sat on the wedge of a mountain range. Paddy fields, green in early summer and golden by autumn, surrounded the cluster of mud-and-brick houses. In winter, snow slid slowly from our roof and fell on our lawns with a thud. My younger brother and I made snowmen using pieces of charcoal for their eyes. And when our mother was busy with some household chore and Grandfather was away, we rushed to the roof, broke icicles off it, mixed them with a concoction of milk and sugar stolen from the kitchen, and ate our homemade ice creams. We would often slide down the slope of the hill overlooking our neighborhood or play cricket on the frozen waters of a pond. We risked being scolded or beaten by Grandfather, the school headmaster. And if he passed by our winter cricket pitch, he expressed his preference of textbooks over cricket through his dreaded shout: "You good-for-nothings!" At his familiar bark, the cricket players would scatter in all directions and disappear. School headmasters were feared like military and paramilitary men are, not just by their grandchildren but by every single child in the village.

On winter afternoons, Grandfather joined the men of our neighborhood sitting at the storefronts warming themselves with *kangris*, our mobile fire pots, gossiping or talking about how that year's snowfall would affect the mustard crop in the spring. After the *muezzin* gave the call for afternoon prayers, they left the shop fronts, fed the cattle at home, prayed at the neighborhood mosque, and returned to the storefronts to talk.

Spring was the season of green mountains and meadows, blushing snow and the expanse of yellow mustard flowers in the fields around our village. On Radio Kashmir, they played songs in Kashmiri celebrating the flowers in the meadows and the nightingales on willow branches. My favorite song ended with the refrain: "And the nightingale sings to the flowers: Our land is a garden!" When we had to harvest a crop, our neighbors and friends would send someone to help; when it was their turn, we would reciprocate. You never needed to make a formal request weeks in advance. Somebody always turned up.

During the farming season, Akhoon, the mullah who refused to believe that Neil Armstrong had landed on the moon, complained about the thinning attendance at our neighborhood mosque. I struggled to hold back my laughter when the villagers eager to get back to farming coughed during the prayers to make him finish faster. He compromised by reading shorter chapters from the Quran. Later in the day he would turn up at the fields to collect a seasonal donation—his fee for leading the prayers at the mosque.

In summer, after the mustard was reaped, we planted rice seedlings. On weekdays before we left for school, my brother and I took samovars of *kahwa*, the sweet brew of saffron, almonds, and cinnamon, to the laborers working in our fields. On weekends, I would help carry sacks of seedlings from the nurseries; Mother, my aunts, and other neighborhood women bent in rows in the well-watered fields, planted, and sang.

Grandfather kept an eye on a farmer whose holdings bordered our farms. We would see him walking toward the fields, and Grandfather would turn to me: "So, whom do you see?" "I see Mongoose," I would reply. And we would laugh. A short, wiry man with a wrinkled face, Mongoose specialized in things that led to arguments—diverting water to his fields or scraping the sides of our fields with a shovel to increase his holdings by a few inches.

Mongoose, Grandfather, and all the other villagers worried about the clouds and the rainfall. Untimely rain could spoil the crop. If there were clouds on the northern horizon, they said, there would be rain. And around sunset, if they saw streaks of scarlet in the sky, they said, "There has been a murder somewhere. When a man is killed, the sky turns red."

Over more cups of *kahwa*, the rice stalks were threshed in autumn. Grains were stored in wooden barns, and haystacks rose like mini-mountains in the threshing fields, around which the children played hide-and-seek. The apples in our orchards would be ready to be plucked, graded, packed into boxes of thin willow planks, and sold to a merchant. Village children stole apples; my brother and I would alternate as lookouts after school. Few stole from our orchard; they were too scared of my grandfather. "If they steal apples today, tomorrow they will rob a bank. These boys will grow up to be like Janak Singh," Grandfather would say. Many years ago, Janak Singh, a man from a neighboring village, had killed a guard while robbing a bank. He had been arrested and sent to prison for fourteen years. Nobody had killed a man in our area before or since.

On the way home from school on those mid-eighties afternoons, I would often stare from the bus window at Janak Singh's thatch-roofed house as if seeing it once again would reveal some secret. My house, a three-floor rectangle of red bricks and varnished wood covered by a cone of tin sheets, was just a mile up the road. I would stand on the steps and watch the tourist buses passing by. The multicolored buses carried visitors from distant cities like Bombay, Calcutta, and Delhi; and also many *angrez*—the word for the British and our only word for Westerners. The *angrez* were interesting; some had very long hair, and some shaved their heads. They rode big motorbikes and at times were half naked. We waved at them; they waved back. I had asked a neighbor who worked in a hotel, "Why do the *angrez* travel and we do not?" "Because they are *angrez* and we are not," he said. But I worked it out. They had to travel to see Kashmir.

Father had bought me an American comic book dictionary, which taught words using stories of Superman, Batman and Robin, and Flash. I would often read it by the jaundiced light of our kerosene lantern and think that if Flash lived in Kashmir, we could have asked him to fix our errant power supply. I preferred reading the comics to the sums my grandfather wanted me to master. They added new stories to the collection of Persian and Kashmiri legends I heard from my grandmother and our servant Akram—legends such as the tale of Farhad's love for Shirin. Akram always began the story by saying, "It is said that once upon a time in Iran, there was a most beautiful queen called Shirin . . ." The young sculptor Farhad was enamored of her and loitered around, seeking a glance of Shirin. Over time Shirin began to develop a liking for him. Her husband, King Khusro, was furious, and his advisers suggested a plan to be rid of Farhad: They told Farhad that Shirin would be his if he could dig a canal from a distant Behistun mountain to the palace. Shirin told Farhad about his impossible task and the artist-lover set off for the mountains with his spade. Farhad toiled alone for years, molding the mountains, crying out the name of his beloved, sculpting Shirin's face on the rocks along the canal.

Farhad had survived the impossible task, and the canal was nearing completion. King Khusro was worried by the thought of keeping his promise and letting his wife marry another man, a commoner. His advisers had a plan: An old woman should be sent to the mountains to tell Farhad that Shirin was dead. It would break Farhad's resolve and make him leave the canal unfinished. Farhad was toiling away when an old woman arrived, crying, choking on her words. "Mother, why do you cry?" he asked. "I cry for a dead beauty," she said. "And I cry for you, brave man!" "For me?" a surprised Farhad asked. "You have cut the mountains, brave man! But your beloved, the beautiful Shirin, is dead!" Farhad struck himself with his spade and fell, his last cry resounding through the mountains: Shirin!

My family ate dinner together in our kitchen-cum–drawing room, sitting around a long yellow sheet laid out on the floor, verses of Urdu and Farsi poetry extolling the beauty of hospitality painted in black along its borders. Dinner often began with Grandfather leaning against a cushion in the center of the room and turning to my mother: "Hama, looks like your mother will starve us today." Grandmother would stop puffing her hookah and say, "I was thinking of evening prayers. But anyway, let me feed you first." And she would amble toward her wooden seat near the earthen hearth above which our tin-plated copper plates and bowls sat on various shelves. Mother would leave aside her knitting kit or the papers of her students and briskly move to arrange the plates and bowls near Grandmother's throne. I would fill a jar with water and get the bowl for washing hands. "Call the girls," mother would say, and I would go upstairs to announce to my aunts that dinner was ready.

Two of my younger aunts—Tasleema and Rubeena—lived with us; the others were married but visited often with their kids and husbands. Tasleema, the geek, was always poring over thick chemistry and zoology texts or preparing some speech for her college debating society and practicing her hand gestures in front of a mirror. Rubeena didn't care much about textbooks but had great interest in women's magazines, detective fiction, and Bollywood songs, which always played at a low volume on her transistor, strategically placed by her side, to be switched off quickly if she heard someone climbing the stairs.

We would form a circle with Grandfather at its center and eat. Almost every time we cooked meat or chicken, he would cut a portion of his share and place it on my plate and tell Tasleema to bring a glass of milk for Akram, who would be visibly tired after a long day of work at the orchards or the fields.

In the morning, we would gather around a samovar of pink salty milk tea, and then Grandfather and Mother would leave to teach, and my aunts, my brother, and I would leave for our colleges and schools. My school, a crumbling wooden building in the neighboring small town of Mattan, was named Lyceum after Plato's academy. Saturdays meant quizzes, debates, and essay competitions. Once I got the first prize—three carbon pencils and two notebooks wrapped in pink paper—for writing about the hazards of a nuclear war. Hiroshima and Nagasaki were just names to memorize for a quiz, as were the strange names of those bombs—Little Boy and Fat Man. I concerned myself with learning to ride a bicycle, playing cricket for my school team, grabbing my share of *fireen* (a sweet · pudding of almonds, raisins, milk, and semolina topped by poppy seeds and served during a break in the nightlong prayers at our mosque before Eid), or trying to stretch the predawn eating limit during Ramadan.

We woke up long before dawn during Ramadan. Grandmother and Mother heated the food and the traditional salty tea. Grandfather read the Quran; my younger brother, Wajahat, and I yawned till we ate. We ate quickly because you had to stop eating after you heard the call for prayers. Often we would take a few more bites after the *azaan*, the call for prayer, peeping out of the kitchen window and turning back to say, "You still can't see the hair on your forearm without artificial light." The expression dated back to the times when there were no watches. People determined daybreak by looking at their arms. If they could see the hair on their forearms, they decided it was dawn and stopped eating. Despite Japanese electronic watches, the tradition came in handy when you were trying to gulp down some more tea or eat another morsel. Grandfather, who ate little, would remind us of the purpose of fasting: "To understand what hunger means and to learn to be kind to the poor."

Toward the end of Ramadan, the talk about the meanings of fasting would lessen, and my brother and I would grow excited about the festival of Eid. On the twenty-ninth evening, everyone searched the sky with great hope for the silver sliver of a new crescent announcing the end of fasting. But the orange sun seemed to slide behind the jagged mountain peaks with great reluctance, as if it were being imprisoned for the night. All the neighborhood children would stand in the courtyard of our house staring at the horizon as it changed from shades of red and orange to a dark blue. We looked and shouted at each other, "You saw it?" "Not yet." Soon we would run up the stairs of our houses, continuing our search from the windows; our shouts grew louder as we moved from the first floor to the second to the third. If the crescent remained evasive, my brother and I would scuttle back to the kitchen, where Grandfather would be jumping from one radio station to the other, hoping for reports of crescent spotting.

Every morning on Eid, Mother would prepare *kahwa*. My brother and I followed Father and Grandfather to a clearing on the slope of the mountain overlooking the village shaded by walnut trees, which served as Eidgah, the ceremonial village ground for Eid prayers twice a year, and marked as such by an arched pulpit in a western corner from where the imam led the prayers and read his sermon. We met relatives and friends on the way. Everybody dressed in new clothes and smiled broadly. We sat in long rows on jute mats brought from our mosque. The prayers lasted only a few minutes, but a very long sermon followed. The preacher gave the same sermon every year, and my friends and I would look for ways of slipping away. Our parents, relatives, and neighbors gave us *Eidyaneh*, or pocket money, to spend on toys and crackers.

Young men and adolescents from our village would hire a bus and go to the Heaven cinema in the neighboring town, Anantnag, and watch the latest Bollywood film. I wasn't allowed to join them, but after they returned, I was riveted by their detailed retelling of the movie. I would populate their stories with the faces from movie posters. The canvases, covered in bright reds, yellows, greens, and browns, hung from electric poles by the roadside or were ferried around the village once a week on a *tonga*, a horse carriage, while an announcer standing beside the *tonga wallah*, the carriage driver, dramatically proclaimed the release of a new movie from a megaphone. Every poster was a collage of hypertheatrical expressions: an angry hero in a green shirt and blue trousers, with a pistol in hand and a rivulet of blood dripping from his face; a woman in a red sari tied to a pole with thick ropes, her locks falling over her agonized face; the luxuriously mustached villain in a golden suit, smoking a pipe or smiling a treacherous smile.

I would spend most evenings doing my homework. One evening I was distracted by the strains of a Bollywood song coming from our neighbor's house. I hunched over my notebooks, but the music made my body restless, eager to break away. I tried to focus on the sums, but the answers kept going wrong. Grandfather slapped me and left the room. Every schoolboy got a few canings and slaps for not doing the homework properly. Grandfather tried to ensure that no music was played in our house; anything that he considered un-Islamic was forbidden. Strict interpretations of Islam do consider music—except at a wedding—un-Islamic. Mohammed Iqbal, the great Urdu poet and philosopher of Kashmiri ancestry who had studied philosophy in Munich, was influenced by Nietzsche, and propagated the ideal of superman-like Muslim youth, was welcome. Bollywood actresses dancing around trees, singing songs of love and longing, could lead to bad grades and worse: a weakened faith. Once I did not come first in class and hid under my father's bed to escape a beating. "Spare the rod and spoil the child," Grandfather loved to say. He spent about two hours every evening giving me lessons, checking my notebooks, smiling if I lived up to his expectations, scolding me if I failed. He wanted me to be like his best student: my father.

In the late-1960s, Grandfather was teaching in a high school in a neighboring village when he noticed an eighth-grade student. Ahmad was the brightest in the school and also one of the poorest—an orphan being raised by his cousins, who wore ill-fitting hand-me-downs and wore torn bathroom slippers instead of shoes. Grandfather felt that with a good education and family support, Ahmad could go far, and he would often mention him to my grandmother. "Go, talk to his family. We can support him," she told her young husband. And thus my grandfather became a mentor and a de facto father to young Ahmad.

Ahmad taught at a private school while in college; after graduation he got a high school teacher's job, like my grandfather. Then some of my grandfather's friends suggested that he should marry Ahmad to his eldest daughter, Hameeda, who also had graduated from college and become a teacher. Ahmad and Hameeda had known each other since school. They agreed to the proposal and were married. A year later, Ahmad qualified for the competitive selection test for the Kashmir civil service and was appointed a magistrate. And then I was born, their first son, in the winter of 1977. Father's postings in various towns across Kashmir kept him away most of the time.

On most Saturday evenings throughout my childhood in the mid-eighties, a blue Willys jeep would drive to my village in southern Kashmir. It would follow the black ribbonlike road dividing vast expanses of paddy and mustard fields in a small valley guarded by the mighty Himalayas. Two- and three-floor mud-and-brick houses with tin and thatch roofs faced the road. Most were naked brick, and though a few were brightly painted, dust and time had colored their rough timber windows and doors a deep brown. A ground-level room in every third house had been converted into a shop. Villagers sat in the wooden storefronts gossiping, talking politics and cricket, waving at the jeep. A not-so-tall man in his early thirties, almost always wearing a suit, a matching tie, and brown Bata shoes, would raise his right hand in greeting. He had deep brown eyes, a straight nose, plump pink cheeks, and the beginnings of a belly. The Willys would slowly come to a halt in a village square, not far from a blue-and-green milestone that gave the name of our village: SEER, 0 KILOMETERS.

Father would step out of the jeep and walk toward us, past a grocery store and a pharmacy. People at the storefronts would say, "Peer Sahib is here." They would rise from their seats, and a chorus of greetings and hands would welcome him home. The first hand Father shook was that of my grandfather, who would blush with pride. I would run toward Father and grab the piles of books, newspapers, and office files he carried. He would sit in his usual corner in our drawing room, facing the road. I would run to the baker next to the pharmacy and get fresh bread. Mother would bring a boiling samovar of *noon chai*, the salty pinkish Kashmiri tea.

Father would tell me stories from the papers and encourage me to read the newsmagazines, answering my questions over more cups of tea. In one of those sessions, he told me that he wanted me to join the Indian civil service when I grew up. It had a professional exam tougher than that of the provincial Kashmir civil service, which led to higher positions in the bureaucracy than my father's. "He didn't have the resources and time that you will have," Mother said. Father began preparing me, bringing me children's books about politics, history, and English literature, books such as *Tales from Charles and Mary Lamb's Shakespeare* or *One Hundred Great Lives*. We would read them together every time Father came home. One of his heroes was Abraham Lincoln, and he talked a lot about how Lincoln read by candlelight and, through his hard work and honesty, became the president of America. In a few years we had made the transition to spending Sundays reading *Othello, Hamlet,* and *The Merchant of Venice.*

Despite the apparent tranquillity of our lives, I was beginning to get a vague sense of the troubled politics of Kashmir. In 1986 India and Pakistan were playing each other in the finals of a cricket tournament in the United Arab Emirates. On the day of the match, the atmosphere on the bus I took home from school was charged. Men, women, and children—some standing in the aisle and others on seats—huddled around radios, straining to catch every word of the commentary. Pakistan was chasing a difficult score set by India, and the number of balls they could play was running out fast. I stood in a corner behind the driver's seat and watched the driver push harder on the accelerator and continually take a hand off the wheel to raise the volume of the transistor on the dashboard. Everybody wanted to get home for the final phase of the match. Every time Javed Miandad, the Pakistani batsman, missed a ball, the bus erupted in a chorus of swearing. Every time he hit the ball and scored a run, we let out loud exclamations of joy.

The bus stopped in the tiny market near my house. Excited crowds had gathered at the pharmacy and the butcher's shop. The match was about to end. Abu, the old butcher, was biting his lips. I rushed to drop my school bag at home. In our drawing room, my grandfather, my aunts, and my mother sat in a circle around the radio. Grandmother faced Mecca on a prayer mat, seeking divine help for the Pakistani team. I dashed outside and heard the radio commentator say, "Pakistan needs three runs on one ball to win this match. Chetan Sharma will be bowling to Javed Miandad from the pavilion end of the stadium." The crowd was silent, tense. Abu's hands fell at his sides. "There is no chance. Just no chance!" He seized his radio and smashed it on the road. We watched the pieces scatter, and then we gathered around the pharmacist's radio. Chetan Sharma, the Indian bowler, was about to bowl the last deciding ball of the match to the Pakistani batsman, Miandad. The commentator told us that Miandad was scanning the field, deciding where to hit the ball when it reached him. Then he bowed west toward Mecca in prayer. He rose from the ground and faced Sharma, who was running toward the wickets. Sharma was close to the wickets, and a tense Miandad faced him. The stadium was silent. Sharma threw the ball. It was a full toss. Miandad swung his bat. Almost everyone stepped back and waited. Silence. Amin pushed his shirtsleeves up to the elbows; Abu continued biting his lips; and I boxed my left palm with my right fist. The commentator shouted, "It is a six! Pakistan has won the match. They have scored three more runs than required." People hugged, jumped around, and shouted over the din of the celebratory firecrackers.

Kashmir was the largest of the approximately five hundred princely states under British sovereignty as of 1947. Kashmir was predominantly Muslim but ruled by a Hindu maharaja, Hari Singh; the popular leader, Sheikh Mohammed Abdullah, preferred India to Pakistan and an independent Kashmir to both. When India was violently partitioned in 1947, both Singh and Sheikh Abdullah sought time before deciding Kashmir's fate. In October 1947, however, tribesmen from the northwest frontier province of Pakistan, supported by the Pakistani army, invaded Kashmir, forcing their hand. Singh decided to join India, and Sheikh Abdullah, who was a friend of the new Indian prime minister, Nehru, supported him. In January 1949 the fighting stopped after the UN intervened. The UN endorsed a plebiscite for Kashmiris to determine which country they wanted to belong to, and created a cease-fire line. The line still divides Kashmir into Pakistan-controlled and India-controlled parts, and it is now known as the Line of Control (LoC).

The agreement of accession that Hari Singh signed with India in October 1947 gave Kashmir great autonomy. India controlled only defense, foreign affairs, and telecommunications. Kashmir had its own constitution and flag; the heads of its local government were called the president and the prime minister. Gradually, this autonomy disappeared. In 1953 India jailed Sheikh Abdullah, who was then Kashmir's prime minister, after he implemented a radical land reform and gave a speech suggesting the possibility of an independent Kashmir. In the following decades,

India installed puppet rulers, eroded the legal status of Kashmiri auton-omy, and ignored the democratic rights of the Kashmiris. Sheikh Abdul-lah remained in jail for around seventeen years; when he was released, he signed a compromise with the Indian government in which he gave up the demand for the plebiscite that the UN had recommended. He spent the remaining years of his life in power, and the period (also of my childhood) was relatively peaceful. In 1987, five years after his death, the Indian government rigged state elections, arresting opposition candi-dates and terrorizing their supporters.

In the summer of 1988, a year after the troubled elections—when I was eleven—Father sent me to a government-run subsidized boarding school in Aishmuqam, a small town five miles from my village. I was bad at sports and spent long happy hours in the library reading Steven-son, Dickens, Kipling, and Defoe. I saw less and less of Father, as he had been transferred to Srinagar, the Kashmiri capital. But when we were home together, we took our usual places, and Father taught me poetry. He would recite a few verses from a poem and say, "If you explain the meaning, you will get two rupees." It was a lot of pocket money, and I tried hard.

In December 1989 I returned home for my winter holidays, hop-ing to join Father for the winter vacations in Srinagar. A week later, a group of armed young Kashmiris, led by a twenty-one-year-old named Yasin Malik, kidnapped the daughter of the federal Indian home minis-ter. Malik and his comrades demanded the release of their jailed friends. After negotiations, the Indian government gave in. People cheered for the young guerrillas.

Yasin Malik, who led the militants of the Jammu and Kashmir Lib-eration Front (JKLF), had been one of the polling agents arrested and tortured after the rigged elections of 1987. The bottled-up resent-ment against Indian rule and the treatment of Kashmiris erupted like a volcano. The young guerrillas led by Malik and his friends, challeng-ing India, were seen as heroes—most of them had received training in Pakistani camps between early 1988 and late 1989, and they had in turn secretly trained many more within Kashmir. In the next two months, the Indian government responded ruthlessly. Hundreds were killed and arrested after Indian troops opened fire on pro-independence Kashmiri protesters. It was January 1990. I was thirteen.

The war of my adolescence had started. Today I fail to remember the beginnings. I fail to remember who told me about *aazadi*, or freedom, who told me about militants, who told me it had begun. I fail to remember the date, the name, the place, the image that announced the war—a war that continues still. Time and again I look back and try to cull from memory the moment that was to change everything I had been and would be.

The night of January 20, 1990, was long and sad. Before dinner, my family gathered as usual around the radio for the evening news on BBC World Service. Two days earlier, Jagmohan, an Indian bureaucrat infamous for his hatred of Muslims, had been appointed the governor of Jammu and Kashmir. He gave orders to crush the incipient rebellion. Throughout the night of January 19, Indian paramilitary men slammed doors in Srinagar and dragged out young men. By morning hundreds had been arrested; curfew was imposed. Kashmiris poured out onto the streets in thousands and shouted slogans of freedom from India.

One protest began from a southern Srinagar area where my parents now live, passed the city center, Lal Chowk, and marched through the nearby Maisuma district toward the shrine of a revered Sufi saint a few miles ahead. Protesters were crossing the dilapidated wooden Gawkadal Bridge in Maisuma when the Indian paramilitary, the Central Reserve Police Force, opened fire. More than fifty people were killed. It was the first massacre in the Kashmir valley. As the news sank in, we all wept. The massacre had occurred a few hundred meters from my father's office. Mother was certain he would be safe. "He wouldn't have gone to work on a tense day like that. He will be fine," she said. "And he would never go near a procession," Grandfather added. But there was no way to get the same assurance from Father by hearing his voice for a few minutes: There were no phones in our village. Grandfather walked out of the room onto the lawn; we followed him. Our neighbors had come out as well. We looked at one another. Nobody said much. Later that night I lay in my bed imagining the massacre in Srinagar.

Kashmiri mornings are full of activity. I would wake up to the banging of utensils in the kitchen; the sounds of chickens running around in the courtyard after Grandmother let them out of their coop; one or another of our neighbors herding their cattle out to graze on the mountainside; the brisk footfalls and chatter of village women passing by on their way back from the forest, carrying bundles of fir and pine branches they'd gathered for timber; the repeated honking of the first bus leaving the village calling passengers; the newsreader's words in a flat monotone floating from our black Phillips radio on a windowsill in the kitchen.

The village was unusually silent that morning. Hasan, the neighborhood baker who always made wisecracks as we waited for him to bake fresh *lawasa*, looked sullen as he slapped round loaves of dough with ferocity. He stared at the flames leaping out of the oven, turned toward me, and said, "Those murderers will burn in a fire far brighter than this. I cried when I heard it on the radio last night."

The shops did not open, and the buses did not leave the village. There was no way to reach Father. Like most people in Kashmir, we relied on the public phone at the district post office in the nearby town of Anantnag. But the post office would be closed because of the protests. Father had called a friend in Anantnag, who visited us the next day with the news of his safety. Villagers stood around repeating how they'd heard the news on the radio. I felt anger spread in me. A young man raised a slogan: HUM KYA CHAHTE? AAZADI! (We want? Freedom!) He repeated, and we repeated after him: We want? Freedom!

The protest gathered momentum. Voices that were reluctant and low in the beginning became firm and loud. The crowd began a slow but spirited march along the main street of the village. Old and young women appeared at the windows of the houses. New chants were created and improvised. A young man raised an arm toward a group of women watching the procession from a communal tap and shouted, "Our mothers demand!" The crowd responded: *Aazadi!* He repeated: "Our sisters demand!" The crowd: *Aazadi!* A rush of adrenaline shot through me, and I marched ahead of my friends and joined the leaders of the procession. Somebody who was carrying his young son on his shoulders shouted: "Our children demand!" *Aazadi!*

By February 1990 Kashmir was in the midst of a full-blown rebellion against India. Every evening we heard the news of more protests and deaths on the BBC World Service radio. Protests followed killings, and killings followed protests. News came from Srinagar that hundreds of thousands of people had marched to pray for independence at the shrine of the patron saint of Kashmir, Nooruddin Rishi, in a town an hour away from Srinagar. All over Kashmir, similar marches to the shrines of Sufi saints were launched. Another day I joined a procession to the shrine of a much-revered Sufi saint, Zain Shah Sahib, at Aishmuqam, near my school. A few young men led us wearing white cotton shrouds. They seemed to be in a trance, whirling like dervishes, singing pro-independence songs. I walked behind them, repeating their words in complete wonder. Men, women, and children stood on the sidewalks, offering food and beverages and showering flower petals and *shireen*—round white balls of boiled sugar and rice—on us, a practice held in shrines and at wedding ceremonies.

The crowd itself was a human jumble. The contractor who carried whiskey in a petrol can and the uptight lawyer who waited for passersby to greet him, the tailor who entertained the idle youth in his shop with tall stories while prodding away on his sewing machine and the chemist who would fall asleep behind the counter, the old fox who bragged of his connections with congressional politicians in Delhi and the unemployed graduate who had appointed himself the English-language commentator for the village cricket team's matches, the Salafi revivalist who sold plastic shoes and the Communist basket weaver with Stalin mustache all marched together, their voices joining in a resounding cry for freedom. Amid the collision of bodies, the holding of hands, the interlocking of eyes in affirmation and confirmation, the merging of a thousand voices, I had ceased to be a shy, bookish boy hunched by the expectations of my family. I wasn't scared of being scolded anymore; I felt a part of something much bigger. I let myself go fly with the crowd. *Aazadi!* Throughout the winter, almost every Kashmiri man was a Farhad, ready to mold the mountains for his Shirin: freedom!

WAR TILL VICTORY was graffitied everywhere in Kashmir; it was painted alongside another slogan: SELF-DETERMINATION IS OUR BIRTHRIGHT! The Indian government seemed to have deployed hundreds of thousands of troops to crush the rebellion. Almost every day the soldiers patrolled our village in a mixture of aggression and nervousness, their fingers close to the triggers of their automatic and semiautomatic machine guns. Military and paramilitary camps sprouted up in almost every small town and village.

It became harder for Father to visit home on weekends. He stopped traveling in his official vehicle, as that made him conspicuous. The journey from his office in Srinagar to our village, once a lovely two-hour ride, had become a risky, life-threatening affair. Almost every time he came home, it took him around five hours. On a lucky day, his bus would be stopped only every fifteen minutes, and at each military check post, he and other passengers would be made to stand in a queue, holding an identity card and anything else they carried. After a body search, Father would walk half a mile from the check post and wait in another queue for the bus to arrive. On various other days, he barely escaped getting killed.

Father worked in a colonial castlelike office compound a few minutes from the city center, Lal Chowk, and the adjacent Maisuma area, the home of JKLF commander Yasin Malik. Gun battles between the JKLF guerrillas and the Indian soldiers, and hand grenades exploding near the paramilitary bunkers and patrols, were becoming a routine near Father's office.

One afternoon he stepped out of his office compound with a few colleagues, a group of middle-aged bureaucrats in suits and neckties carrying office files. They crossed the military check post outside their office gate and began walking toward Lal Chowk to catch buses home. Suddenly, the shopkeepers by the road jumped from their counters, pulled down the shutters, and began to run. Rapid bursts of gunfire resounded in the alleys behind the office; louder explosions came from Lal Chowk. As a burning passenger bus rushed down the street, Father and his colleagues stood in a huddle close to the massive stone-and-brick pillars of the office gate, waiting for the gunfire to stop.

A stern bark from the road startled them. "Hands up!" A group of angry Indian paramilitaries stood across the narrow road, their guns raised at Father's group. Some policemen guarding the office compound stepped forward and shouted at the soldiers, "Don't shoot! They are government officers! They work here!"

A week later, Father and a friend of his were walking toward Lal Chowk after work when a grenade exploded across the street. They wanted to rush back to the office, but heavy gunfire seemed to come from all directions. Father and his friend ran toward a roadside tea stall. His friend slipped and fell into a manhole. Father dragged him out, and they hid in the tea shop, under wooden tables. They lay on the dusty, mud floor for a long time.

That winter began my political education. It took the form of acronyms: JKLF (Jammu and Kashmir Liberation Front), JKSLF (Jammu and Kashmir Students Liberation Front), BSF (Border Security Force), CRPF (Central Reserve Police Force). I learned new phrases: *frisking, crackdown, bunker, search, identity card, arrest,* and *torture.* That winter, too, busloads of Kashmiri youth went to border towns and crossed over to Pakistan and Pakistan-administered Kashmir for arms training. They returned as militants carrying Kalashnikovs, hand grenades, light machine guns, and rocket launchers issued by Pakistan.

My friends were talking about a novel, *Pahadoon Ka Beta,* the story of a young Afghan boy who fought the Russians. I wanted to read it and found a copy with a cousin toward the end of my winter vacation. It was a slim paperback, with a green cover featuring a boy with a gun. It read like a Frederick Forsyth thriller. Ali, its young protagonist, was both James Bond and Rambo. He seemed to have destroyed hundreds of Russian tanks, undertaken espionage missions within Russia, and even rescued his father from a Russian prison. Its charm and fame seemed to lie in its obvious romanticizing of a guerrilla fighter at a time when almost every young person in Kashmir wanted to either be a guerrilla fighter or get to know one.

And there was a movie everybody wanted to watch: Arab-American filmmaker Mustafa Akkad's *Lion of the Desert*. Father had bought a black-and-white television set, but we didn't have a video cassette player. One of our neighbors had one, and his son promised to let me watch *Lion of the Desert* if I could get a copy of the film. I couldn't find it. But one day I heard the men sitting at a shop front near my house talk about it. Rashid, a bus driver who often ferried passengers from Anantnag to Srinagar, was talking about having seen *Lion of the Desert* many years ago. He had watched it at the Regal Talkies in Lal Chowk. He narrated the story of Omar Mukhtar, an aging Libyan tribal chief who fought the occupying Italian army of Mussolini till he was arrested and hanged. "He was fair and tall and had a short white beard," Rashid described Mukhtar, played by Anthony Quinn. "After the Italians arrest him, the Italian commander asks him to organize the surrender of his men. Omar Mukhtar is old and in chains but he tells the Italian general that they will never surrender, that the Italians have no right to be in Libya, that no nation has a right to occupy another nation. The Italians hang Omar Mukhtar."

Those animated conversations at the shop fronts would come to a sudden halt every time we saw a column of soldiers or a convoy of trucks and armored cars pass by. The Indian government seemed to have deployed hundreds of thousands of troops to crush the rebellion. Morning to evening, the soldiers patrolled the road through our village. They walked in long lines on both sides of the road in uniforms and bullet-proof helmets, their fingers close to their triggers. Some of them carried big cylindrical guns that fired mortars. Every time we saw a soldier with a mortar gun, someone would talk about how the soldiers used the mortar guns to burn houses wherever they came under attack from the militants. Rashid talked about a town called Handwara, near the border, that was burned by Indian troops. "They throw gunpowder over the houses and then fire mortars, and an entire village is burned in an hour."

Military and paramilitary camps sprouted up in almost every small town and village. A camp was set up near my village, too: Sandbags fortified its windows and doors, coils of barbed wire formed a boundary around the camp, empty liquor bottles hung from the barbed wire, and grim-looking soldiers who stood in the sandbag bunkers along the fence held on to their machine guns. Every pedestrian and automobile had to stop a hundred meters from the camp; people had to raise their hands and walk in a queue to a bunker, where a soldier frisked them and checked identity cards. No farmer, shopkeeper, or artisan had official papers except for maybe a ration card with his address and the names of family members written on it. Only the few men like my father or grandfather who worked for the local government had state identification cards.

My school was closed for the winter holidays till March. I bought an identity card from our neighborhood stationery store. The shopkeeper had bought a big bundle of identity cards from a dealer in the nearby town of Anantnag. He boasted that the identity cards he sold worked best with soldiers. They said INDIAN IDENTITY CARD and had an impression of the Indian emblem: a pillar with four lions on four sides, a wheel, and a pair of oxen on its base. I got my identity card signed and stamped by the local magistrate and promptly pulled it out whenever I was stopped by soldiers on the street or was walking past one of their numerous check posts. It became a part of me.

In our mosque, after prayers and before the recitation of *darood* a song praising the Prophet Muhammad—people made spontaneous speeches and shouted slogans of *aazadi*. I specifically asked God to give us freedom by the next year. But there were also moments of frivolity. One day a young man from our village who worked in Srinagar gave a speech at the mosque. He grabbed the microphone and shouted in Arabic, *"Kabiran kabira!"* The slogan meant "Who is the greatest?" But no one understood. None of us spoke Arabic. He shouted again, and again there was silence—then the adolescents in the last row, the backbenchers of faith, began to laugh. Embarrassed, the young man explained that in reply to the slogan we were supposed to shout, *"Allah-o-Akbar!"* (God is great). He shouted again, *"Kabiran kabira!"* He was answered with a hesitant, awkward *"Allah-o-Akbar."* For about a year after, we teased him.

2 ⮒ Freedom Songs

The winter of 1989–90 was the longest, most eventful winter in Kashmir, a season of conflict and rebellion that still remains. January and February 1990 had changed Kashmir in profound ways. On the first day of school, I was struck by the number of empty chairs. Five of our Kashmiri Hindu or Pandit classmates were not there. I felt a little numb. "They have left," someone said. The words exploded like a tracer, dazzling the whitewashed walls of the classroom, the bare blackboard, the varnished wooden surfaces of the desks where the ones who were absent and the ones who were present had scribbled their initials in a suggestive, romantic arithmetic. Our eyes were fixed on the empty chairs for a long time.

Along with killing hundreds of pro-India Muslims, ranging from political activists to suspected informers for Indian intelligence, the militants had killed hundreds of Pandits on similar grounds or without a reason. The deaths had scared the Pandits, and thousands, including my classmates and their families, had left the valley by March 1990 for Jammu, Delhi, and various other Indian cities and towns.

The talk was of war. During the lunch break, my friends and I shared stories of militancy. We began drawing maps of Kashmir on our school notebooks and painted slogans like WAR TILL VICTORY and SELF-DETERMINATION IS OUR BIRTHRIGHT on the school walls. One of my classmates, Asif, a boy with big black eyes and careless curly hair who was popular with the girls, talked about seeing a militant. "I saw one walking near the bus stop. He was wearing a green military uniform and had a badge on the chest that said: JKLF! And he had beautiful blue sports shoes." "Force 10 shoes?" I asked Asif. Force 10 was a popular running shoe from an Indian company. "No! No! It was Warrior! Warrior is Chinese. It is much better than Force 10." Asif began to smile and tell me how the guerrilla's hairstyle was similar to his own: long curly locks. I hoped at least one guerrilla commander had short, straight, spiky, oiled hair like mine.

The best story was about the magical Kalashnikov. Made in Russia, a gift from Pakistan, it was known to have powers greater than Aladdin's lamp. I remember standing outside our dining hall after lunch and getting into an impromptu discussion about Kalashnikovs. "It is as small as a hand and shoots two hundred bullets," said Shabnam, my cousin, who was a year senior to us. "No! It is as long as a cricket bat and fires fifty bullets in a minute," retorted Pervez, my roommate and an enthusiastic footballer whose village was a major stronghold of JKLF. "My brother touched a Kalashnikov," said Showket, who was a few years younger. "He says it is very light. Yes, it is as long as a small cricket bat. He told Mother that he wanted to become a militant. She cried, and Father slapped him."

Pervez told me there were many militants in his village who wore beautiful green uniforms. One afternoon we were on the football field when a militant passed by. Even our snooty games teacher went up to him, smiled, and shook hands. Encouraged, we gathered around. "Can we see your gun, please?" Pervez said. He was the center forward, beaming in his blue tracksuit. The militant took off his loose *pheran*, a cloak-like woolen garment, and showed us his gun. "We call it Kalashnikov, and Indians call it AK-47," the militant said. We were enraptured and clapped in delight. From then on we all carried our cricket bats inside our *pherans*, in imitation and preparation.

The next morning before the school assembly, the seniors told us not to chant the Indian national anthem: "We are Kashmiris, and now we are fighting for independence. We cannot go on chanting the Indian songs, even if the principal might like us to." At the assembly, the students refused to chant the Indian anthem. Our teachers, who would routinely answer disobedience with corporal punishment, remained silent. Nobody threatened to dismiss us from the school; they knew our world had changed, and so had the rules governing it. The school principal, a short, bald man from Rajasthan who promoted laughter therapy, was not laughing. "If you don't want to sing it, we can't force you to. Singing a song does not mean much if you don't believe in the words you speak," he said in a grave voice.

Outside our small world, there were endless gun battles between the soldiers and the rebels; grenades were lobbed, and mines were exploded—death, fear, and anger had taken over Kashmir. By the summer of 1990, thousands of young Kashmiri men had crossed the Line of Control for arms training in the Pakistan-controlled part of Kashmir. When they returned as militants, they were heroes—people wanted to talk to them, touch them, hear their stories, and invite them for a feast. Many more were trained in local apple orchards and meadows, earning them the nickname *dragud*, or meadow. Like almost every boy, I wanted to join them. Fighting and dying for freedom was as desired as the first kiss on adolescent lips.

In the autumn of 1991, when I was fourteen, I walked with four boys from my dorm to a nearby village, looking for guerrillas. We saw a group of young men dressed in fatigues, assault rifles slung on their shoulders, coming from the other side of the road. They were tall and seemed the most glamorous of men; we were awestruck. The white badges on their green military uniforms read JKLF. Standing there in our white-and-gray school uniforms, I blurted out, "We want to join you." The commander, a lean youth with stubble, laughed. "Go home and grow up, kids!" I was furious. "If you do not take us with you, we will join HM." Hizbul Mujahideen, a new militant group, was an ideological rival to JKLF and supported the merger of Kashmir with Pakistan. The guerrillas burst into laughter. We continued our meek protests as they left.

We returned to our dorm sulking, talking about a better way to join. We could talk to Students Liberation Front (SLF), the student wing of the JKLF. Some of the JKLF and SLF guerrillas had begun staying in our dorm. They would join us for a game of volleyball, leaving their guns lying casually on the grass by the volleyball court. Or they would be sitting on the dorm veranda, cleaning the Kalashnikovs as I left for classes. A small, curious crowd would grow around them. One of them, who was barely eighteen, did let me hold a Kalashnikov. I felt its cold steel barrel, ran my fingers along its banana-shaped magazine of bullets, posed with its aluminum butt pressed against my right shoulder. It felt fascinating! But then he took it back the next minute and asked me to move on.

One of the commanders was from my village. He was about six feet tall and had a broad forehead and wavy hair. He was a jovial man who had three daughters and used to work as a plumber in the hotels at a nearby tourist resort, Pahalgam. The villagers called him Tonga because he seemed as tall as a horse carriage. He was a lovable rogue and the stories of his adventures were often told at the village shop fronts. During the tourist season in Pahalgam, he was in great demand. He would fiddle with the supply pipes and insert blockages that stopped the water to hotel rooms. The desperate hoteliers would then pay him a desired price to fix things up. But the tourists stopped coming to Kashmir after the winter of 1990, the hotels shut down, and Tonga joined the JKLF. Every time I would see Tonga, he would ask about my family and tell me to study harder. "I will ask your teachers how you are doing." And "Give my greetings to Peer Sahib and Masterji."

But my friends and I were still dreaming up ways to go for arms training. Groups of boys left for training camps in Pakistan every other day. We needed some money for the bus fare to the border towns, we needed winter clothes and good shoes for a potential trek through snowy mountains, but most of all, we needed a guerrilla commander who didn't know our families and would let us join a group leaving for the border.

One day we were interrupted in geometry class by a knock. The teacher went out and returned to tell me that my uncle was here. A bank manager in his early thirties, Bashir was a fashion icon for my brother and me. I admired his baggy jeans and checked shirts and slicked-back hair, like John Travolta's in Grease, and the mysterious accent of his English, which he had picked up from some German friends.

I shouted a loud greeting, and we hugged. He was carrying a bag, and I promptly volunteered to carry it. "That is our lunch! Your mother made chicken for us." He threw an arm around my shoulder. "Let's go to your room and eat." The thought of home-cooked chicken after the bland lentils and rice that dominated our hostel menu filled me with great joy.

My room was small, bare except for two beds, two small bookshelves, and two closets for clothes. I laid out a cotton sheet on my bed, and we began eating. Uncle stopped between morsels to watch me devour the pieces of chicken.

I shrugged. "I am hungry."

He laughed, but something seemed wrong.

"Everything fine at home?" I asked.

"Yes. All is well."

We continued eating, and I asked, "Why didn't you go to the bank today?"

"Nothing! I was talking to your father last night, and then I thought I should come and save you from the lentils."

After lunch we walked about the campus and sat near a rose bed. We talked about my studies. He said my father dreamed of seeing me in the civil service. "Your father struggled very hard to get where he is. He has great hopes for you. I know you will do us proud," he said. "I met your school principal and he had great things to say about you." I shook my head.

Uncle stared at the school buildings for a long time. "You will be done here in two years."

"Yes, 1993."

"You know what? You must go to Delhi." He went on to paint a romantic picture of the colleges and universities in New Delhi. "You would have a great time there. Your father and I were talking about it last night."

I shook my head. Yes. Maybe. "How is Baba?" I asked of Grandfather.

"He is getting older by the day. And he misses you a lot. You should come home for a few days. He will be happy."

I quickly packed my bags, and soon we were walking to the nearest bus stop. A scrawl of graffiti on the wall of a nearby house read: WAR TILL VICTORY—JKLF. "So that is the group you want to join," my uncle said, smiling.

"JKLF? Me?" I denied everything.

He shook his head slowly. "We know all about it," and he told me about the meeting waiting for me at home.

The bus passed a few villages separated by empty paddies and conical haystacks, almost golden in the autumn sun. We crossed an old bridge over a stream rushing toward my village. I saw the familiar peaks of the village mountain and a medieval canal running alongside. Before moving to my school, I rarely left the village except for occasional visits to Anantnag or Srinagar. When I went away even for a day, on my return I would be impatient for the sighting of a landmark: an old shingle-roofed hut on the slope of the village mountain. I saw it again.

The bus stopped in the village square. Uncle continued his journey to the next village, where he lived. I grew a bit stiff, dreading the encounter at home. Standing by the bus stop, I took in my house—the one with the green windows stacked with five others in a row on the right side of the road. Abu, the cricket-obsessed butcher, was chopping pieces of lamb; Amin, the short and wiry chemist who always wore an Irish cap, stood outside his shop; Kaisar, the tailor who regaled the village boys with ribaldries, was bent over his sewing machine; Hasan, the baker famed for his wisecracks, sat behind a stack of sesame-seed bagel-like *chochevaer*; old Saifuddin, my grandmother's cousin who noted every new presence and kept a severe eye on the goings-on in the neighborhood from his grocery, was watching people alight from the bus; a group of boys I used to play cricket with hung around the stationery store next to the grocery; and a few older men sat at an empty storefront next to Amin's pharmacy, talking.

It felt like standing on a familiar stage, facing a familiar audience. I shouted greetings at people on the far side of the road and shook hands along the storefronts on our side. Anxious about the encounter at home, I made my greetings a little more elaborate at every stop: the baker, the pharmacy, the butcher, the tailor, and finally, a hop across the road to hug Saifuddin, and repeat the same litany:

"*Assalamualikum!* How are you?"

"*Valikumsalam!* I am happy. I am well. How are you?"

"I am happy. I am well."

"You just arrived?"

"Yes, I just got off the bus."

"How is school?"

"School is good."

"Are you working hard?"

"Yes, very much."

"You must work very hard. You are the future."

"I will. Thanks."

"How is business?"

"Thank God! It is all right."

"How is everyone at home?"

"They are well. You should come for tea."

When I arrived home, Grandfather made me sit beside him. Father was on his way back home from work in Srinagar. Uncle, Grandmother, and mother formed a semicircle around us. I was silent, unsure what to say. "May I have a cup of tea, please?" I tried. Mother had already poured me one from the samovar. I traced the pinkish flowers embossed on the white porcelain cup in between sips. Grandfather turned to Mother. "Hama, you remember his first day of school."

She looked up with a forced smile. "Yes! I had dressed him in a white shirt and gray shorts and his red necktie. And then you took him along."

Grandfather seemed to stare into a distant time for a long moment, and then he laughed a bit and said to me, "I dropped you at your school and went to teach at my school. You had cried and shouted so much that an hour later, your teacher brought you to my office."

"Most children cry," I said.

Then he repeated the oft-told story of how, inspired by my Superman comics, I once jumped from the first-floor window. My younger brother helped me tie my *pheran* like a cape. I broke my right arm. This buildup to the real question was irritating me. I was thinking of walking out. They could see it.

Mother looked at me and said nothing. Grandfather fixed his watery green eyes on me. "How do you think this old man can deal with your death?" he said. His words hit me like rain on a winter morning.

I had nothing to say and stared at the carpet. I imagined myself lying dead on a wooden board on our lawn, surrounded by our neighbors and relatives. My mother had fainted, and someone was throwing water on her face. Father was holding the board, his head was buried in his arms, and his shoulders were shaking.

"You don't live long in a war, son." Grandfather's words brought me back. He had tears in his eyes.

A *muezzin*'s voice came from the mosque loudspeaker, calling the faithful to afternoon prayers. Mother adjusted her casually worn head scarf, and Grandfather rose to leave for the prayers. "Think about your father! He is coming all the way from Srinagar only because he is worried about you. God knows what will happen on the way," Mother said.

"I will keep an eye on the buses," I said, and walked out.

I had been talking to a few neighborhood men for an hour when Father got off a bus, wearing one of his blue suits and carrying a bundle of books. We all stood up; I reflexively rushed to get his books and files. A chorus of greetings followed. "How are you?" "How are things in the city?" "Hope the journey was fine. The highway has become very dangerous." Father seemed tired but calm.

At home, we took our usual places, and another round of tea followed. Father sorted the books and picked up a commentary on the Quran in English. "You must read it. You will understand religion and improve your English. You must also read the Bible, which is very good for your language skills." Father went around in circles, talking about the story of Ishmael and Isaac. "You need the permission of your parents even if you want to be a KLF commander," he said in a half-serious voice. He made it easy somehow.

"I know," I replied.

"Especially if you are fourteen." He smiled. "That is four years short of the voting age."

I said nothing.

He looked directly at me and said, "I won't stop you."

I couldn't hide my astonishment.

"I won't stop you," he repeated. "But maybe you should read and think about it for a few years and then decide for yourself. At that point I will not say that you should or should not join any group."

I found myself nodding in agreement. "From what I have read, I can tell you that any movement that seeks a separate country takes a very long time. It took India many decades to get freedom from the British. The Tibetans have been asking for independence from China for over thirty years. Czechoslovakia won its freedom from dictatorship; even that took a long time."

Father continued to argue that rebellions were long affairs led by educated men. "Nehru and Gandhi studied law in England and were both very good writers. You have seen their books in our library. Václav Havel is a very big writer. The Dalai Lama has read a lot and can teach people many things. None of them used guns but they changed history. If you want to do something for Kashmir, I would say you should read."

I stayed in the classroom. But the conflict had intensified. Fear and chaos ruled Kashmir. Almost every person knew someone who had joined the militants or was arrested, tortured, or beaten by the troops. Fathers wished they had daughters instead of sons. Sons were killed every day. Mothers prayed for the safety of their daughters. People dreaded knocks on their doors at night. Men and women who left home for the day's work were not sure they would return; thousands did not. Graveyards began to spring up everywhere, and marketplaces were scarred with charred buildings. People seemed to always be talking about the border and crossing the border; it had become an obsession, an invisible presence.

School was quiet, mundane. Breakfast. Classes. Lunch. Classes. Football. Cricket. Homework. The guerrillas occasionally took shelter in my dorm and occasionally joined us for a game of football. Familiarity had shorn off their glamour somewhat.

Shabnam, my cousin, was one of the finest volleyball players on the school team. I began taking volleyball lessons from him and spent more time on the field trying to perfect a serve and a smash. Shabnam had learned his cricket and volleyball from his older brother, Tariq, who had recently finished college. Every time I visited them and my uncle Rahman, I would see Tariq playing cricket on the enormous field near their house, with Shabnam hanging out on the sidelines.

My father was very attached to Uncle Rahman, his oldest cousin, who had raised him after his parents died. Uncle Rahman was a police officer, a tall, dark man with big black eyes who often talked about his long stint as a bodyguard of Sheikh Abdullah. He ironed his uniform immaculately and polished his brown police boots till they shone. He had recently retired and, in his civilian days, donned the seventies double-breasted suits and fezzes that Sheikh Abdullah wore. "You should be an all-rounder. Be the best in the classroom, and be the best on the playground," he would tell me.

He would walk to the field occasionally to see Tariq play. "Tariq would look good as a police officer," he often said. Tariq had graduated in mathematics and chemistry, but he was more of a sportsman. He saw me as a bookworm and entertained himself by asking me random questions: How many astronauts were onboard *Apollo 13*? What is an F-16? What is the symbol for sulfuric acid? I knew all the answers. Shabnam didn't care much about such things, but he would try to teach me a few things about cricket and volleyball.

With Shabnam's help, I was swaggering a bit on the school volleyball field. One late autumn day just before a game, I saw Shabnam walking out of the dorm with his bags. He was quiet, and there was a darkness in his eyes. "What is wrong?" I asked.

He dropped his bag on the lawn; his face was pale. "Tariq has gone across the border!"

I knew that crossing the border to be a guerrilla meant being killed.

Shabnam went home. A few days later I visited my aunt and uncle. Tariq had left suddenly without telling anyone; Uncle Rahman was chain-smoking his hookah. He seemed to have aged in a few days. My aunt was in shock and trying to deal with it by busying herself with unnecessary chores such as arranging and rearranging the plates and bowls on the kitchen shelves, flitting out to fix the clothes drying on the line in the courtyard, and then disappearing again to buy sugar when there was already sugar in the house. Uncle Rahman watched her in silence and then laughed a little laugh that seemed to scream all his love and all his pain. I fought my tears; he puffed on his hookah again. "When I was in the police, nobody in my jurisdiction dared disobey me. My son has crossed the border without even telling me." A rivulet of tears escaped his eye and rolled down his rough, wrinkled face. I had never seen him cry.

Soon somebody connected to the group that Tariq had joined sent a message to the family that he had crossed the border and was in Muzaffarabad, the Pakistan-controlled capital of Kashmir, where most arms-training camps for Kashmiris were run. But one could not be sure, and there was no way to confirm that Tariq had indeed safely crossed the border.

Back at school, Shabnam hoped that Tariq was safe and eagerly awaited his return. In his hostel room, Shabnam listened to the Muzaffarabad-based *Sada-e-Hurriyat* (Voice of Freedom) radio. Every evening the separatist radio station ran a popular show of songs interspersed with propaganda and messages from listeners. When a militant in training wanted to let his family know how he was, he requested a song, and a message was played along with it. The messages said things like: "Tahir Mir from Soura, Srinagar, likes the program and requests this song be played." His family and relatives heard the message and knew he was safe.

Shabnam and I were sitting on a bench outside our dorm. He had brought out his black Phillips radio, and we listened to the songs and messages. The show's hosts were notorious for over-the-top rhetoric and propaganda. One of the hosts, who called himself Malik, would prophesize about Kashmir getting independence in a week and how he would travel across the border from Pakistan-controlled Kashmir to the

Indian-ruled Kashmir and drink *kahwa* at the Jehangir Hotel, a prominent hotel in Srinagar, the next Friday.

But Shabnam and I were tense when we listened to the program. We heard the messages and waited for familiar names. For months there was no message from Tariq. Every day Shabnam listened for a message from his older brother; every day he hoped for news and fended off rumors: "Tariq was arrested on the border." "Someone said he was killed on his way back." "A boy from Pulwama who returned met him in a training camp." Every time someone from a neighboring village returned after completing his training, Shabnam or one of my other cousins visited his family seeking news of Tariq. Word of mouth was the only source of news.

One day after dinner, Shabnam was lying on his bed, holding the radio like a pillow, and listening to the show. I was talking to his roommate. The usual songs played: "The Daughters of Srinagar! The Brave Daughters of Srinagar!" A few minutes of messages and another song: "Wake up! The morning is here! Martyrs' blood has bloomed! The flags of victory are flying! Wake up! The morning is here!" The hosts' voices droned a litany of names and addresses; I continued talking. And then a sudden loud thump startled Shabnam's roommate and me; Shabnam had jumped off the bed and stood a few feet away, holding the radio in his left hand. "It is Tariq! It is Tariq! Basharat, he really is alive! It said, 'Tariq Peer from Salia, Islamabad, likes the show and requests this song.' "

Around a year after he had crossed the border, Tariq returned home. Friends, relatives, and neighbors had descended on Uncle Rahman's old, decrepit house. I couldn't even find a place to take off my shoes. The veranda and the corridor had turned into a multicolored jumble of sandals, loafers, and sneakers. I walked into the large room with green walls. A new floral rug had been laid out; men, women, and children sat against cushions along the walls. Shabnam carried a gleaming tin-plated copper samovar, pouring *kahwa* into the porcelain cups placed in front of every guest; another boy carrying a wicker basket served *chochevaer*. A hundred eyes were focused on a single face: Tariq's. He was sitting on a velvet-covered cushion, the one used for Kashmiri grooms. "*Mubarak*

Chuv! Mubarak Chuv!" (Congratulations! Congratulations!) every new guest shouted from the gate. *"Shukr Khodayus, Sahee Salamat Vot!*" (Thank God! You made it back safe.) Men shook his hand and hugged him. Women embraced him and smothered his forehead with kisses. *"Miyon Nabi Thayinay Vaarey!*" (May my Prophet protect you!)

Uncle Rahman sat next to Tariq; he seemed to have accepted the difficult truth that Tariq had become a militant and was on a path of great danger. I walked up to Tariq and hugged him. "You have grown taller!" he said. I smiled. "You have grown thinner," I replied. His round face seemed sunken; he had cut his long curly hair short, like a soldier's, but his big black eyes had retained their familiar spark. He looked neat in white *kurta* pajamas, almost like a groom. My eyes wandered to his fatal bride, the Kalashnikov hidden under a thick green sport coat by his side. Outside, neighborhood boys strained their eyes and ears for signs of military vehicles; the family was afraid that the military might raid if they got word of Tariq's homecoming from an informer.

The militant son talked. The retired-police-officer father listened, as did the roomful of people. They listened as if Tariq were Marco Polo bringing tidings of a new world. He told us about his journey to Pakistan and back. He and his friends had taken a bus for Srinagar. A point man from the militant group waited for them at the crowded Batamaloo bus station in southern Srinagar. There they boarded a bus for the north Kashmir town of Baramulla. The bus was full of employees returning home after work. The driver played Bollywood songs, and the passengers talked about the militant movement. Some passengers seemed to recognize Tariq and his friends as boys out to cross the border and smiled at them. There were neither checkpoints nor military patrols. The boys spent the night in Baramulla at a stranger's house with two more groups of young men wanting to cross the border. The next morning the three groups boarded a bus to Kupwara, the town closest to the LoC. The ticket collector refused to accept a fare from them. Kupwara teemed with young men from every part of Kashmir, waiting to cross the border.

Tariq and his friends were introduced to a man who was to take them across the mountains. Men like him were referred to as guides. They were often natives of the border villages who knew the terrain well. Wearing Duck Back rubber shoes, carrying rucksacks full of clothes and food, they left Kupwara in a truck. By evening, they had reached the village of Trehgam, a few miles from the LoC. They waited in a hideout till night fell. In the darkness, they followed their guide. They climbed ridges, crawled past the bunkers of the Indian troops, climbed again throughout the night. The guide had instructed them not to light a cigarette or litter. Cigarettes could invite fire if noticed by a soldier's binoculars; biscuit wrappers in the jungle could expose their route. They held hands and walked in silence. Dawn came, and they hid in the brush, behind the fir and pine trees growing on the mountains forming the border. They passed the day, apprehensive of being spotted by Indian troops. Night fell. They trekked again till the last Indian check post. It was still dark when they crawled beneath the Indian post overlooking them and reached the Pakistani post on the other side. The next day Tariq was in Muzaffarabad. He was taken to an arms-training camp run by the Pakistani military. For six months he trained in using small arms, land mines, and rocket-propelled grenades.

Tariq wandered around in Pakistan for a few months, waiting for his turn before returning home a year later. "They have Indian movies there," he said. "I watched some. And you can buy the cassettes for all new songs." "Really, in Pakistan!" someone said. "Did you watch any?" another person asked. Shabnam and I looked at each other and smiled. A few minutes later, someone asked about the journey back across the mountainous border. Tariq said, "The snow was melting, but still there was a lot of it." He was bolder on his way back; every guerrilla in his group carried a bagful of ammunition and a Kalashnikov. The trek took three days. The ammunition bags were heavy. "Whoever was tired would lighten the bags. We buried food packages and some bullet magazines in the snow." Thousands of boys like Tariq had passed through the snows since his journey to Pakistan a year before. He saw the evidence of their encounters with the Indian border troops on the way: skeletons lying under the fir trees; a pair of shoes lying by a rock. They almost got killed when they came face-to-face with a group of boys crossing from Srinagar. They were dressed in military fatigues, as was the fashion among the militants those days. Tariq and his group thought they were Indian soldiers. Their guides whistled, a code signaling they were on the same side. The Srinagar guide responded; the boys shook hands and moved on. Tariq and his friends had an encounter with Indian paramilitaries near the border town of Kupwara. "Three in our group were killed," he said. "One of them was from Kupwara. He would have been home in half an hour." The mood changed, and the room was filled with exhortations: "Life and death are in the hands of Almighty God." "Those who die for the truth always live." "Thank God! You got home safe." "My Prophet will protect you!" A bullet had grazed Tariq's leg, tearing a hole in his trousers. Later, Shabnam showed me the trousers.

Visitors kept arriving, among them an emaciated woman in a loose floral *pheran*. She stood a few feet from Tariq, staring at his face for a long time. He rose from his seat and hugged her. She was from a neighboring village. Her son had crossed the border for arms training. She had been told he was killed while crossing back. Families whose sons had died while crossing the LoC, where the bodies could not be recovered, held funerals in absentia. People offered funeral prayers with an empty coffin or without a coffin. This woman had had such a funeral for her son, but she had not reconciled herself to the news of his death. She sat in front of Tariq and held his hands. "Tariq, my dear, my son, they told me he was martyred on the border!" The room fell silent; every eye stopped on her sad, grieving face. "My heart doesn't agree. Tariq, my dear, tell me they are lying. Tell me you saw my rose! You were there, too. You must have seen my rose!"

Tariq embraced her. "Yes, I saw him. He is waiting to cross back. He is waiting for his turn."

I am unsure whether he told her the truth, but she kissed his forehead again and again and broke down. "My son will come home."

Homecomings for militants were short-lived. Tariq would visit his parents once or twice a month, but his visits were always hurried and stealthy. He lived in unknown hideouts with other guerrillas, planning attacks on Indian military camps and convoys. Though I had seen guerrillas his age walking around or even preparing to attack a military convoy near my house, I failed to imagine Tariq in battle, firing a gun, hurling a grenade, exploding a land mine, killing. But that was the life he had chosen. And Indian soldiers were looking for him. They often knocked at Uncle Rahman's door, looking for Tariq, beating Uncle Rahman and Tariq's two older brothers, seeking information about his whereabouts and telling Uncle Rahman to ask Tariq to surrender or be ready to die the day the soldiers found him.

I saw Tariq for the last time in August 1992, a few hundred meters from my uncle's house on a plateau that served twice a year as the venue for ceremonial Eid prayers, and the rest of the time as a cricket field.

August 14 and 15 are the Pakistani and Indian independence days. Pro-Pakistan militants hold celebratory parades on August 14, and a day later, the Indian Independence Day is declared a Black Day. On August 15 traffic stops, shops close, schools shut down, identity checks by Indian troops increase, and life freezes. In Srinagar, however, pro-India politicians who form the local state government herd groups of their supporters and force government schools to gather contingents of schoolchildren on a cricket field guarded by hundreds of Indian paramilitaries. Then the politicians hoist the Indian flag. Outside the stadium, the streets remain empty.

On August 14, 1992, Shabnam and I watched Tariq and other guerrillas celebrate Pakistani Independence Day on the cricket field. Thousands had gathered for the spectacle. We sneaked through the crowd to the front row for a better view. Militant leaders made fiery speeches in favor of Pakistan and raised separatist slogans. We stared at the militants in their green uniforms, holding their rifles. They performed military stunts and sang battle songs to a clapping audience. A militant leader raised the Pakistani flag after the songs. His men fired into the air. Then someone said that an army patrol was approaching the village, and the gathering vaporized.

A year after I saw Tariq in the parade, soldiers stopped knocking on his parents' door. They had killed him in a raid on his hideout.

3 ⌒ Very Long Miles

The fighting had changed the meaning of distance. I came home almost every weekend from school. The black sliver of the road made its way through an expanse of rice and mustard fields, willow groves, grand Iranian maple or chinar trees alongside a flamboyant stream, and the huddled houses of a few small villages. But the six-mile ride on a local bus was dangerous. Military and paramilitary trucks drove on the same road, carrying supplies between various camps or going on raids in the villages. Guerrillas hiding in the fields by the road would often fire at the military convoys or detonate mines planted in the road. Soldiers would retaliate after such attacks, firing in all directions and beating anyone they could lay their hands on.

One weekend on my way home, I was standing in the bus aisle near the driver. Kashmiri buses are like noisy cafés; almost everyone knows everyone else, and voices of varying pitches fill the vehicle. The driver played a Bollywood song, its melancholy lyrics floating over the din. A mile into the journey, a paramilitary convoy overtook our bus and hovered just ahead of us. The voices in the bus lowered, and the driver turned off the music. Soldiers had realized that driving close to a civilian bus would keep guerrillas from attacking them. Anxiety filled the bus. Our driver began praying feverishly: "God, I have three small children, please don't make them orphans today. Please get us safely to our homes today." We drove in silence, waiting. The minutes passed, and the paramilitary convoy gathered speed. Our driver slowed, and the distance between us grew. We were in a village called Siligam, midway between my school and my house, when I heard a loud explosion. The driver slammed on the brakes, and in the distance, we saw a paramilitary truck skid off the road and land in the fields. I heard a barrage of bullets—the lighter sounds Kalashnikovs; the heavier, retaliatory bursts, light machine guns. The driver swung the bus around and sped back as fast as he could. Everyone crouched under the seats.

I sat on the floor, gripping a seat. The roar of the engine rose above the sound of bullets being fired. I was thinking where a bullet might hit me; I desperately hoped it would not be my face, my head, or my right hand. I became intensely aware of my body. I felt the tension in my spinal cord, the nakedness of my neck, the stiffening of my legs. Where would a bullet hurt the most? I buried my head in my knees and closed my eyes.

We were driving away from the battle. I began listing the guns that could still hit us. We seemed out of the killing range of an AK-47 and a carbine submachine gun, but a self-loading rifle, a light or heavy machine gun, and a 51 mm mortar gun could easily hit us. A little while later, the driver stopped the bus. I stood up in a quick, involuntary motion. Two men hugged the driver. "You saved our life," another man said, and shook his hand. An old man began to cry. A woman patted his back and consoled him. I smiled at everyone. We got off the bus and drank from a roadside stream. The driver and a few other men smoked cigarettes.

We had just gotten back on and begun to drive back to the bus yard in the village of Aishmuqam, near my school, when a convoy of paramilitary trucks hurtled toward us. The convoy stopped, and so did we. Armed soldiers circled the bus, and an angry paramilitary officer ordered us out. We stood in a queue on the road. I was close to the door and the first one to get down. I was in my school uniform and carried a school bag. The officer raised his gun like a baton. I waited to be hit by the weapon. I could not remove my eyes from his. He lowered the gun and pushed me with his other hand. I knew he was going to shoot me. But then he grabbed my arm and shouted, "You are from the school near our camp. I see you pass by every day. Now get out of here." He let the bus and everyone on it go. As we arrived at the bus yard, a crowd gathered.

Two hours later, another bus arrived, and its driver told me, "You are lucky that no soldier was killed by the land mine. The road is open now, but they have begun a crackdown in the surrounding villages." Fifteen minutes later, we passed the spot where the mine had gone off. I saw no soldiers, no military trucks. There were only the willow trees lining the road, the paddy fields, the tin roofs of a village beyond the fields, and a large crater on the right corner of the road, carved out by the explosion. We drove past a few villages where the shops had been closed and the streets were empty except for patrolling paramilitary soldiers. Fortunately, they let our bus pass.

A few weeks later, I was home again. That weekend we expected Father to visit from his office in Srinagar, which was wracked with violence. Each day on BBC World Service, we heard reports of scores of deaths there. The solemn voice of Yusuf Jameel, the BBC's Srinagar correspondent, rang through our radios each evening: "I am hearing the sound of gunfire." The fatal sound of bullets would play on the radio for a few seconds, and Jameel's stoic voice would follow: "Yet another unidentified body has been found in the river Jhelum in Srinagar."

Late in the afternoon Mother sent me to buy lamb chops for the dinner she was making for Father. I stepped out of the house and saw Mother's grand-uncle, the white-haired Saifuddin, sitting by his grocery counter and scanning the market. He didn't do much business but knew everything that happened in the neighborhood, as he spent most of his time watching who went where, and asking relentless questions. He waved at me and asked, "Today is a Saturday! Is Peer Sahib coming home?"

"Yes, he should be here soon," I replied.

"I only asked because I haven't seen Masterji [my grandfather] at the butcher's shop yet. He usually buys meat by this time on a Saturday. I was wondering if everything is fine. God knows this is a dangerous time."

I assured him that Grandfather was busy with some chore, and I was buying the meat. I walked toward the butcher, and the few neighborhood men hanging about the pharmacy and the tailor's shop called out, "How was the interview?"

"Oh! The usual. He hadn't seen Grandfather buying meat yet," I said.

Everybody laughed. Abu, the butcher, was looking our way, smiling. "This neighborhood won't be the same without Saifuddin. At least he asks about everyone." He began cutting lamb chops for me, instructing me along the way about the parts Grandfather would ask for. And then: "Masterji must have gone to check the apple orchard. Or the fields."

"No, he is home, fixing some electrical stuff."

Then I noticed a group of young men with guns standing near the bus stop. Tonga, the tall JKLF man from our village, was with them. Some village boys had begun calling him Rambo, but the elders still called him Tonga. A small crowd of villagers had gathered around Tonga and were arguing about something. Abu and I looked at each other. "God knows what Tonga is up to," he said, sighing. I rushed to find out. Tonga and his cohorts were planning to attack a convoy of Indian troops supposed to pass by our village. The villagers were trying to persuade them against it. They were addressing Tonga by his real name. "Mohiuddin Sahib, you are our son, you are from our own village. You have to stop this attack." "Mohiuddin Sahib, you know what the soldiers do after an attack. Do you want your own village burned?" "Have you forgotten we have young daughters? Do you want soldiers to barge into our homes? Have the fear of God, this is your own village!"

Tonga moved away from his sullen comrades to explain himself to the villagers. "I know! I know! I swear by my mother, I can't do anything. Every time my commanders plan an action here, I fight with them. Don't I know? My old mother lives here; my three daughters live here."

Hasan the baker held Tonga's hands. "Please! Do something."

Abu joined in. "Mohiuddin dear, please. You can save the village. Please."

Even the old Saifuddin left his perch and came up to him. "Mohiuddin Sahib, you are my son. Rahet, your mother, is like my sister. Remember that! And look at my white hair and white beard! Where will I run?"

Tonga held his hands. "You are like my father, and I am like your son.

But I can't stop it today. Please, close the shops and leave! Please, we don't have much time."

The villagers gave up. The shopkeepers pulled their shutters. I ran home. "Mummy, KLF people are outside. They are going to attack a convoy," I shouted. "Tonga is there, too, but he can't stop his commander. We have to run." Everybody panicked. Mother folded the sleeves of her *pheran* and asked everyone to shut up. She was in schoolteacher mode, and everyone listened to her. She hid the jewelry of her sisters that was kept in our house. Grandfather got a bag of the family's academic degrees, professional documents, cash, and passbooks. We were ready to leave through the door opening onto the vegetable garden behind the house. Then Mother said, "What about the books?" We looked at one another.

Father had built his library over the years. Each book had his name and a book number on the first page in either his scrawly handwriting or in Mother's neater letters. I had spent long hours in his library. There were the great Russian writers in thick People's Publishing House hardbacks that were sold in the mobile bookshops run by the Communist Party of India; there were the American and European novelists in slim paperbacks; there were the great Urdu writers Premchand, Manto, Ghalib, Iqbal, and Faiz. And there were histories, law books, commentaries on religion and politics in South Asia. The most beautiful of my father's books was *The Complete Works of William Shakespeare*—a thick edition, leather-bound, with gold-tinted pages. His books were those of a self-taught man, books that had shaped him, helped him build his life; they made him stand out when he talked about worlds and ideas that few men in our world could talk about. Touching their spines, running my fingers along their fonts, feeling the smoothness of their paper, and being mesmerized by their stories made me feel closer to Father and that I shared his connection to a magical world.

But there was nothing to be done; we had to leave the books in the house. We stepped into the backyard. Grandmother kept looking toward the house. "Sahib must be here anytime," she repeated. The sun was sinking in the sky, and we expected Father to arrive at any moment.

"God will keep him safe. There is nothing you can do by staring," Mother shouted at her, and bolted the locks.

Our neighbors were standing on their lawns with a few bags. Yusuf and his sons, Manzoor, Khalid, and Asif, were there. "Now what are we staring at!" Grandfather roared, and we began walking away. Amin, the chemist, was walking with his family; Abu, the butcher, was there with his wife and sons. A little ahead, I saw Kaisar, the ribald tailor, helping his father to safety. And Gul Khan, the old farmer who gave the call for prayers, was carrying his tiny granddaughter on his shoulders. Soon our walk turned into a run. I hoped that Father would hear about the attack and stay away; I hoped that nobody would be killed in the attack and the soldiers would not set our house on fire. I thought of some of my most beloved things: books, the black-and-white television, the Sony radio, the Polaroid camera.

Our village was emptying fast, almost everyone running toward Numbul, the adjacent village. It lay across some paddy fields and the Lidder, our local stream. The blue-green waters of the Lidder rushing through the fields bubbled over the stones. The wild grass grew by the stream, the willows swayed, and the paddies were ripening. The mountains stood witness. In the open sky, crows and eagles wandered and whirled. Indifferent. They continue with their own seasons.

We were half a kilometer from the Lidder when the first bullet was fired. Yusuf tried running faster, Grandfather stopped, and Gul Khan lay on his stomach in the fields, holding his granddaughter. I had an urge to laugh when I saw that Yusuf was running with his left hand covering his left cheek as if it could stop a bullet. Every few seconds, we heard the crackle of bullets. Kalashnikovs used by the militants sounded different from the machine guns and other rifles used by the soldiers. Yusuf's son Manzoor tried to tell from the sounds who was shooting. "Now the military is firing back. The militants seem to have stopped firing." His normally calm father slapped him.

The guns were still booming when we reached Numbul. Every door there was open to us. I do not know whose house we rushed into. We were ushered into a room. People from our village were already there, sitting silently along the wall, with half-empty cups of tea. As my family followed Grandfather into the room, two young men stood up and offered him and Grandmother their places; another took the cushion he was leaning against and placed it against the wall for Grandfather. "This is not a time for formality," Grandfather protested. Tea followed. Nobody said much. We listened to the faint sound of gunfire.

After a while, Grandfather and a few other men stepped outside. I followed. We stood looking toward our village; all I could see were distant treetops, a few minarets, and the village mountain. Nobody said it, but each of us was searching the horizon for flames and smoke. Gunpowder doesn't take long to burn a village. But I saw no smoke, only a slowly darkening sky.

I imagined people stopping a local bus in a neighboring village, telling the driver about the attack and turning it back. I imagined Father holding his newspapers and office files, getting off the bus, and staying with an acquaintance. But I could not ignore thoughts of the bus driving toward our village or getting caught in cross fire. I fully understood for the first time that he was making dangerous journeys week after week to see us.

The guns fell silent some time later. We stayed in Numbul that night. The next morning we headed back, anxious and edgy. Our walk home was brisk, punctuated only by short greetings to acquaintances and curious looks at village houses, searching for signs of the last evening's battle. We came to a sudden stop when we reached our backyard. My grandparents, Mother, my brother, my aunts, and I were transfixed for a moment, staring at our untouched home, as if we had sighted a new moon. I rushed into our courtyard. Father was standing on the veranda. "I heard about it on the way and stayed in Islamabad at Mohammad Amin's." He spoke casually.

I shook his hand. "Were you all right?"

Father smiled. "Yes! We were fine."

Grandfather repeated the details of our flight and our stay at Numbul. I joined in and gave the account of seeing the militants on the road and the conversations villagers had with Tonga. My younger brother couldn't be silent either. "Daddy, Basharat was crying when we were in Numbul." Father looked away, pretending not to hear him. "Let's go inside!" he said.

We went around checking each room facing the road for signs of damage. A few bullets were stuck in the ceiling in Father's room, and a few more had pierced the walls in the drawing room and the guest room facing the road. Grandfather pulled out the cartridges with pliers. We looked at them for a few moments and then threw them away.

By late afternoon, Father was sitting in his usual corner in our drawing room, a few books and a boiling samovar of tea by his side. My brother and I sat facing him. Every now and then, a friend or a relative would drop by, and tales of the previous night were recounted. In between these tellings, Father would recite a verse or two of Urdu poetry or a passage from Shakespeare and then turn to my brother and me: "Whoever explains this verse will get five rupees."

4 ⌒ Bunkeristan

Over the next few months, there were various crackdowns in my village and the neighboring villages. More Indian military camps were being set up in Kashmir. Military vehicles, armed soldiers, machine guns poking out of sandbag bunkers were everywhere; death and fear became routine, like going to school or playing cricket and football. At times we forgot about the war around us; at times we could not.

In the summer of 1992, my aunt was pregnant, and Mother constantly worried about a militant attack or a crackdown in our village. "What will we do if something happens?" she often mumbled. One June afternoon, my aunt's labor pains began. Her husband, Bashir (the uncle with the mysterious English accent), Grandfather, and Mother talked about moving her to the hospital in Anantnag. But there was a general strike, or *hartal*, that day to protest something—a very frequent occurrence those days. The shops were closed, and there were no vehicles on the roads. Neighborhood boys played cricket with a tennis ball on the road. There was no way to get to the hospital but to persuade one of the two taxi drivers in the village to drive my aunt there. Grandfather found Dilawar Khan, one of the two drivers. Uncle Bashir, Mother, and Grandfather were accompanying my aunt to the hospital. As they began to leave, an acquaintance arrived on his scooter and asked them to wait.

Militants had attacked a military convoy near the hospital in Anantnag, and an intense gun battle was being fought. My aunt was in great pain. Mother tried to calm her. Uncle Bashir walked in and out of the house nervously. Grandfather prayed.

After a while, we could not wait any longer. Mother and Uncle sat with my aunt in the backseat of the taxi. Grandfather sat in the front seat. Dilawar, the tall, bald driver, sat behind the wheel, solemn and purposeful. He revved up the engine and turned to Grandfather. "Masterji, she is my daughter, too. Even if they have brought out tanks, I will get her to the hospital." The cricket players left their game and stood by the car. Almost everyone in the neighborhood had assembled to see them off. Children tried to get closer to the car windows and see her. Women reached through to pat her head and hold her hand. Men made noises about hurrying up and being brave and patient. The car drove away. Scores of hands rose and a chorus of voices broke into prayer: *Miyon Khoday Thaeyinav Salamat! Miyon Nabi Kariney Raecchih!* (May Allah keep you safe! May Muhammad guard you!)

Three hours later, Dilawar pulled up outside our house. "It is a boy!" he shouted.

I shook his hand. "Is my aunt all right?"

"Yes, yes, she is fine. I drove really fast. And at the check posts, I called every soldier 'Major sahib' and told them the girl was about to give birth. After all, even they are human beings. We got there on time." I thanked him, and he smiled. "She is like my own daughter. It is a beautiful boy!" We named the boy Murtaza—the brave one.

One autumn day a few months later, I was with a few friends in the small market near my house. A patrol walked in, and our hands went to our pockets for our identity cards. A soldier stopping near you meant trouble. It meant an identity check, a possible beating, or a visit to the nearest army camp. Or he might simply order you to carry a bag of supplies to his camp. Soldiers forcing civilians to work for them was common.

The soldier who walked toward my friends and me only wanted to purchase batteries for his radio. I directed him to the shop of Bashir Lala, my mother's second cousin, a good-natured man somewhat famous in the extended family for his cowardice; we often sought a laugh at his expense.

One day Bashir was visiting relatives in Anantnag. The locals mostly referred to Anantnag by its traditional name, Islamabad. The soldiers would beat anyone who used Islamabad, as it was also the name of the Pakistani capital. Bashir had been reminding himself to say Anantnag and not Islamabad if a soldier asked where he was headed. His bus was stopped at a check post outside the town, and a soldier demanded, "Where are you going?"

Bashir forgot his rehearsed answer, "Islamabad." The soldier's baton stung his left arm, and Bashir cried out, "Anantnag, sir! Anantnag, not Islamabad."

It was rumored that Bashir took the next bus home and visited neither Anantnag nor Islamabad for the next few months.

The soldier wanting batteries took the few steps to Bashir's shop. I saw Bashir rise from his wooden seat and walk to the stairs leading to the shop, sweating and shivering. He addressed the soldier. "Sir! What have I done? Do not believe these idiots, they have no other work but to tease me. I am their father's age, and still they scare me. I am only a small shopkeeper." The soldier laughed and asked for batteries. Bashir fumbled through the few wooden shelves of his shop, found nothing, and apologized again. "You should keep batteries here," the soldier said. Bashir said, "What brand, sir?"

The soldier moved on to another shop. Bashir watched the column of soldiers till they disappeared. Only then did he dare to shout: "You swine! You joke with me! You dogs!" He kept shouting at us. Then he hid his head between his knees, covered it with his hands, and broke down. "Why do you do this to me? I have a heart problem, and these guns terrify me. Yes, I am a coward. I don't want to die. I have two daughters. I have to marry them off before I die." He held his round, bald head and cried. "You, too! And you are my sister's son," he said, looking directly into my eyes.

I soon understood his fear better. One winter night my younger brother Wajahat and I were watching *The Three Musketeers*. War or peace, one couldn't let a chance to watch a movie slip by. Pakistan Television screened clean versions of various Hollywood classics. The reception on our television was bad, so Wajahat and I would spend hours adjusting the antennae. I would carry the antennae attached to a wooden staff from our roof to the lawn, to the cowshed, revolving it slowly. Wajahat would run breathlessly between the drawing room and my position to report the progress. Sometimes the TV would catch the images, but the sound would be muffled with static; sometimes we could get clear sound, and people would appear on the screen as if in a negative. Eventually, we would come upon the right place for the antennae, and the image and sound would synch up.

I lowered the volume to a bare minimum, lit a night lamp, and lowered the curtains to avoid attracting any attention. Outside, the curfewed night lay in silence like a man waiting in ambush. *The Three Musketeers* fought, frolicked, and entertained us for a while. Then the rumble of military trucks outside blurred the duels. We switched off the TV and peeped through the curtains; the headlights of the trucks lit up the empty road and the surrounding houses. After the convoy had passed, there was silence, and a wistful moon reclined on clouds.

Morning came abruptly, with a loud announcement over the mosque's public announcement system: "*Asalam-u-alikum!* This is an urgent announcement. The army has cordoned off the village. Every man and boy must assemble on the hospital lawns by six. It is a crackdown. Every house will be searched. The women can stay at home." Gul Khan, the farmer who lived in a hut of sun-baked bricks next to the mosque and gave the call for prayer, repeated the announcement several times. Few responded to his early-morning calls for prayer. But announcement of the crackdown gave his voice a new power. Within minutes my family had gathered in the kitchen. After a quick breakfast, Grandfather, Father, my brother, and I stepped outside on the road. Small groups of men and boys from our neighborhood were already standing by the closed storefronts.

Soon Mother and my aunts would be opening the doors of every room and cupboard for the soldiers looking for militants, guns, or ammunition. Kashmir was rife with stories of soldiers misbehaving with women during crackdowns. But there was nothing we could do.

A small crowd of freshly washed faces began a reluctant journey through the empty market toward the hospital compound. The light mustard sun, half hidden behind the mountains, touched the tin roofs of the houses. We walked in the misty light between rows of soldiers in greenish metal helmets cradling assault rifles and machine guns, past the forlorn shops. I reluctantly followed my father. Soldiers barked at us to walk faster. We obeyed. Another group asked us to pull out our identity cards and raise our hands. Within seconds, a long queue formed at the hospital gate. Two parallel lines of raised hands, the right hand holding firm to the identity card a few inches higher than the empty left hand. There was no distinction between the farmhand and the judge, just one man behind the other.

I entered the hospital compound, where several hundred men were sitting on the cold, bare hospital ground. Father, Grandfather, my brother, and I sat with a group of our neighbors. A military officer ordered visiting relatives and guests to stand in a group away from the residents of the village. They were ordered to walk in a queue past an armored car. Each man was asked to stop near the window and show his face to the masked *mukhbir*, a Kashmiri man who had become a collaborator and identified militants and their supporters.

Some *mukhbirs* were suspected militants who had been beaten into submission. Some were volunteers who worked for money. Some had joined the troops to seek revenge on militants for the killing of a family member. Some time ago, militants had taken an alleged *mukhbir* to the canal running along the mountain towering over our village and shot him. They had thrown the injured man into the canal and left him to die. Fortunately, the injured man, who turned out to be an unemployed former student of my grandfather from a neighboring village, survived. Two bullets had hit him near his neck, but the canal's cold water coagulated his blood and saved him.

Over the next few hours we were told to form queues and walk past the *mukhbir*. If the informer raised his hand, the soldiers pounced upon the suspect and took him away for interrogation. My turn came. My heart galloped, but I tried not to look nervous. The *mukhbir* waited for a moment and asked me to move on. But Manzoor, my neighbor's sixteen-year-old son, was taken away for interrogation. His father used to run a hotel at a nearby tourist resort. After the fighting began and the tourists stopped coming to Kashmir, they locked up the hotel. His father opened a grocery shop after modifying a room on the ground floor of their house. Manzoor went to school, but on the frequent days of *hartals* against an arrest, arson, or custodial killing by the soldiers, he manned the shop when the schools remained closed. He was a gregarious and talkative teenager. Occasionally, the militants passing by would stop to buy something or simply sit and talk. Manzoor loved the attention and being able to talk to many commanders. The army seemed to have heard that the militants stopped by his shop.

I returned to my place on the lawns and sat near Father and Grandfather, who were consoling Manzoor's distraught father. Then two soldiers came toward us. "Is someone called Basharat Peer here? He is a ninth-class student." They had the name of my school. I stood up. "Come with us," one said. "But . . . I am a student," I tried protesting. "We know. We just need you to identify somebody," the soldier said curtly. They walked toward the doctor's-residence-turned-interrogation center. I followed them, not turning back to see how my father or grandfather were reacting. We entered the three-room building. I had been there many times to see the doctor, who was a family friend. I was told to sit in the storeroom, and the soldiers slammed the door behind me.

The room was empty and had a single window facing the village mountain. I stood near the window and stared at the door. It was a plain wooden door, painted in the regulation bluish-green of hospital buildings. I stared at the door and looked at my watch. I turned to the window and looked at the mountain, at the pine trees standing in bright morning light, at the rough track skirting up the slope to the canal, and at the lone old hut in the clearing beside the canal. I looked at my watch again and turned toward the door. It stood still, wooden. I sat down on the floor

and stared at the door. I was somewhat numb. The anticipation of interrogation is worse than the interrogation.

Loud cries and shrieks from the rooms next door startled me. Over
and over I heard the words: *Khodayo Bachaav* (Save me, God!) and *Nahin
Pata, sir!* (I don't know, sir!). They were torturing the men and the boys
who had been taken away after the *mukhbir* had pointed them out. I
thought of Manzoor. How would his reedy body endure anything?
I thought of the boy from my school whom they wanted me to identify. I muttered all the prayers I had ever known. The door stood still.
I stared at the dusty bare floor and waited. The shrieks continued, with
brief intervals of silence.

Around two hours later, the door opened violently. Two soldiers
stood there with their guns pointed at me. I stood up. I was stiff, scared,
and staring into their faces. But they did not hit me. One of them began
questioning me. "What is your name?"

"Basharat, sir!"

"Full name?"

"Basharat Ahmad Peer, sir!"

"Father's name?"

"Ghulam Ahmad Peer, sir!"

"What does he do?"

"Government officer, sir!" Quickly adding for the effect, hoping it
might help, "Kashmir Administrative Services officer, sir!"

He didn't seem to hear me. "Where in the village do you live?"

"Down the road, sir! Next to the pharmacy."

I continued looking at him and then briefly at the other soldier. But
their stern, impassive faces gave away nothing.

Suddenly: "Which group are you with? KLF or HM?"

"With nobody, sir! I am a student."

He paused and looked at me. "Everyone says he is a student. "How
many of your friends are with them?"

"None of my friends, sir! They are all students." I took out my student
identity card from my shirt pocket and presented it.

He scanned it, turned it around, and returned it. "Where are the weapons?"

"I have no weapons, sir! I am a student."

"Come on, tell us. You know we have other ways of finding out."

"I know, sir! But I am only a student!" I pleaded.

"Think harder. I will come back in a few minutes," said the interrogator, and left.

The other soldier stood there in silence. I tried to persuade him that I was merely a student. "Talk to the officer when he returns," he said, and maintained his frightening silence. After a while, the interrogator returned and asked the same questions again. I had the same answer: "I am a student."

"All right," he said, "I know you are a student." He seemed to soften a bit. He asked me about a student from my school who was still enrolled but didn't come to school much. He was Pervez, my best friend from school, bad singer of Bollywood songs, center forward on the football team, and a boy with pink cheeks and a blue tracksuit. I answered quickly and gave Pervez's father's name, profession, and the name of their village. I also mentioned that he had relatives in our village. Pervez had been visiting his relatives and had been arrested in the crackdown. They had wanted to cross-check his identity. The interrogator looked at me for a moment and said, "All right! You can leave."

I thanked him and walked out of the storeroom. I could feel hundreds of curious, sympathetic eyes on my face. I became very self-conscious, took measured steps, and tried to smile. Father and Grandfather rose and walked toward me. I hugged them. "Did they beat you, Commander in Chief?" Father tried to joke. Grandfather's eyes were moist; he threw an arm around my shoulders and said nothing. After a while Manzoor appeared, limping. Later, when the crackdown was lifted, my friend from school was released as well. Pervez came limping toward me. We hugged. I asked him to come home: "I have to get home. Thanks! You saved me today." I watched him go, his cinnamon-checked shirt disappearing in the crowd.

I never saw him again. A few years later, I heard that he had joined the JKLF and was killed in a gun battle.

The day passed in a flurry of visits to the houses of men and boys who had been arrested. Manzoor had bruises all over his body from the beatings. His father forbade him from manning the grocery shop. Back home, my family talked about the traces of mustache and beard that had begun to grow on my face. The soldiers were particularly suspicious of anyone with any kind of facial hair. Some of the older men of the village—including Manzoor's father—who used to dye their hair black had stopped. Gray hair made you less of a suspect. "This bit of beard is not good for you," Father said to me. "You must shave." Grandfather smiled. Mother laughed. I felt very shy. Father brought his shaving kit. "Come, I will teach you. It is easy." I had always watched Father shave. I stood in front of the bathroom mirror; he stood near me. I rinsed my face with water and put some of his Old Spice shaving cream on a brush. "Move the brush slowly in circles on the skin," Father said. Soon my face disappeared in white lather. The entire family was watching me. Father gave me his razor. "Glide it slowly. Don't press hard or you will cut yourself." I shaved.

5 ⁀ Shalimar Express

One afternoon in the spring of 1992, I saw a convoy of military trucks drive on the dirt track connecting our school to the village of Aishmuqam. I walked toward the row of willows and poplars near the aluminum fence of the school to get a clearer view. The trucks screeched to a halt at the gate of my school. The soldiers were moving in. The complex was owned by the Geological Survey of India, but they had shut the offices soon after the fighting started, and our school had rented some of the buildings. In a few hours, the trucks had been unloaded and the compound turned into a military camp.

Over the next few days, they built watchtowers and sandbag bunkers along the school fence. Scores of machine-gun nozzles and stern-looking soldiers stared from the rectangular firing slats of the bunkers, draped with wire mesh aimed at deflecting potential grenades. Soon we had new rules to follow. Parts of the school complex, including half of the main school building, became off-bounds. We had to carry identity cards on us and show them every time we entered or left the school. A sign ordering visitors to prove their identity was put up near the checkpoint on the school gate. Visitors wrote their names, addresses, and other details on a register and would enter the school after a body search by the soldiers.

The soldiers never bothered us. We went to our classes, played football and cricket, and on our part of the campus, continued talking about what everyone else was talking about in Kashmir: the war. We feigned being utterly apolitical if a soldier spoke to us. The soldiers set about their work of "area domination"—patrolling the road passing by the school, leaving early in the morning for crackdowns in neighboring villages. In a few weeks, my schoolmates and I became used to the sight of military trucks returning from raids and crackdowns with suspected militants—young men tied with ropes being taken into the part of the school building occupied by the military. At night in our rooms, we would hear the cries of the prisoners being tortured. Small crowds of students would gather outside, speculating about the forms of torture our uniformed neighbors were employing. We talked about helping the prisoners escape but had neither the means nor the will.

The military camp and its operations were an invitation for a guerrilla attack. We awaited the inevitable. The soldiers told our teachers to restrict us to our dorms after sunset.

One evening I was sitting in my room after dinner talking to Shabnam, now my roommate. The electricity had gone out, and I had lit a candle. A sudden bang! Another. Rapid, continuous bursts. "Kalashnikov!" I shouted. And then the louder, retaliatory bursts of light machine guns positioned in the bunkers along the school boundary. "LMG!" I snuffed the candle, and we squatted under our windowsill. We listened to the varying gunfire. There was an element of adventure, thrill. But within a few minutes the gunfire turned very intense, and the excitement melted into fear. Shabnam whispered the Quran prayer most Muslims read in the face of danger. I repeated the prayer known as *Aayat-ul-Kursi*, or the Verse of the Throne, after him: *Allah! There is no god but He—the living, the self-subsisting, the eternal. Neither slumber can seize Him nor sleep. His are all things, in the heavens and on earth. His throne extends over the heavens and the earth. And He feels no fatigue in guarding and preserving them. For He is Supreme.*

Our eyes were drawn to the window. The row of green-roofed, white-walled cottages housing the girls, our wide cricket field, and the apricot and poplar trees forming a sort of a border between us, the asbestos-sheet garage for the school bus, the white cotton net hanging from the poles of the volleyball court, and the mountains in the distance were shining in a lovely white light. The rough music of gunfire played on. A boom would sound and a sun would rise, exploding in a blinding flash of light. I stood in a daze by the window and stared at the sky: A thousand small suns seemed to have bloomed.

The attack on the school rattled my family; they arranged for me to move out of the dorm and commute from home. Mother talked about placing me in Wajahat's school in Anantnag, but that wasn't much safer. And most schools remained closed almost all the time. One day it was a protest against an arrest or a killing of an arrested person in an interrogation center; another day it was a gun battle or a crackdown. The troops continued setting up camps in school buildings; militants burned down many others they feared might be converted into military camps. Going to school was fraught with danger. Wajahat had a close call one day. He had been playing Snakes and Ladders with a friend in the back row of their mathematics class when they heard heavy gunfire. The shots were being fired in the market close to their school. Their teacher decided to carry on and finished his lecture ten minutes later. Some of the students were scared and some were excited on hearing gunfire. After a two-hour lull in the firing, they were allowed to leave the school, which had been closed for the day.

The school gate was opened, and the students pushed each other to get out only to find an Indian army tank looming in front of them. The soldiers instructed the students to run and waved them away. Wajahat and his friends ran through the empty market toward a bus stop a mile down the road. Tense soldiers patrolled the area. Wajahat reached a footwear showroom managed by a friend of our father's whom everyone called Good Luck. He heard a strange mechanical sound and turned around to find a tank moving slowly behind him. Alone on the road and scared, he began walking faster, but the tank rode alongside him. The barrel of its gun was rotating, pointing at him and then pointing away. "I thought the soldiers would fire a shell at me. Then I saw the machine gun mounted on the tank and thought they were more likely to shoot me with a bullet," Wajahat told me. The tank stopped, and he stopped. The tank commander shouted at him, "Run! Or do you want to die?" He ran.

Parents wanted to get their children out of Kashmir. The rich were sending their sons and daughters to Europe and North America; the middle and the lower middle class chose colleges and universities in Indian cities and towns. Most students were going to medical and engineering schools; physics, chemistry, and biochemistry were also popular. In August 1993, when I had passed my tenth-grade exams, Grandfather accompanied me to Aligarh Muslim University, three hours from Delhi. I was supposed to study physics, mathematics, and chemistry for two years at a school run by the university, then join the college there and graduate in a social sciences subject that helped earn good marks on the civil services exam. My brother would follow two years later. When I left home with Grandfather, my family members, relatives, and neighbors stood outside our house for the farewell. We walked toward a taxi with a beige VIP suitcase. I didn't feel sad or troubled. I did not know how long it would take before I would return home. Every one of my departures ever since has been a continuation of that moment.

The state transport bus struggled on the narrow highway along the mountain ridges that overlooks deep gorges and connects Kashmir to the Indian plains. Halfway into the trip, the bus halted for lunch at a highway market. It was full of eateries that were called hotels and had strange names. Hindu Hotel. Sikh Hotel. Muslim Hotel. We ate at the Muslim Hotel. After a day's journey, we arrived at the nearest railway station in Jammu. I had never been on a train. An orange sun was setting over barren plains as we entered the redbrick railway station. Coolies in khaki shirts, trousers, and red overalls buzzed about us. The platform spilled with people—enthusiastic youths, heavily made-up middle-aged women, their husbands carrying polythene bags and briefcases, relatives seeing them off. Hawkers with tin flasks of lukewarm tea and coffee ran toward every potential customer and shouted *Chai garam!*—hot tea. A nasal voice speaking in broken English blared out of a railway megaphone, saying that it regretted the inconvenience caused to the passengers by a train delayed for ten hours. Ten hours. Inconvenience regretted.

Our maroon train rolled in, and we got into our compartment. Grandfather told me that the most expensive ones were air-conditioned and only the rich could afford them; then the slightly less expensive first-class compartments; then the sleeper class, which we could afford. The sleeper class was an overcrowded oven. Each section of the compartment had three berths facing one another and two others across the aisle. We took our reserved seats, and a few minutes later, I began my first train journey.

I was uneasy, awkward, and conscious of my ignorance of simple things like closing a train window or unfolding a berth. The weather was brutal: hot and humid. My face burned, and my sweat-drenched shirt stuck to my back. Grandfather's lips were so dry that I could see a layer of salt on them. The heat became a little more bearable as the Shalimar Express left the station. "You can drink tea on the train and the cup will not shake," a friend had told me once. I did, and he was right.

A few hours into the journey, as the Shalimar Express entered Punjab, two soldiers entered our compartment. Like me, the soldiers had made a twelve-hour journey through the high mountains to the railway station in Jammu. Ahead of us was a fourteen-hour train ride to Delhi. The soldiers smiled and dropped their bags in the aisle. "Will you please make room for us?" one of them asked a middle-aged man reading a newsmagazine. "We are going home after a year in Kashmir and don't have any reservations." The man was unmoved. The soldier repeated his request, and as I squirmed in my seat, another passenger pointed at the dirty floor and said, "You may sit there." I was stunned. Grandfather and I looked at each other. Unlike people in Kashmir, our north Indian fellow passengers had no reason to be scared of the soldiers: They ordered them around, and the soldiers obeyed.

After a while the conductor arrived. He wore a white shirt, a black coat and trousers, and a steel badge near his coat pocket with his name and the inscription: TRAVELING TICKET EXAMINER. "What are you doing here?" he barked at the soldiers. "Sir, there is no room in other compartments. Sir! Please accommodate us somewhere," they pleaded. He asked the soldiers to leave the coach and began to walk away. They followed him. A few minutes later, they returned and installed themselves on the floor. "How much did he charge you?" someone asked. "Fifty rupees each," a soldier said. My co-passengers laughed and chatted about corruption. "This is India," declared the man with the newsmagazine.

We reached Delhi in the morning, and by late afternoon, we were approaching the small town of Aligarh. I watched slumlike clusters of houses, gray industrial areas, vast empty fields, more slums and villages where women in saris dried piles of mud cakes in the sun by the railway track. Two and a half hours later, we walked out of the redbrick railway station at Aligarh. Outside the station, there were no taxis or local buses but hundreds of rickshaws pedaled by emaciated men. Grandfather was reluctant to be pulled by another human being, but it was too hot to walk the two miles to the university. We felt guilty being pedaled by a poor man pushing hard against the load of his two passengers and their bags. "There is terrible poverty here," Grandfather said. He paid the rickshaw puller twice the fee.

We met some Kashmiri students at the university who helped me with admissions. The university was overcrowded, and there was no room in the dorms. But my new Kashmiri friends took me to their hostel and made some space for me. One of my friends and I saw Grandfather off at the railway station the next day. I was sad to see him go but also excited to be in a new place with new friends. I began it well: by walking out of the railway station with a friend and going off to watch my first Bollywood movie in a theater.

On my first day, I walked toward the school building with books and expectations. Sir Syed Ahmad Khan had founded the university in 1920 to provide modern education to Muslims. It was once known as the Oxford of the East. But it had fallen on bad times and was dying, like most provincial universities in India. It was no real *aazadi* from the misery of Kashmir. The political context of the university made things worse: It was one of the foremost institutions for Indian Muslims, and their anxiety and frustration about their position within India was palpable. I had heard about the sectarian violence and tensions in northern India, but that had remained a distant abstraction.

In December 1992, about a year before I joined my school in Aligarh, an extremist Hindu mob had demolished the Babri Masjid in Ayodhya, a few hundred kilometers from Aligarh. The Hindu right, led by the Bharatiya Janata Party (BJP), argued that the mosque had been built after demolishing an ancient temple. They wanted to construct a Ram temple on the site of the demolished mosque. The demolition triggered religious violence throughout India, and thousands were killed. Hilal, a Kashmiri friend at my new school, had witnessed the violence. Two days after the demolition of the medieval mosque, Hilal and ten other Kashmiri students boarded a train from Aligarh to Delhi, where they planned to catch a bus for Kashmir. *Karsevaks*, the Hindu right activists who had demolished the mosque in Ayodhya, were traveling on the same train. They wore regulation saffron headbands and carried saffron-painted crowbars, tridents, and daggers.

Karsevaks asked the students their names and places of residence. "Most students gave their real names and said they were from Kashmir," Hilal told me. Then he saw frenzied groups of *karsevaks* calling them Kashmiri Muslim terrorists and attacking them with crowbars and daggers. Hilal heard screams and realized the *karsevaks* were pushing the injured students off the moving train. A group of *karsevaks* approached him and asked his name. His surname, Bhat, is common to both Muslims and Hindus in Kashmir. "I am a Hindu. My name is Praveen Bhat. My father's name is Badrinath Bhat," Hilal lied. He feared they might want to check his identity card or, worse, ask him to drop his trousers so they would see whether he had a foreskin. Muslims are circumcised; Hindus are not. Rioters often did that. Fortunately, the group seemed to be in a hurry and let him go. He wanted to jump off the train at the next stop but saw a mob on the platform running after Rafiq Sofi, an undergraduate chemistry student. Hilal hoped his friends in the other compartments had survived.

The train reached Delhi two hours later. Hilal and another boy waited outside the Delhi station for the others. They met some, but many were missing. Later, Hilal learned that his friend and fellow ninth-grade student Farhat Razak had been stabbed to death. His body was found on the railways tracks by the police. Another student, Javed Andrabi, was missing for a month. Reports of an unidentified body found on the tracks near a town half an hour from Aligarh reached the university. People who had collected and buried his body had saved his trousers. The tailor's label on the dead boy's trousers gave the name of the Andrabi family tailor and town in Kashmir. Andrabi's brother was able to confirm the dead boy as his brother.

Despite their insecurity and despair in an India witnessing the rise of Hindu nationalism, most of my Indian Muslim friends were Indian nationalists. They disagreed with me and other Kashmiri students about our ideas of an independent Kashmir. They were afraid that the secession of a Muslim-majority Kashmir from India would make life worse for India's Muslims. Whenever a cricket match was screened in the television room of our hostel, my Indian Muslim friends cheered, sang, and rooted for the Indian cricket team. Kashmiris cheered for Sri Lanka or Pakistan, or whichever team played against India.

But the rhythms of student life and the confusions and longings of early youth kept us busy. After two final years of high school, I joined college in the autumn of 1995 to study political science, sociology, and English literature. College was mostly uninspiring. No teacher ever bothered to connect the textbooks to the social and political upheaval outside the classroom.

I preferred the literature classes. The teacher who taught us Hemingway spoke in a mixture of Hindi and English, which Hilal told me was called Hinglish. Few students attended classes, and of those who did, fewer were able to speak or write a proper sentence in English. Student politicians strutted around with henchmen carrying country-made revolvers. Every other week there were shootings on the campus, and gang members would beat up other gang members. When the student politicians did not scuffle with rivals, they nourished dreams of making it in Indian politics.

I hung out mostly with other Kashmiri students. We shared stories of our experiences of the war back home. A boy from Srinagar talked about learning to play bridge and chess during days and nights of curfew. A boy from a northern Kashmir town talked about hiding in a storeroom for hours with his family after the Indian soldiers came under attack. Somebody talked about the boredom of having to stay inside the house after sunset, which reminded someone else of the orders from the Indian troops that anyone stepping out of the house at night should carry a lantern or a torch, which reminded others of incidents when people were killed at night after the troops mistook them for militants. Someone told a story about a madman who used to walk around his town at night and was shot by a patrol. On phone calls home and visits during the summer and winter holidays, we heard of and saw more tragedies. One of those days, on a visit to a friend in the nearby town of Bijbehara, I had stopped near a graveyard where scores of protesters killed after the paramilitary had fired on a procession were buried. The age of the dead on most tombstones was eighteen.

I heard echoes of Kashmir in the pages of Hemingway, Orwell, Dostoyevsky, and Turgenev, among others. I returned to Hemingway and began to reread *A Farewell to Arms*. He had written about a faraway war and yet I saw only Kashmir in his words. Hemingway's narrator, Frederic Henry, the American ambulance driver for the Italians, said of gunfire: "I could not see the guns but they were evidently firing directly over us." It reminded me of the day when I had to escape to a nearby village with my family after the militants attacked Indian troops in our neighborhood. Further ahead in the novel, when the British nurse Catherine Barkley told Henry that her fiancé had been blown to bits and his unit had sent her the thin leather-bound stick he'd carried, I thought of militant groups in Kashmir sending copies of the Quran to families of slain militants.

When I came across an old copy of George Orwell's *Homage to Catalonia*, I developed an obsession with his merging of the personal and the political, the small details and the big ideas, his sparse, powerful prose. *Homage to Catalonia* brought back many memories of Kashmir and made me believe that writing similarly about my own war might be possible someday. I saw the walls of Kashmiri towns when I read Orwell's writings about Barcelona during the 1936 uprising against the Fascists:

"The revolutionary posters were everywhere, flaming from the walls in clean reds and blues that made the few remaining advertisements look like daubs of mud." I heard the songs from the loudspeaker of my local mosque when he wrote: "Down the Ramblas, the wide central artery of the town where crowds of people streamed constantly to and fro, the loudspeakers were bellowing revolutionary songs all day and far into the night."

When he wrote, "There was much in it that I did not understand, in some ways I did not even like it, but I recognized it immediately as a state of affairs worth fighting for," I found him giving voice to my attraction to the Kashmiri rebellion as a teenager, which was rooted more in emotional truths than in theories of politics and knowledge of history.

I saw similar windows of understanding opening up in the *Red Cavalry* stories of Isaac Babel. And when I read about Babel's own disappearance and murder, I thought again of the arrests and custodial murders of thousands of young men in Kashmir. In John Steinbeck's chronicle of displaced farmers, *The Grapes of Wrath*, I saw Indian military camps taking over orchards and paddy fields around my village in Kashmir. A little later, the essays of James Baldwin reminded me of the ghettos of Indian Muslims and lower castes.

I wanted to write like that about Kashmir but kept the thought to myself. I was not going to be the bureaucrat my family wanted me to be. Aligarh didn't have much to offer me. I had seen reports of book launches, film festivals, and theater workshops in Delhi papers. My brother, Wajahat, was already studying German literature and philosophy at a university in Delhi. I called Mother and told her about my unwillingness to prepare for the civil services examination. Arguments and discussions continued for several months. We arrived at a compromise. I could train as a lawyer, prepare for the civil services, and write in my spare time.

I ended up at the law school at Delhi University. It was a way to be in Delhi and explore possibilities for writing.

6 ⮑ A Close Call

On my first day in the city, I walked through Connaught Place, an elegant circular arcade in the center of Delhi. I was overwhelmed. The buildings seemed too big, the roads too busy. It was a scorching June day; there was no breeze, no shade. Diesel buses left clouds of smoke. But I had a sense of freedom, a feeling that I could teach myself what I needed to learn. I spent most of my first year at the law school reading literature and journalism. Delhi had numerous libraries and a fabulous used-book bazaar on Sundays. In mid-2000 I left law school and found my first job with a news website. After my very first week, with some lessons from my editors, I was sent out to cover Delhi. I tried, failed, tried again, and began learning to survive as a reporter.

My reporting job required me to travel a lot throughout the city. I was losing my patience with the crowded Delhi buses. After receiving my first paycheck, I bought an old motorcycle from a colleague. "You have to be quick. It is breaking news," my news editor would shout. Delhi was all about running faster than everyone else. I often thought of Ruskin Bond when I stopped my motorcycle at a traffic light. "In Delhi you are either the first or you are lost," Bond wrote. I did not want to be lost. As the traffic lights turned green I would release the clutch, wind the accelerator to the maximum, and shoot ahead of the crowd.

I lived in a garret on the roof of a South Delhi house, a mile away from my office. After work, when I was not reading, I hung out with friends at a university near my rented room. The university was and remains one of the few politically tolerant spaces in New Delhi. The Delhi police had over the years earned a reputation for fake encounters with Kashmiri terrorists. I understood why I had been sent to the decaying provisional Muslim university and not to a college in Delhi.

Slowly, I learned to like Delhi. I was also beginning to understand the various Indias that existed, Indias that I liked and cared about, Indias that were unlike the militaristic power I'd seen in Kashmir. India had opened its economy in the early 1990s. Round-the-clock channels broadcast news, and the number of magazines was growing. Young anchors and reporters asked victims of tragedies questions like "So, how does it feel?" in a faux American accent. The newly moneyed capital of India began to pride itself on its special DJ nights and malls featuring Levi's showrooms and Nokia outlets. Thousands of Toyotas ferried call-center executives for night shifts at the suburban BPO offices, among them a flatmate of mine, a boy from a small southern Indian town who had been told to jettison his Indian name. He would tell me about his job and begin acting out his calls: "Hi! This is Jack Smith calling from JCPenney!"

The old India and its power structures did not disappear. My neighborhood was full of students from small towns and villages, living very austere lives and preparing for the competition, or the "civils"—the Indian civil services examination. They dredged through tedious manuals and textbooks for four, five, even six years, fortifying themselves with cheap Old Monk rum and staring at the whitewashed ceilings of those claustrophobic rooms and dreaming of sitting behind the chair of a district magistrate, surrounded by armed guards, servants, drivers obsequiously lapping to attention at every whim, a bungalow, a white ambassador car with a siren and flashing red light, and in a few years holding the power to administer an entire district—often with hundreds of villages and more than a million people. In the heart of Delhi, near Jantar Mantar Street, I saw almost every day groups of India's powerless—people sitting on the footpaths with cloth banners or cardboard placards, seeking official attention for their woes, for the injustices they lived with. India was grotesque and fascinating.

Delhi was beginning to be a second home. Maybe a city feels like home when you know there will be a person or two who will come to the airport or the railway station to greet you, when you know there are people you want to meet as you arrive. I might have forgotten Kashmir—it might have turned into a place I visited every two or three months—but I could not. Kashmir was the text and subtext of my professional, personal, and social worlds in Delhi. Kashmir was the death count in the newspapers: Almost every day I woke up to the news of a mine blast, a gun battle and the rubble of a destroyed home, a protest against a custodial killing in Kashmir. I hoped I would never have to read the names of people I loved the most in those reports of deaths.

One day I almost ran out of luck. I was covering Delhi courts for the news website I worked for. On May 14, 2001, the London-based Indian business tycoons the Hinduja brothers were being tried in India for their alleged involvement in the Bofors scam, a 1980s graft scandal involving the purchase of arms for the Indian military. The hearings were held in a North Delhi court complex, Tis Hazari. It was a very hot day. I was sweating the minute I stepped outdoors. The courtroom was pretty far, and my editor had asked me to take an office cab instead of my rickety motorcycle. The air-conditioning in the car made the prospect of going to the court appealing. An hour later, the driver parked outside the monstrous concrete court complex. I walked in to find the familiar crowd of reporters whiling away time with cups of tea and the retelling of court reporter jokes. The hearing began around one-thirty, after two hours of waiting in the heat.

I found a place near the witness box where two of the Hinduja brothers stood in their gray suits and square seventies-style spectacles, sweating under the leisurely, noisy motions of an antique ceiling fan. A reporter joked about equality under law, how the ill-paid reporters and the billionaire Hindujas sweated under the same fan. As the case proceeded, a vague sadness overcame me. I was restless, uninterested in the trial. I tried taking notes and failed. I felt breathless and decided to leave. Fifteen minutes later, I made my way through the crowd and sneaked out of the courtroom.

My office was in a crowded shopping complex dominated by huge Benetton, Reebok, and Adidas stores. A TGIF stood next to a new multiplex. A small independent bookstore was almost hidden in this glitter of billboards and the nonchalant noise of Delhi's rich kids. I walked past the shop and took the stairs to my office on the top floor. "How was the story, Basharat?" said Ramesh, my editor and mentor, the moment I entered the office. I told him I'd had to walk out.

"Don't worry. It is the goddamn heat," he said. Ramesh fidgeted with some files, then put a hand on my shoulder. He seemed disturbed, trying hard to be composed. "There was a call for you from Mukhtar [the Srinagar reporter]. Please call him back right away."

I dialed the number. Mukhtar picked up the phone on the second ring. He made some small talk about my work. And then: "Basharat, your parents were traveling back from a wedding at your uncle's village. There was a mine blast on the road. Thank God they are safe. I just spoke to them. Please call them."

Parents. Mine blast. Safe. I registered the words and held the receiver. Ramesh stood in silence. *Parents. Mine blast. Safe.* It was as if someone had punched my heart. I sat on the office floor and rested my head against a stack of newspapers. I cried. My colleagues stood around me, silent, sad. I gathered myself in a few minutes and called home. I spoke to my parents for a long time. I was going home.

There were no flights till the next morning, and I had to take an overnight bus. First I had to meet Wajahat. His university was a few minutes from my office.

I walked toward my rust-colored Kawasaki motorcycle, parked in a long line of scooters and motorcycles, and turned on the gas and the ignition. I tried to kick-start it, and nothing happened. I kicked again, and the machine whined. I tried harder, and the old engine groaned to life briefly. I felt I would fall; my hands were shaking, and my legs felt very weak, as if some giant syringe had sucked every ounce of blood out of me. I struggled with putting the motorcycle back on the stand

and holding my helmet in my lap and sat on a cemented parking divider, smoking, thinking how to tell Wajahat.

As I navigated the streets on my bike, images of my parents came to my mind: leaving a hospital with an arm in a cast and getting a bottle of Campa cola and a Five Star chocolate from Father; walking with him to the Royal bookseller near his office and buying Batman comics; drinking tea and talking poetry at home; receiving a seven-page letter from him upon publishing my first story in a Delhi newspaper. And Mother: staying awake throughout the nights I had fever; finding a packet of cigarettes in my trousers when I was home from college and keeping my secret; insisting that I wear proper clothes, making half-serious inquiries about marriage after I began working.

I stopped at the open-air café near Wajahat's dorm. Small groups of young people sat along the road and on blocks of concrete along the slope of the café. Many more stood in a line waiting for tea and snacks at the counter and at the tiny cigarette and betel nut shop next door. Others hung about the public phone booth. I lived across the road from the university and often met Wajahat and a few other friends there. He was with a group of people closer to the café counter. I walked slowly past groups of students immersed in loud, passionate discussions about politics, casually laughing and flirting.

Wajahat and his friends sat in a circle; half-empty paper cups lay on a block of stone in the middle, and smoke rose from a few cigarettes. Wajahat held a cotton towel in his left hand. His long, wavy hair was soaked with sweat. He always had a towel on hand to keep sweat from dripping onto his contact lenses. He saw me from a distance and said something; his friends laughed. They often made lighthearted comments comparing my "pedestrian" reporting job to their critical readings of Hegel and Kant in the air-conditioned library.

Wajahat grinned. "Mr. Reporter, what's up?"

"Oh! The usual grind!" I sat down and took a few moments to fortify myself. "We have to call home." My voice was uneven, shaky.

His face stiffened, and he stood up. "What happened?" His eyes were grave, apprehensive. His friends circled us.

"Everyone is fine. Mummy and Daddy were coming back from a wedding at Salia. There was a mine blast on the road. They are safe at home now, but it was very close." Wajahat sat down. I held him. "We should call them now."

I put my arm around his shoulder and pushed him into the phone booth from where one could make long-distance calls. A fan hanging from a wall whirled in vain against the blistering May heat. Wajahat held the door ajar, and I dialed home. The phone began to ring. I gave him the receiver and stood behind him, my hand on his shoulder. He talked on the phone as if in a daze. When he hung up, we embraced.

"We have to go home," he said.

"Yes. We have to," I replied.

Wajahat had an exam in a few days.

"I will go now," I said decisively. "And you will come after your exam."

He was silent, thinking, tears welling up in his eyes. "I will come with you," he said. "I will drop the exam."

"No! You can't. They are safe. You will come after the exam. Let's talk to Mummy again. If she says yes, you can come."

"You know she won't let me."

"Let's call her."

Mother and Father insisted that Wajahat take his exam. I took an overnight bus to Jammu, a flight from there to Srinagar, and a cab home from the airport. I remember nothing else.

The cab stopped outside the house. Many cars were parked along the road; I stood there for a moment, looking at our house, at the mountains in the distance, seeking assurance in the familiar. I walked in. Father was surrounded by friends, relatives, and neighbors on the lawn. A samovar and a few trays full of cups and plates of bread and cakes lay around. Mother was standing next to him. I was tired with the relief of being able to see them again, grateful that I didn't have to walk into a house without them. I felt no anger—that came much later, after weeks. I walked toward them, and silence fell upon the group. Father smiled from a distance and rose from his place; Mother remained where she was. I walked up to her and hugged her.

I said nothing. What do you say when your parents nearly get killed?

Eventually, Mother asked about Wajahat's preparation for the examination. Father asked about my journey. We shook hands. Then we looked at each other and hugged. There was no need to say anything.

We drank some tea. "You must take a shower and change," Father said.

"Later." I sat with them, drinking tea, saying nothing much.

"It was a miracle," Father said.

They were at a relative's wedding in Uncle Rahman's village, three miles from our ancestral home. The ceremonies were over by one P.M., and after lunch, they left in the car with two of my cousins. The car moved out of the village, and they traveled on a narrow dirt road running past clusters of houses built on a plateau on their right.

"I saw these two young men sitting on the plateau across the stream. They were looking at us," Father said. "Your mother pointed at one of them. He had something like a calculator in his hand."

The car slowed down. "We were crossing a concrete water pipe running through the road."

Then there was a loud explosion.

"It was like a strong blast of air lifting the car."

The force of the blast pushed the car off the road. Bricks and stones torn from the road fell on the car roof.

For a few minutes they lay huddled, waiting for possible gunfire. The calculator Father had seen was a detonator; the two young men across the stream had planted the mine inside the water pipe. Luckily, they had forgotten to block one end of the pipe. The force of the explosion had veered off toward the unblocked end of the pipe, and the car tossed in the other direction. They escaped with minor bruises. Physics had saved my family.

"But why you?" I asked him. He had no answers. I heard him repeating the same question on the phone. Militants had been killing pro-India politicians, police, or anybody whom they perceived as working against them. But civil servants like my father, whose job was to look after daily administration, were rarely targeted.

Over the next few days, friends and relatives brought news and the name of the man who had convinced the militants to kill my father. He was a man with political ambition whom my family had known for a long time. I shall call him Iago. A month before the attack, he had met my father in his office. Father was the head of administration for the district and had to decide various disputes between organizations and individuals. One of Iago's rivals, also a man with political ambition, had applied in my father's office for a certain permit. Iago wanted the permission denied. Father told Iago that, legally, his rival had the right to that permission. "But you can skirt around that if you want. It is a little-known law," Iago told Father. Father disagreed, and Iago left, sullen.

Iago was the characteristic ambitious operator from a conflict zone, flirting with pro-India groups during the day, feeding, sheltering, donating money to the separatist anti-India militant groups by night. One of the commanders in the biggest militant group operating in the area, Hizbul Mujahideen, was from Iago's village. While the militant was on the run, Iago had supported his family. After his meeting with my father, Iago sent word to the militant commander through one of his men: "Peer is dangerous for you. He is working hard to ensure that village-level elections go smoothly." Militant groups had called for a boycott of all elections—village, district, state—which they saw as an exercise in strengthening Indian rule in Kashmir.

Iago's men convinced them that if the militant boycott of the village elections were to work well, they had to get my father out of the way. A month later, the land mine went off. In the weeks following the attack, hundreds of people visited our house, and the phone never stopped ringing. Iago did not call. Much later, I bumped into him on the street. He shook my hand, complained that I didn't visit his family, asked about Father's well-being, and paid him many compliments. I kept up the pretense, smiled back, and asked about his family.

Father was scared and even stopped making the twenty-minute journey from his official house in Anantnag to our village. A few months later, he left Anantnag for a new job in the relatively safe Srinagar.

I had somehow believed that my family would always be safe. I mentioned this to my father. We had talked earlier about people dying but never about death per se. "I, too, had this faith that we would be fine and survive it all. Maybe people don't really believe that they can be killed or come close to death," Father said.

7 ⪕ Situation

I n the winter of 2001, I was in a meeting with my editors at the Bombay headquarters of my news site. The air around the conference table was charged. Reporters were tossing around ideas: scoops, big interviews, detailed stories on complex subjects. Editors argued back, agreeing, disagreeing. Performances were being evaluated, decisions made about assignments. Economy. Elections. Environment. Urban politics. And Kashmir!

I had worked as a police reporter and a court correspondent; occasionally, I wrote about fashion, cinema, and television—anything my editors asked for. But after work, I obsessively read about armed conflicts around the world. I was training myself for the one story I had to tell. And then my editor said, "Basharat! You are going to Kashmir."

One early December afternoon, I was on a flight from Delhi to Srinagar. I was finally going home as a reporter to tell the stories of Kashmir. I had never flown home and continually stared out the window. Frozen crusts of snow on mountain peaks brought the first intimation of home. A silver-gray blanket of fog hid the arcs of steep mountains framing the valley. The plane began to descend. Silhouettes of village houses and leafless walnut trees appeared amid a sea of fog. On the chilly tarmac, the fog formed rings of smoke.

When my car left the airport gate, it was as if I had emerged in the midst of a siege. Scores of olive military trucks with machine guns on their turrets lined the road. Solemn-faced soldiers in heavy overcoats slinging assault rifles hung around the trucks and check posts. In summer they would swagger on the roads in dandyish bandanas, but the bitter chill of Kashmiri winter had subdued them a bit.

In Srinagar the streets were quieter; the naked rain-washed brick houses seemed a little shrunken; men and women walked leisurely on the sidewalks in loose wool *pherans*, their pale faces reddened by the cold.

I dropped my bags at the house my parents had rented in southern Srinagar after the land mine blast. I ate a quick lunch with Mother, and then prepared to step out. "Where are you going?" she asked. "I have to find stories," I told her. "I am on deadline." She smiled. I walked onto the street, almost quixotic, my notebook and pen ready to record, my gaze at times a restless dart, at times clouded by despair.

A short ride in a rickshaw brought me to a small enclave in Lal Chowk, where most newspapers had their offices. The Press Enclave, two opposing rows of staid white and redbrick buildings, had been renamed Mushtaq Ali Enclave. A little ahead of the marble plaque engraved with that name, I passed the whitewashed house of the celebrated BBC radio reporter Yusuf Jameel. One September afternoon in 1995, Jameel had walked into his office with a younger journalist, Mushtaq Ali. An unknown veiled woman had left a parcel for him. As Jameel began to open the parcel, the phone rang in an adjoining room. He rushed to take the call. Mushtaq opened the package. It exploded. Jameel was injured, and Mushtaq died three days later. Everyone believed that the Indian army had sent the package to silence Jameel.

A little ahead of the house, I entered the modest redbrick office of *The Kashmir Times*. Smoke billowed out of a charcoal heater, or *bukhari*, in the tiny newsroom. Four men sat behind old wooden tables, typing on ancient computers. Piles of press releases and notebooks cluttered their desks. A file of old newspapers hung from a wooden stand, and a seventies-style black telephone sat on the window. Masood, a veteran reporter and friend, welcomed me. "The first Kashmir assignment!" he shouted, and hugged me.

I sat on a wooden chair by the charcoal heater. I was excited and nervous and wanted his advice. "It all depends on how you write, how you choose your words," he said slowly. "Thirty-seven words is all you need to know to be a reporter here." He laughed the weary laugh of a man who had witnessed a lot. It was a grim list: fear, arrest, prison, torture, death, Indian security forces, separatists, guerrillas/militants/terrorists, grenades, assault rifles, sandbag bunkers, army installations, hideouts, crackdowns, search-and-destroy operations, frustration, tension, anxiety, trauma, democracy, betrayal, self-determination, freedom, peace talks, international community, mediation, breakdown, despair, and rage.

One of Masood's colleagues joked about a wire service reporter in Srinagar who, it was rumored, had written the basic format for his news stories years ago. He kept altering names and figures in his basic reports, which read: "At least seven protesters were killed and fifteen injured, three of them seriously, when paramilitary forces opened fire on demonstrators at X village in south Kashmir." Or: "Five civilians were killed and twenty injured when militants hurled a grenade at troops in the north Kashmir town Baramulla. The grenade missed the target and exploded on the street. The injured have been rushed to a local hospital." "Don't follow that example," Masood said.

We drank tea and talked a little more about stories. Masood checked his watch. It was quite late in the afternoon. "Who is doing the situation today?" he asked nobody in particular. One of his younger colleagues rose and checked a chart that read: SITUATION. "It is my turn," he said. A reporter was on duty to check the day's death toll. The young reporter dialed the police-control number. "I am from *The Kashmir Times*. Could you please give me the situation for the day?" He scribbled the names of the dead and the injured.

Outside, it was already getting dark. Shopkeepers were pulling down shutters. Buses didn't linger, conductors hurriedly shouted the names of destinations. Rickshaw drivers were alert, ready to leave with a passenger. The twilight seemed pregnant with a fear that descended on the city every evening. Few lights were switched on in my neighborhood after dinner, fewer vehicles ventured out. Check posts, searchlights, and curfew owned the night.

Mornings came late. The hills surrounding Srinagar remained hidden in a thick fog, and every color faded and made way for a stark gray. The air in tea shops in Lal Chowk was thick with cigarette smoke and talk of politics. America, bin Laden, 9/11, Tora Bora, the war on terror. Everyone had a theory. The world has changed. The world has not changed. America will be interested in Kashmir. America will not be interested in Kashmir. I interviewed people, wrote my stories, hung out with journalist friends in tea shops and newspaper offices, and took care to get back home by sunset. Nothing extraordinary happened during my two weeks in Srinagar, but I met a man I can never forget: Maqbool Sheikh.

In his late forties, slightly plump, Maqbool was a paramedic at the police hospital in Srinagar. He had straight black hair and a face that could have belonged to any other middle-aged man on his way to work in Srinagar. Yet he was the most intimate witness of the costs of armed conflict. He was the only autopsy expert at the police hospital, where most of the people killed in and around Srinagar were brought. Between 1990 and 2001, he had conducted autopsies on more than eleven thousand bodies of civilians, militants, and soldiers. Maqbool worked for under two hundred dollars a month and didn't have a telephone in the house. Policemen knocked on his door every time the mortuary received a body at night. "Every time I hear a knock, my heart seems to stop beating," Maqbool told me. "I know someone has been killed. Throughout the ride to the mortuary, I keep thinking who will it be: a child, a woman or another young man."

He dreaded the encounter with every new body, hated cutting it open to find out how the person had died, what weapon was used, and what distance it was fired from. The law of the land requires such details be recorded; judgments are pronounced on the dead, and those judgments affect how their families live and are treated by the law. Which side was the dead man on? Was he a guerrilla? A police informer?

A soldier? A bystander? Or just a man who had been arrested and killed? Maqbool's scalpel sought answers in the wounds and ruptures of bodies.

The knowledge that a major part of his job alleviated the pain and shock of grieving families helped him go on. Blasts killed many and tore the bodies into pieces. Families arrived at the mortuary looking for their missing children. "I imagine the face of a father who is waiting to receive the body of his young son. The least I can do is to stitch together the scattered parts and hope that it lessens the shock," Maqbool told me. My eyes wandered to his rough, calloused hands. He noticed that and smiled sadly. "At times after mine blasts, I find myself standing in a heap of torn limbs, and then it is a struggle to ensure that the fingers I stitch to a hand are of the same person."

Some years back, after a grenade blast in a Srinagar suburb, five bodies were brought to the police hospital in a truck. Maqbool was sifting through them, when he saw an arm move. "I pulled him out. He was young and he was alive." A little later, Maqbool found the boy's father waiting to collect his son's body. "I told him that his son was alive." The old man began whirling and shouting, "He is alive," and then he stopped and sat on the hospital floor and cried and cried.

"Nothing is harder than the death of one's child," Maqbool said.

One afternoon he walked toward the autopsy table with his surgical kit. He read verses of the Quran and sought forgiveness from the dead for touching their bodies, which is forbidden in Islam. Reciting the Quran gave him courage. Maqbool raised his scalpel, but he felt the eyes of a five-year-old staring at him. "His eyes seemed alive. It felt as if he could see me." Maqbool refused to do the postmortem. "It makes me think of my children."

Maqbool has a daughter and two sons. One of his sons drove an auto rickshaw, and the other had dropped out of high school. The dropout son seemed to be getting angrier by the day about the brutal ways of the Indian military. Maqbool feared he might join a guerrilla group. "I was worried where his anger could lead him."

His was a fear most parents shared in Kashmir. The entire generation that grew up in the nineties is far too intimate with violence. It reminded me of a ten-year-old cousin who plays a game called army-militant. Cricket bats become wooden guns, and broken plastic balls stuffed with cloth turn into hand grenades. My cousin and his friends take combat positions. A child shouts "Fire!" and they pretend to be guerrillas and soldiers shooting each other. When it snows and the guns turn quiet, they still make snowmen, using charcoal pieces for eyes.

Maqbool took the angry son to the mortuary. "I thought maybe I could persuade him to assist me, and I would also get to keep an eye on him." His son couldn't bear standing through an autopsy. "He vomited and did not eat for three days." The boy stayed away from trouble. Twenty-five years earlier, when he'd gotten the job with Kashmir Medical Services, Maqbool considered himself lucky. "Only yesterday after work, I took some fruits for my daughter. She dropped the packet and shrieked that my clothes stink of blood."

Writing about such violence-stained lives was painful, but the writing partially liberated me. A few years earlier, a young army captain posted near our village had harassed my grandfather because he was not carrying an identity card. I was angry but couldn't do anything about it. As a reporter, at least I could tell the stories. Yet the two weeks in Kashmir had shredded my initial euphoria at being home. Listening to people talk about death, fear, and humiliation was hard. It made me angry and sad. It made me cry. I had to come back and spend more time in Kashmir.

Before returning to Delhi, I went to spend a night with Grandfather in the village. Winters mean a heavy snowfall and a slower pace of life. Even the militants and the soldiers took it easy; less blood was spilled. We were leisurely drinking tea and talking, indifferent to the television droning on, when the news anchor's voice turned shrill and loud. "Terrorists have attacked the parliament!" I was startled by a chaotic barrage of sounds and images on the screen: the sirens of police cars, soldiers and policemen running, ducking, and firing at the terrorists in military fatigues running inside the parliament building, smoke rising from exploding tear-gas shells, the resounding echoes of their gunfire, the body of a dead terrorist on the stairs of the parliament building, and a little later, the shaken legislators being led out. I feared that a war might erupt between India and Pakistan. "This winter the snow will turn red." Grandfather sighed. I quickly said goodbye, rushed to Srinagar, and called my editor. "Stay there. You will have a lot to report from Kashmir," my editor said.

The details of the attack became clearer: In the morning legislators had gathered in the domed central hall of the circular colonnaded building of the Indian parliament, a majestic presence in the heart of New Delhi. They were arguing about the involvement of the Indian defense minister in an arms scandal. White Ambassador cars were lining up on the concourse. At about eleven-thirty A.M., policemen at the main parliament gate saw a white Ambassador approaching with five men inside. It appeared to have the necessary entry pass on the windshield; they stepped aside. The car accelerated as it moved past the red sandstone wall of the parliament. The next moment it had collided with one of the cars in the motorcade of the Indian vice president, who was expected to emerge from the parliament at any moment. As policemen ran toward the Ambassador, its doors opened, and five men with guns started firing at the police. They scattered onto the parliament's large grounds before anyone could retaliate. The speaker abruptly adjourned proceedings in the debating chamber. Emergency messages crackled across police radios: Terrorists had attacked the parliament. More police and paramilitaries were urgently summoned. A fierce battle was fought outside the building. Inside, around two hundred trapped and terrified legislators listened for half an hour to gunfire and grenades. By noon it was all over. The five armed men had been killed. Eight policemen and a gardener were also dead.

In the days following the attack, hostility rose as India ordered half a million soldiers to the India-Pakistan border. On television, analysts talked about a nuclear war; newsmagazines calculated the extent of devastation Indian and Pakistani nuclear bombs were capable of. Kashmir was debating whether India or Pakistan would go to war. A lot of Kashmiris I interviewed on the streets in Srinagar wanted a war. "It will be better than dying slowly every day!"

Indian and Pakistani gunners were continuously firing mortar shells at the villages along the border and the Line of Control. Yet I somehow didn't believe they would go to war.

Like most journalists, I drove to the villages along the border. Families of refugees lived in tents and school buildings in various towns near the border. Many were in hospitals with legs and arms torn by shrapnel.

One early morning, a photojournalist and I drove to Banglar, a village on the border. We drove on an empty road, passing deserted villages. Thousands of Indian soldiers were already on the border, and hundreds of their olive-green trucks were headed that way. The soldiers struck battle-ready poses for the photographer.

Banglar was a few dozen bare huts and houses among fields of wheat, mustard, and wild grass. The border was simply a barbed-wire fence, abandoned fields full of land mines, wild grass, and bunkers. We met the few men who had stayed behind to guard and feed their cattle. We took pictures of destroyed houses. A policeman who had just arrived from his posting in a faraway town to check on his destroyed house was telling me how tired they were of the cross-border shelling every time relations between India and Pakistan became embittered. "They should fight a war now and settle it. We are tired of dying every day." As we spoke, the shelling began again. I could hear the hiss of a mortar going over our heads and falling a few hundred yards away. The policeman rushed the photographer and me into a cowshed. We sat on cow dung for the next hour, praying. Then the shelling stopped for a minute. We ran out of the village.

• • •

Delhi had changed after the attack on the Indian parliament. The residents of the city scanned every stranger's face. I was looking for a place to stay. I met about a dozen people who had advertised in a local daily for a tenant for a two-room flat. Mr. Sengupta, a lawyer, was happy to know that I was comfortable with arranging the whitewashing and repairing the broken electric switches. In his living room full of law journals and imitations of Indian miniature paintings, we talked about the rent, my work, and my income. He patted his dachshund pup as he spoke. "So, your parents are posted in Kashmir?"

"They live there; we are Kashmiris. I studied here and work here."

"Oh! You are a Kashmiri. A Kashmiri Muslim." He asked me to call him the next day. When I did, he said, "You are like our own son. But my daughter called, and a friend of hers has to stay in Delhi. We will have to house her. I cannot rent out the flat."

Over the next few months, I continued hearing similar responses from landlords and real estate agents. The armies were still on the borders; the war clouds were still hovering. I responded to a few dozen advertisements, but I was still spending nights on my friends' couches. The first words I spoke to the last real estate agent I met were: "I am Muslim, and I am from Kashmir. Now, do you have a place to rent?"

Naresh Chandra, an elderly property agent with a slight build and a slighter mustache, was sympathetic. "They do not understand. All the five fingers are not the same. You are a Kashmiri, but you are not what they think of you." He added, "Sikhs could not rent an apartment for ten years after the 1984 riots." Another month passed. The generosity of my friends was heartwarming, but the city was changing for me. In newspaper advertisements, police warned against possible attacks by Kashmiri militants. Security checks and barriers outside theaters, railway stations, and markets added to the paranoia. I was scared to say I was a Kashmiri. But it was impossible to hide; people could tell from my long nose and pale complexion. I carried my press card with me all the time. Even then I avoided busy markets and entertainment complexes.

Someone suggested an address in a Muslim ghetto at the other end of the city. Muslims in Delhi lived mostly in the squalor of the old city near the Red Fort or in the overcrowded, dingy Okhla area in the southern corner of the city. It was hard for Muslims to rent or buy a place in the mostly Hindu middle-class or upper-middle-class areas. HSBC and Citibank, which had hundreds of branches in Indian cities, refused to entertain requests for personal loans from the Old Delhi or Okhla areas; Pizza Hut would not deliver a pizza there.

I was considering leaving Delhi when a broker called. "I have an old lonely lady who wants a paying guest." It meant being in by ten at night, sharing the bathroom with her, and having no guests. As we entered her apartment, I saw a frail woman in her seventies talking in Kashmiri on the phone. I smiled at the broker. The elderly woman was a Kashmir Hindu who had moved to Delhi with her husband some forty years ago. "Where are you from?" she asked in Hindi.

I answered in Kashmiri and told her that I was a journalist, that my mother was a schoolteacher, that my father was a bureaucrat, that my brother studied German at the university close to her house. "My husband was a bureaucrat, like your father." She smiled and talked about some of her relatives who were bureaucrats in the Kashmir government. My parents happened to know them. "You are a journalist. You write in English. That is very good." She offered me a seat in her drawing room, where pictures of her husband and Kashmiri Hindu deities hung from the walls. I paid the rent and the advance; there was no contract to sign. "He is from a good family. He will be like my own son," she said to the broker.

I fought my tears; after months of suspicion, I was being welcomed.

8 ✒ The Trial

The Indian government believed that a Pakistan-based jihadi group, Lashkar-e-Taiba (the Army of the Pure), which drew its cadre mostly from the rural poor of Pakistan's Punjab province, which claimed to fight to end Indian rule in Kashmir, had attacked the Indian parliament. Hardliners inside and outside the Hindu right's Bharatiya Janata Party, or the Indian People's Party (BJP), claimed that December 13 was India's 9/11. They demanded that Indian soldiers cross the Line of Control and attack the terrorist camps in the part of Kashmir held by Pakistan. Leading the hardliners was the Indian home minister, L. K. Advani, who had engineered the rise to power of the BJP in the 1990s.

Within hours of the attack, the Delhi police claimed to have recovered from the body of Mohammed—an allegedly Pakistani terrorist killed in the parliament complex—a mobile phone, three SIM cards, and some telephone numbers. Two days later, they arrested three Kashmiri men and a pregnant housewife and charged them with conspiring in the attack on the parliament. The police claimed that the telephone numbers had led them to the Kashmiris. The first to be arrested on December 15 was a thirty-two-year-old Delhi University Arabic lecturer, Syed Abdul Rahman Geelani. The police said they had picked him up outside his rented house in North Delhi.

The news of his arrest shocked me. I had met Geelani one evening

in autumn 1999 at Delhi University. A mutual acquaintance from Kashmir had introduced us. A short, handsome man, Geelani was warm and
bookish. He told me that he had left Kashmir before the insurgency. He
had studied in other parts of India before coming to the university in the
early 1990s. He seemed happy to see me at the university and lamented
the collapse of the educational system in Kashmir. "Delhi will teach you
a lot and open your horizons," he said. "Here, the bigger world opens
to you. Work hard." Geelani had talked a lot about his teaching job at a
Delhi University college. He spoke with the pride of a small-town boy
who had worked his way up to the faculty of a prestigious university. We
walked to the hostel cafeteria for tea. His easygoing manner contrasted
with the nervousness that I had seen in many other young Kashmiris in
Delhi. When we talked about Kashmir, he showed none of the raw pas-
sion or emotion that most Kashmiris did. He seemed to have accepted
Delhi as his world. I saw Geelani occasionally after that, but we did not
progress beyond the usual pleasantries.

In Srinagar, the police arrested two other Kashmiri men: Mohammed Afzal, who had joined a Kashmiri militant group in the early 1990s,
then laid down his arms and apparently started a business; and Shaukat
Guru, his businessman cousin. They lived in Delhi but had left for the
valley on the day of the attack. The police also arrested Afshan Guru,
Shaukat's wife. All three arrested men were from Baramulla, a border
district in North Kashmir; they lived in the same area in Delhi and knew
one another. They were booked under the draconian Prevention of Terrorism Ordinance (POTO), introduced a month after the September 11
attacks. In March 2002 the ordinance became a law. Indian opposition
parties and civil rights groups such as Amnesty International opposed it,
but the global war against terror was taking its toll on civil liberties in
India.

The arrested men were interrogated. The police claimed that Afzal,
the main accused, had confessed to his involvement. Rajbir Singh, the
assistant commissioner in the anti-terrorism cell of the Delhi police,
had invited television crews to record Afzal's public confession, which
was then broadcast across India. A tall, sturdy man with rugged fea-

tures, Singh had risen from being a lowly subinspector to his present prestigious position in just a few years. His role in six separate killings of alleged terrorists and gangsters had provoked questioning by various Indian newspapers and magazines. Singh was already under a cloud when the home ministry, under Advani, appointed him to head the investigation into the attack on the Indian parliament. It was under Singh's direction that Geelani was arrested.

Soon after Geelani's arrest, I left Srinagar for Baramulla. I drove for two hours past miles of leafless poplars and apple trees, past soldiers huddled in small groups around fires of twigs, past gray hills rolling in the distance. Baramulla began with the striking redbrick complex of a colonial high school run by British missionaries facing an enormous Indian military garrison. A little farther on, it was a noisy bazaar of hundreds of similar shops selling groceries, clothes, stationery, carpets, cement— almost anything. Signs for math tutors or computer-programming classes competed for attention with models drinking Coke or balancing precariously on new bikes. The town seemed to live up to its reputation of relative wealth and high education.

Baramulla stretched along the two banks of the Jhelum River on its westward journey to Pakistan and the Arabian Sea. I drove across a wide wooden bridge spanning the river. Thousands of naked brick houses spread out from the riverbank to the massive arc of mountains forming the northern limits of the town.

"Where is Professor Geelani's house?" I asked a shopkeeper.

"Are you from the press?" he replied, quickly stepping out of his shop and shaking my hand. "Geelani is being framed, sir! We know him. He is no terrorist!" His voice grew louder with every word. "We know him very well," an older man said. He placed his hand on my shoulder and looked gravely into my eyes. "He has nothing to do with the parliament attack." "That is what I was saying." The shopkeeper raised his voice higher. A small crowd had circled me within seconds. "That boy is an angel," the old man concluded. I extricated myself. A teenager jumped into my car and directed the driver to the Geelani house.

We stopped outside an old house of limestone and red brick. A mur-

mur rose from the crowd in the courtyard, and scores of eyes stared at me. A frail old man in an elegant sheepskin cap led me inside. "I am Habibullah. Professor Geelani is my son-in-law," he said. A dozen visitors reclined against pillows placed along the walls. Everyone rose to shake our hands. *"Salam-u-alikum Haz! Salam-u-alikum Masterji!"* The same greeting that people gave my grandfather the schoolmaster. Habibullah had retired as a school headmaster some years earlier.

Somebody brought tea. Habibullah explained slowly, like a teacher. "Geelani Sahib's father died when he was very young. Life hasn't been easy for him. But he worked hard for years till he got to teach at Delhi University." Habibullah insisted that I drink my tea before he continued. I did. "He is a responsible man. I gave him my daughter in marriage. They have a boy and a girl. He is a responsible father and a responsible husband." The visitors drank tea in silence, nodding in agreement. "It is impossible. He has nothing to do with the parliament attack." Despite his grief and shock, Habibullah maintained a dignified air. "Hundreds of people have been coming to the house to express support. They want to protest on the highway against his arrest. But I have to stop them." He feared that demonstrations, as they typically did in Kashmir, would lead to anti-India sloganeering, which would anger the government and damage the chances of his son-in-law's release. "We will fight for his release in court."

I then sought out Geelani's younger brother, Bismillah, who lived in Delhi with Geelani's wife and children. Bismillah told me that he had visited his brother a week after his arrest; he was living in a cagelike room at a Delhi police interrogation center. Geelani was limping and had wounds on his ankles; nylon ropes had left blue marks on his wrists. Bismillah had brought him some food, but the torture had left Geelani without the appetite or energy to eat. The brothers met again a week later, this time in jail, where Geelani was in solitary confinement and denied access to books, paper, or the jail library. Criminals looked upon him as a terrorist and an anti-national and had assaulted him several times. Around that time, university officials suspended Geelani from his teaching job.

In May 2002 the police filed a charge sheet against him. At the same time, his landlord evicted his wife and children, who had to find refuge in a Muslim ghetto in another part of the city. It was not until July that Geelani's trial began. It proceeded not under the usual Indian law but under the controversial new Prevention of Terrorism Act. Amnesty International questioned whether a fair trial was possible. The Indian law ministry appointed Shiv Narayan Dhingra as a special judge. Dhingra had specialized in cases of terrorism and had earned the nickname the Hanging Judge.

I was assigned to report on the trial. Policemen with automatic rifles guarded the courtroom; they checked my identity card and frisked me before allowing me inside. I had expected a crowd of reporters but was surprised to see very few there. Policemen, both uniformed and plainclothed, occupied most of the chairs, along with the lawyers in black gowns. Geelani stood in the dock with the other accused. I thought of our first meeting at Delhi University in 1999. He now stood before me, accused of conspiring in the attack on the Indian parliament that had almost triggered a nuclear war between India and Pakistan. I couldn't stop looking at his handcuffs and at the three armed policemen watching him. Over the next few months, I kept going back to the trial. Each time Geelani's brother, Bismillah, and father-in-law, Habibullah, sat in the courtroom with gloomy faces. And each time Geelani stood in the dock with the same serene expression. I often wondered why he appeared so unfazed.

Perhaps he was given hope by the Indian intellectuals who believed that he was innocent and had come together under the banner of the All India Defense Committee for Syed Abdul Rahman Geelani. Many teachers and journalists had written letters of protest to the chief justice. Initially, there was no criminal lawyer ready to defend him in court. Finally, Seema Gulati, a well-known, sought-after criminal lawyer, agreed. Her high fees were paid by contributions from university teachers, lawyers, and civil rights activists.

The prosecution presented the evidence. It said that Geelani had received a call on his mobile phone on December 14, 2001, from Kashmir, in which he had supported the previous day's attack on the parliament. This two-and-a-half-minute telephone conversation in Kashmiri with his younger brother was the main evidence against him. The police had it translated by a semiliterate Kashmiri youth, Rashid Ali, who worked as a fruit vendor in North Delhi. The incriminating evidence, according to the police translation, was this: Caller (Faisal): "What is this you have done in Delhi?" Receiver (Geelani): "This was necessary."

The conversation, police said, revealed the role of the teacher in the conspiracy to attack the parliament. Seema Gulati produced two respected Kashmiris as defense witnesses: Sampath Prakash, a veteran trade union leader from Srinagar; and Sanjay Kak, a well-known film-maker. The witnesses maintained that the call was an innocent conversation between two brothers that had been mistranslated. Kak's translation of the same conversation was markedly different. Caller: "What's happened?" Receiver: "What? In Delhi?" Caller: "What's happened? In Delhi?" Receiver (noise, laughter): "By God!" Giving evidence in court, Kak said, "The Kashmiri equivalent of 'What's happened?' is *Yeh Kya Korua*. It is a broad term used in all kinds of circumstances, such as when a child spills a glass of milk or when there is snowfall or a marital dispute. Geelani's brother had called simply to get a syllabus and a prospectus." Kak translated that portion of the call as: Receiver (Geelani): "Tell me what you want?" Caller (Faisal): "Syllabus and prospectus." The boy was preparing for the medical school entrance examination and wanted a brochure of a school in Delhi.

During the cross-examination, Ali, the police translator, admitted that he could not understand English; he was also shaky in Hindi, the language into which he had translated the call. That day I saw Bismillah and Habibullah smile. Testimonies by independent witnesses seemed to tilt the balance in favor of Geelani's innocence.

One day a fellow reporter, Shams Tahir Khan, who worked for Aaj Tak, a popular Hindi-language Indian news channel, took the stand. He was one of the television reporters invited by Singh, the Delhi police officer, to record the confession of the main accused, Mohammed Afzal, after his arrest. The full version of the video interview was played in the courtroom. Afzal was seen saying that Geelani was a professor and that he, Afzal, "never shared any of this [terrorism-related] information with him." Khan told the court that Assistant Commissioner Singh had requested the media not to relay that part of the interview. Geelani, his relatives, and his lawyer seemed more relieved; their smiles were broader.

Other days revealed other flaws in the case against Geelani. By November the witnesses had testified, the accused had given their statements, and the final arguments in the case had begun. The Delhi high court had ordered that Geelani's handcuffs be taken off, though armed policemen still filled the courtroom. Barring a few reporters, the media continued to ignore the trial. The prosecution argued for Geelani's conviction for conspiring in the attack on the Indian parliament. The grounds were that he had supported the attack while talking on the phone; he knew the other accused; his phone number was found on their phones; and he had received calls from one of the accused on the day of the attack. Geelani did not deny knowing the co-accused and speaking to them on the phone.

On December 16, 2002, when the judge was to deliver the verdict, Habibullah did not come to the court. Instead, led by Singh, personnel from the Delhi police's anti-terrorism wing—who had arrested Geelani and conducted the investigation—filled the courtroom. The policemen, who were usually unshaven and shabbily clothed, were dressed in expensive suits with matching neckties. They would look good in the newspaper photographs tomorrow, I thought. The courtroom was for once crowded with reporters. I stood close to the judge's table, hoping to hear every word of the verdict. It was very humid. A reporter shouted at an attendant to switch on the air conditioner. It did not work. A reporter standing behind me placed his notebook on my back for support to take notes.

Judge Dhingra walked in. There was a long silence in the courtroom. Nobody moved while he pronounced the verdict. He held the accused teacher, Geelani, guilty of "conspiracy to attack the parliament, wage war against the government of India, murder and grievous hurt." The two other men were also found guilty. Geelani remained silent. I kept looking at him. He seemed to see me, but his eyes said nothing. Two days after the verdict, Judge Dhingra sentenced Geelani to death, along with the co-accused Kashmiris, Mohammed Afzal and Shaukat Guru.

Geelani was stoic and sought the judge's permission to speak to the journalists. Judge Dhingra granted it. "Without justice, there will be no democracy. It is the Indian democracy that is under threat," Geelani shouted.

Policemen whisked Geelani and the other convicted men toward prison trucks. Television crews jostled for close-ups. Bismillah watched him being taken away and burst into tears. In Baramulla, hundreds of protesters burst out onto the streets as the news spread.

One of India's most respected lawyers and a former federal law minister, Ram Jethmalani, agreed to defend Geelani in the higher courts without payment, prompting activists of the Hindu extremist Shiv Sena (the Army of Shivaji, named after a medieval Hindu chieftain who fought the Mughal rulers of India) to burn the lawyer in effigy as a traitor and threaten him with consequences if he honored his promise. Jethmalani stood his ground. He filed an appeal against Geelani's conviction in the Delhi high court. Its judges began their hearings in April 2003. Hearings and arguments followed. If Judge Dhingra's order was upheld, Geelani would be hanged.

In October the high court pronounced its verdict. Geelani was acquitted of all charges. He was free. He is back at his college, teaching.

Part Two   **Journeys**

9 ⤶ I See You Again

I had begun to think seriously about returning to Kashmir, where far grimmer things were happening. I had shared some stories with a few friends in Delhi, but I could never say everything. I would find myself stopping in the middle of a sentence, rendered inarticulate by memory. The telling, even in the shade of intimacy, was painful. And a sense of shame overcame me every time I walked into a bookstore. People from almost every conflict zone had told their stories: Palestinians, Israelis, Bosnians, Kurds, Tibetans, Lebanese, East Germans, Africans, East Timorese, and many more. I felt the absence of the unwritten books of the Kashmiri experience. The memories and stories of Kashmir that I had carried with me could fade away. I had to find the words to save them from the callous varnish of time. I had to write. And to write, I had to return and revisit the people and places that had haunted me for years.

Among the few literary responses to Kashmir, the poems of Kashmiri-American poet Agha Shahid Ali were the foremost. I often turned to his verses, which evoked the fear, the tension, the anger, and the hopelessness of our experience. I had met Shahid only in his books—*Country Without a Post Office*, *Half-Inch Himalayas*, and *Rooms Are Never Finished*. I had seen him smile from wooden frames in his elegant house in southern Srinagar and watched his father, Agha Ashraf Ali, a retired professor, entertain a constant flow of visitors curious to hear about his poet son. Shahid had died of cancer in 2001 in Brooklyn. Newspapers in Kashmir printed his poems every other day in the autumn of 2001, during his final days. Prayers for him rose from all the mosques of Kashmir.

I caught glimpses of Shahid the man from an essay that his friend the novelist Amitav Ghosh wrote in *The Nation*. One day Ghosh accompanied Shahid and his siblings to a hospital for one of his many unsuccessful surgeries. Shahid tried to walk on his own but fell and had to be put in a wheelchair. Ghosh wrote, "When the hospital orderly returned with the wheelchair Shahid gave him a beaming smile and asked where he was from. Ecuador, the man said, and Shahid clapped his hands gleefully together. 'Spanish!' he cried, at the top of his voice. 'I always wanted to learn Spanish. Just to read Lorca.' At this the tired, slack-shouldered orderly came suddenly to life. 'Lorca? Did you say Lorca?' He quoted a few lines, to Shahid's great delight. 'Ah! *"La Cinque de la Tarde,"*' Shahid cried, rolling the syllables gleefully around his tongue. 'How I love those words. *"La Cinque de la Tarde"*!'"

To me, Shahid continued to speak from the black lettering:

I write on that void:
Kashmir, Kaschmir, Cashmere, Qashmir,
Cashmir, Cashmire, Kashmere, Cachemire,
Cushmeer, Cachmiere, Casmir

One summer afternoon one of my editors called me to discuss possible story ideas. I found myself telling him I was going to resign. He offered me a raise. But I was going home. I was going to Kashmir. My editor wished me luck.

That night I did not set my alarm clock. I spent the next few weeks buying books: books I badly wanted to read, books I had heard about, and books I had never heard about. Discussions with friends and hard goodbyes followed.

A quick look at my savings had ruled out the possibility of flying. A

few weeks later, I left with my bags to catch a bus to Kashmir. The setting sun lit the sandstone domes and minarets of the Red Fort. Local
buses and cars screeched by; cargo-laden rickshaws pulled by sunburned,
sweat-drenched men negotiated their way. The rickshaw driver stopped
by a row of tin shacks with gaudy travel operator signs running parallel
to the ramparts of the fort. Touts pounced upon weary passengers. They
acted with such ferocity that I wondered whether they thought of their
potbellied bosses sitting behind the wooden desks of travel offices as
incarnations of Mughal emperors.

I ignored the touts, lit a cigarette, and took slow, deliberate puffs
while scanning the signs. "Are you a Kashmiri?" a wiry man with dishev-
eled curly hair and a beaklike nose asked. I smiled back. Both his nose
and his question were very Kashmiri. The question asked in Kashmiri
was a greeting, a question one Kashmiri asks another Kashmiri in any
situation, in any corner of the world, the moment he realizes his com-
panion is from Kashmir. I have answered and asked this question. It
comes with an informal smile and more questions aimed at placing you
in Kashmir.

Ramesh was a Hindu from the Budgam district in central Kashmir.
His family had migrated to Delhi in the early nineties. He lived in a slum
in South Delhi. I had been there as a reporter. Ramesh lived in a shabby
municipal building that lay abandoned for years before the Delhi government settled the Kashmiri Pandit migrants there. Tattered curtains, tied
by nylon strings to the nails in the walls, served as partitions between
a dozen or so families of five to six each. Outside the building, women
had erected makeshift kitchens in the courtyard. The stench from the
community toilets could not be kept at bay. Ramesh complained about
the heat in Delhi. He missed his village in Kashmir; his eyes spoke of
the shade of willows, the cold streams, and the apple orchards where he
had grown up. "You are lucky, you are going home," he said. The touts
were lurking, eyeing potential customers. They seemed to remind him
of something; he was not at ease.

"Are you all right?" I asked.

"Yes. We got talking and I forgot about work."

"You work here?"

"Yes. I earn a commission for every passenger I take to the travel agency," he said in a lowered voice. He had hoped to get me to buy a ticket from his agency.

I looked at his somber face. "I want a ticket to Srinagar. Let us get it."

Ramesh got me the ticket for an air-cooled deluxe coach. The bus would arrive in ten minutes and leave in half an hour. I sat on a wooden bench outside the travel agency. We shook hands, and Ramesh left in search of passengers. I watched his lean frame move slowly toward the main road as he looked for potential passengers. He waved at incoming rickshaws, accosted people with travel bags, and disappeared into the crowd.

A battered white bus came in half an hour. The traffic outside had lessened; a dark night covered Delhi, and streetlights rose like artificial moons. We needed five more passengers before the bus could move. I got out of the bus and strolled about. I was worried about how my family would react to my decision to leave my job and my ideas of writing. I went over various versions of my plans to travel in Kashmir, revisit places and people, and write about them. I had my own fear to deal with as well. Maybe I was making a mistake? Maybe I should have waited longer and prepared myself better? The bus eventually took off. It would be a long ride—twenty-seven hours.

I woke up quite late in the morning. By midafternoon, the bus had dragged itself on the serpentine highway running through the high mountains. We were about to enter the valley of Kashmir when Indian army trucks with nets thrown over their roofs began passing by regularly. Soldiers in camouflage and bulletproof jackets and caps patrolled the road, their rifles pointed aggressively at some unseen enemy. Waving the barrel of his assault rifle, a soldier ordered us to stop. A passenger jeered, "Welcome to Kashmir."

We were at the Banihal tunnel, which had been bored through the mountain by Swiss engineers in 1953. Across the tunnel lies the valley of Kashmir. Two soldiers boarded the bus and began checking our luggage; we walked in a queue toward a sandbagged check post. One by one we entered, our hands raised. The soldiers stared at our identity cards and frisked us. There was a strange familiarity to this ritual. It was oppressive and intimate at the same time. In some perverse way, it signaled reaching home.

The bus entered the two-mile-long misty tunnel, barely lit by sodium lamps. The groan of the engine and the song of the tires echoed against the dark, rocky walls. Ten minutes seemed very long. Then the tunnel opening appeared as a blinding semicircle of light.

I opened the window, rose on my toes, and popped my head out the window: Kashmir! There she was: the bluest of the skies over the browns, greens, and blues of the million-inch Himalayas. The bus swerved around a bend, and she was a wide valley spreading out in a gentle wave of paddy fields toward a majestic arc of mountains. The breeze healed me of the Indian summer. I stretched my neck, and my eyes wandered over the peaks, seeking the range I'd grown up with. I saw the mountains that hid my village and the taller, bluer range near my school. The metaled road fell like a black ribbon toward the valley; tall, elegant poplars by the roadside and shorter, greener willows along the wedges of the paddies stood in neat rows as the bus passed village after village of small, tin-roofed brick and wood houses. The dying sun glinted on the roof of a mosque, shopkeepers pulled down their shutters, bus conductors shouted names of villages and called their residents for the journey home, and children waved at the faces half glimpsed through a bus window.

An hour and a half later, I was entering Srinagar. Modern Srinagar began with the largest military camp in Kashmir: Badami Bagh, the garden of almonds, on the highway connecting Srinagar to the southern province of Jammu. It lay facing a shabby market of tea stalls, tailors, and grocery shops and was surrounded by high concrete walls, rows of iron barricades, sandbag bunkers, and alert soldiers in bulletproof jackets. Along the highway stood a row of military vehicles; a little ahead, three stray dogs and a bull fought over the right to sniff the rubbish and look for leftovers. The dogs barked at the bull; the bull swayed his horns at them.

The sun had set, the shops were closed, and soldiers patrolled the roads. The closed iron shutters of the shops stared across Lal Chowk. Flamboyant signs announcing the names of the stores had mellowed in the night. A few rickshaws were parked on the corner of Lambert Lane, branching off the main square. The faint sulfur rays of a streetlight fell on the drivers huddled along the stairs of an astrologer's office. Farther ahead, past an armored military vehicle, the empty avenue bordered by chinar trees led to a watchtower whose clock had stopped working.

I boarded a rickshaw, a green-and-black golf cart–like three-wheeler that thrived in the space between the bus and the cab. The driver switched on a bulb that washed us in a bright yellow light. You always switched on that bulb to let the soldiers see you. The Armed Forces Special Powers Act, a law introduced by the Indian government, gave all Indian soldiers posted in Kashmir the power to shoot any person suspected of being a threat. It also provided them immunity from prosecution in a court of law. Passing by in a rickshaw without a bulb could raise fatal suspicion in a patrol. We drove through empty roads and streets, stopped at check posts, showed my identity card, and opened my bags. The rickshaw drove on through streets without streetlights; faint glows of candles and kerosene lamps lit the houses. Stray dogs barked and whined as I entered my father's house.

Over the next few weeks, I introduced the idea of book writing to my father. He had recently acquired an Internet connection; in the process of teaching him to Web surf, I took him on a virtual tour of various literary magazines and journals. "They make much more sense than the newspapers," Father pronounced after a few weeks. But he was stunned when I told him, "That is what I want to try. I want to write about our life and society like this. In fact, I have quit my job to do just that." He stared at the computer screen, displaying an interview with the great Polish poet-reporter Ryszard Kapuściński in a literary magazine. Father asked me to shut down the computer. "It is quite late now." He walked slowly out of my room. He would have to explain to our nosy relatives and his friends why his grown-up son did not go to an office or have a regular job like most people his age.

I spent my first few days catching up with old friends. One of those days we received an invitation for a wedding. As usual, the words on the card read: MARRIAGES ARE MADE IN HEAVEN; THEY ARE ONLY CELEBRATED ON EARTH. Ashraf, a neighbor's son in my village, was getting married. He'd been a tall, skinny boy when we played cricket in the neighborhood threshing field as children. Now he assisted a contractor who built parapets, roads, and bridges. "He personally dropped the invitation here. You have to go," Mother said.

It had been many years since I had stayed in our house in the village. First my studies and later my work had kept me away. After the mine blast, my parents had moved to Srinagar, and I usually stayed there during my visits.

I caught the bus to Anantnag the next day. The road to my village reminded me of the pictures of Kosovo. The government, in a bid to widen the road and offer better facilities to the tourists visiting Pahalgam—the hill station a few hours ahead—had demolished most houses on both sides of the road. Multicolored marble tiles that had decorated kitchens and bathroom walls stared at me through the hollows made by strokes of the government bulldozers. My village seemed to have changed a lot; new houses had come up on the fields outside the village.

The new house my grandfather had built was one of them. But our mountains—a gently rolling arc of pine a mile away and higher, sharp, rocky cliffs in the distance—were the same, the empty terraces of harvested rice fields, the conical golden haystacks dotting them, and the hum of the Lidder stream beyond brought back the sounds of my childhood. I spent my first evening walking leisurely amid our fields and apple orchards, watched them change shades as the sun moved farther west. Here I had learned to speak, walk, read, write, run, swear, and play. Here I had slept my best sleep.

I woke up late the next morning. In a replay of the scenes from my childhood, Grandfather knocked on the door of my room. His tone had changed from the scary shout to a mellow whisper. After a round of noon chai, we set out for our old neighborhood. "Ashraf is now earning a decent sum, so his family decided to get him married," Grandfather said. We reached the narrow alley leading to his house. The old house of mud bricks and a thatched roof was decorated with miniature lights in green, yellow, and red plastic covers. A shimmering white tent stood in the courtyard.

Ashraf sat on a chair amid a crowd of women and children. He looked elegant in collared *kurta* pajamas over which he wore a black vest. He spotted me standing in a corner. He rose from his seat; we met with a hug and a laugh. "So you are getting married today!" I said. He smiled and said, "One has to marry sooner or later." He held my hand and took me toward his seat. "I am very happy you came. It has been a long time." I sat next to Ashraf on a chair someone brought in a hurry. The girls sang at a high pitch. Boys with pimpled faces shaved with much care kept finding excuses to stand around the groom and steal glances at the girls. Busy-looking men in loose, collared *kurta* pajamas shouted orders that went mostly unheard. Ashraf had to get a haircut before leaving for the bride's house. The local barber arrived with his kit. As the barber set to work, I left to meet the elders.

Behind the house, a narrow alley had been converted into a make-shift kitchen. Food was cooked in copper pots resting on a bonfire lit between two brick rows. The elders had settled themselves in chairs to supervise and chat. My old neighbors and relatives had been permanent characters in my world once. There was Ashraf's father, Khazer, a short, wiry man who always wore a skull cap to hide his bald head and would give me a piece of *jaggery* (candy) whenever I went to their house. There was his uncle Amjad, who always looked about to die and used to ask children to thump his back to relieve him of the backache; I often hit him a bit too hard, running away before he could hit me with his equally aged cane. Among the young men helping out was Nissar, a childhood friend. A bald man sat on a *pategih*, a mat woven from hay, puffing a hoo-kah. It was Bashir, our neighborhood grocer, at whose expense I'd had some insensitive laughs in the early days of the conflict.

I watched Bashir from a distance. I was happy to see him after many years, happy to see he had survived. He almost jumped from his seat when I greeted him. "God! You have grown up, really grown up!" He hugged me and shook my hand repeatedly. We sat together, and he told me about his daughter's marriage. "You did not come for Alia's marriage." He sounded hurt. I explained, "I was in Delhi, tied up with work." He asked about me, and I gave the standard answers. But something worried me; his manner had changed. He used the formal language and reverential manner we used for guests. I went on to meet Khazer, Amjad, Nissar, and others. I had expected the old informality, but they, too, treated me like a guest. Khazer told me to sit in a room reserved for guests. When I volunteered to do some chores, Amjad stopped me. Nissar, who had never left the village, carried plates and served the guests. The chores that neighborhood youth helped with were not for me now.

I had been away in different places and lived a different life. But every time I filled out a form asking for a permanent address, I wrote: *Seer Hamdan, Anantnag, Kashmir.* Though bad with numbers, I never forgot the postal code of my village: 192129. I could not forget the village post office, with its smoke billowing out of the rusted tin pipe of a *bukhari*, the dusty maroon billboard, and the khaki-clad postal clerks. And Ramji, our postman, who I thought had been born old, with his uncombed salt-and-pepper hair falling on his wrinkled face beneath which shoulders drooped over a wiry frame. In the morning he repaired cooking stoves near the butcher's shop, and in the afternoon he went around the village on his bicycle, hanging his jute bag on his left shoulder, ringing the bell and stopping wherever he had to deliver a letter. The village children ran after him, shouting in a chorus, "Is there a letter for me, Ramji?" until he was irritated and chased us away. The letters Ramji delivered had no house numbers, no street names. They had your name, your father's name, and the name of the village. Ramji knew everyone; the letters reached their addressees. I do not get any mail at that address anymore. But still, whenever I fill out a form, faces of that lost world beckon me.

Till the mid-eighties, nobody had a telephone; a couple of families used to have a television. People often gathered at Gani Haji, the *tonga wallah's* house, to watch television. He had been to Mecca for Hajj, the Islamic pilgrimage, and brought back a black-and-white television set. Almost everybody with some weight assembled at Haji's house. The television set used to be in a ground-floor room, and you could see it through a window. Before our families got television sets in the latter part of the eighties, my friend Aafaiz and I often climbed on each other's shoulders to get the view through the window.

Radio told us the news, and newspapers were rare. Then the meaning of news was different. It did not mean the daily body count that it became after 1990. News was not about self-determination, sovereignty, or terrorism; about summits, strategies, and geopolitics; about fundamentalism, tolerance, and secularism. News was made in places nobody from our village had been. News was not about us. I remember returning home one day with a copy of the largest-selling English-language newspaper in India, the *Times of India*, from Anantnag. Before I could get home, a bunch of village elders who idled at a shop near our house called me over. I had to show them the newspaper; they gaped at the printed words and the newspaper pictures. Since it was an English paper, I was asked to read it out loud and translate as well. Over a decade had passed since that day in the mid-eighties. The elders had grown older; the children were young men. Amjad and Uncle Khazer still gossiped at the same shop with other men. Newspapers came regularly to our village. Every rooftop flaunted a television antenna. There were three cable television operators in the village, offering fifty television channels, including BBC, CNN, and various Indian news channels, for ninety rupees a month. People watched the news and read the newspapers. News was about us, too, now. Aafaiz, my friend from the days when there was only one television in the entire village, ran a cable network.

Night fell, and after dinner Ashraf was brought into the tent. It was the night of henna tattoos: *maenziraat*. Women and girls circled him and sang the traditional wedding songs. His mother applied henna to his smallest finger; friends and relatives took pictures with the groom. I decided against sleep; this was an occasion of Kashmiri songs sung with fervor to the beats of a *tumbaknaer*, an earthen drumlike instrument covered with goatskin on one end, which the women beat deftly. The tent boomed with the voices of women and girls in shiny, embroidered clothes, singing a Kashmiri classic:

Hooreh Chayyih Wanwaan Nooreh Mahraazo
Aakho Shahrekih Sheerazo Aakho Shahrekih Sheerazo
(Houris sing for the angel-faced groom,
He is the jewel of the city)

An hour later, some teenagers brought two speakers and a CD player into the tent. Most of them wore knockoffs of Calvin Klein, Lee, and Levi's jeans and T-shirts. Two boys with gym-pumped bodies in acrylic shirts saying HERO and SPORTY set up the system. Loud blasts of Hindi film music drowned out the traditional songs. A few old women protested. Girls blushed with happiness and formed a circle around the boys, who danced to a Bollywood hit. Slowly, the women moved closer and watched with awe the boys gyrating self-consciously to the Hindi songs. The loud music, the mediocre lyrics, and the Bollywood dance moves had overrun the traditional celebration.

In the morning Ashraf's father told me to sit with the men who were to accompany Ashraf to the bride's house, where the *nikah*—the signing of the wedding contract, with two witnesses on each side—was to be held, followed by *wazawaan*, the traditional Kashmiri cuisine of thirty-six varieties of meat. It was meant only for close relatives and special guests.

I wandered for a while through the lanes, catching glimpses of my past everywhere until I found myself in the courtyard of a double-storied tin-roofed house. There were no children on its lawn; there was no cow with black spots on its white hide tied to a peg in a corner, thoughtfully chewing the grass, nor did a blue bicycle lie next to the cowshed. Its cemented boundary wall was new to my eyes. The woman curiously eyeing me from the kitchen window was a stranger. "Who are you looking for?" she asked. I did not know what to say. I was looking for myself; the house she now owned was the house I was born in. It was the home whose memories I carried with me. It was my eternal home in thought, transferred by ownership deed.

Ashraf was preparing to leave for his bride's house. He wore a light brown suit, brown leather shoes, and white headgear embroidered with silver thread. Two marigold garlands and three garlands of ten-rupee notes hung around his neck. The men and women who would accompany him were all hanging around in the courtyard. There was the usual talk about who would be next and how, after the fighting began, the average marriage age in Kashmir had gone from the mid-twenties to the early thirties. Ashraf was thirty-two, his bride thirty. Delays in education and difficulties finding work kept pushing the wedding dates back, much to the annoyance of impatient parents and grandparents. It had become especially worrisome for girls' parents; most of the dead were young men, and thousands more had injuries, depression, and nonexistent careers.

Women and girls formed a circle, held hands, and sang. They moved back and forth, tapped their feet, shook their heads, raised and lowered their voices. It was an old custom practiced before the groom left for the bride's house after sunset, returning after a late dinner. Kashmiris discarded that centuries-old tradition after the evening of May 16, 1990, when Indian paramilitaries fired upon a marriage party and raped the bride.

10 ⤚ City of No Joy

In old pictures, Srinagar is elegant latticed houses, mosques, and temples admiring each other from the banks of the River Jhelum; it is people strolling on the seven wooden bridges and wandering into old bazaars selling spices, lovingly embroidered shawls and carpets, and samovars with intricate engravings, or stepping with a prayer and an expectation into a medieval shrine, flaunting verses of the Quran and poems of mystics on windows and facades, and the gentle greens and blues of papier-mâché interiors. But elegance is granted little space in an age of wars. Those wooden bridges have either collapsed or been torn down. Their skeletons remain in the shadow of new arcs of concrete.

My parents live near the left bank of the Jhelum, a short walk from the eighth bridge, built later and named the Zero Bridge. Lal Chowk, the city center, is right across the river. I walked past the three neighborhood bunkers, an ATM machine, a mosque, grocers, chemists, and stationery shops before reaching the riverbank. Half-dried clothing hung from nylon ropes tied to the masts of white and caramel houseboats waiting for visitors. A few eagles flew over majestic chinar trees on the other bank, circled over the Zero Bridge, and seemed to rise even higher than the mountains drawing a border in the city's east. An old boatman sat in a *shikara*, holding a rough willow branch he used as an oar, waiting for passengers. He urged me to sit toward his end of the boat and leave room for others. I walked with a sense of dread over the decaying planks of timber through which water was seeping in. The boatman switched on his radio and pushed the boat into the river with a thrust of the willow branch against the bank. The passengers clutched the sides of the boat. A song floated over the tense silence.

A few minutes later, we reached the other bank, paid one rupee each, and after showing our identity cards to a group of soldiers patrolling the riverbank, walked over to the city center. Lal Chowk is a busy avenue of sixties-style buildings. Hawkers selling cheap knockoffs of name-brand shoes and electronic gadgets spilled over the footpaths, and carpet shops hung rugs and shawls and made competing claims of being great works of Kashmiri craftsmanship. Small mobs pounced on newsstands to buy newspapers, and bawdy Bollywood lyrics blared from various shops selling pirated videos and CDs. Indian soldiers patrolled the road and looked around like weathercocks. I was struck by a name painted on an armored military truck parked by the roadside. I had seen such names but never paid much attention. The Hindi letters, which few Kashmiris can read, said: MAHAKAAL—literally, great death, and one of the names of Shiva, the Hindu god of destruction.

I walked past Mahakaal to one of the more reliable Internet cafés housed in an old commercial complex. Near the entrance, a crowd of young and old men hovered around a mobile tea shop. Cement flaked off the walls of the building, and dark stairs led to the café. I entered a brightly lit room. Wooden cubicles hugged the garish walls. The young manager and a girl wearing a thick coat of lipstick sat behind a wooden counter. "Sexy Lady" played from an invisible speaker. The cabins had two chairs each, and planks of teakwood revealed only feet: sneakers, sandals; sneakers, sandals; sneakers, sandals. Young couples bought an hour of privacy for thirty rupees. I had barely managed to send a single e-mail when the connection snapped after half an hour. Nobody complained. I thought of my first visit to the café in 2001, soon after it opened. For security reasons, the government had ordered every user to show an identity card and provide his address before using the Internet. At least that had been done away with now.

Outside, the number of cars on the roads had increased. One could barely drive through Lal Chowk without being caught in a traffic jam. Everyone talked about the abundance of easy personal loans and the huge amounts of money both India and Pakistan had pumped into Kashmir to win loyalties—the war economy. The only institution that had thrived in Kashmir throughout the conflict was a bank. Walking around in Srinagar, I would find myself facing a billboard announcing yet another licensee for a stockbroker in Bombay or Delhi. A lot of money was being invested in shares and stocks. On my return, I met Ayaar, an old friend from college. A mechanical engineer by training and a fanatical detective fiction fan, he had turned to stock brokerage after three years of unemployment. We walked to his office in one of the many newly built ugly malls in Srinagar. A billboard announced the office. We walked into a damp half-lit room with bare walls; he checked three flickering monitors. After the customary round of tea, he tried to persuade me to invest in stocks.

After a few minutes, two young men walked in. "We want to invest in shares," one said, "but have no idea how it works." My friend metamorphosed into a stockbroker. He pulled up two chairs, sent his office boy to fetch tea for the guests, grabbed a few brochures, and earnestly began to explain the business to the clueless youth. Fifteen minutes later, he was back at the flickering monitor with another round of explanations. He pointed out the stocks rising and falling, identified blue-chip stocks, and told stories about the man who had made a hundred thousand rupees in five hours. "You keep your eyes open, look for the clues, and this is where you will make money." Like a passionate evangelist, Ayaar continued preaching to strengthen the faith of his converts. The share bazaar seemed like detective fiction: The right clues led to the gold mine. Stocks and shares were words from a language foreign to me: the language of Wall Street, of Bombay, of corporate India. It was here along with the armored cars, funerals, shutdowns/strikes, fear, and despair. Srinagar built memorials for its disappeared young alongside shopping malls with gaudy glass facades.

• • •

I slowly settled down in my parents' house, arranging my books and placing my desk and computer by a window with a view of chinar and mulberry trees. Parrots, sparrows, and eagles flew in and out of the trees into a clear blue sky. It was autumn: the season of golden chinar leaves falling on dried grass, on footpaths, on people passing by. I was happy to be here and spend my afternoons talking to friends in coffee shops near Lal Chowk.

Srinagar is also a greeting, an encounter with a confidant on every street. It is not providing contexts and chronologies to my stories and not explaining the details and the meanings. It is conveying more in a single spoken phrase than in paragraphs and pages in my adopted languages. It is talking endlessly about our shared past, not so much the remote historical past but the recent past—of the fairy-tale childhood of the eighties and the horror of the nineties.

As a schoolboy in the mid-1980s, I had visited Pari Mahal—the Palace of the Fairies—built in the seventeenth century by the liberal Mughal prince Dara Shikhoh. Dara Shikhoh preferred scholarship to statecraft, inviting many learned men to his palace to translate texts of Hindu philosophy, religion, and literature into Persian and Arabic. My father told me these stories over and over because he wanted me to see Pari Mahal as a place of multiple religious traditions. But as a child, I was keener to pose with my classmates for group pictures, play hide-and-seek on the ramparts, or watch the palace—strung, appropriately, with fairy lights—shimmer at night.

One September evening, after showing a visitor's permit and a security check, I returned to Pari Mahal, cresting one of the peaks of the Zabarvan Mountains in eastern Srinagar. Its massive walls of rough stone decorated with arches led to domed chambers, a pattern repeated on its gardened terraces. Below it, the luxurious greens of a forest and an expansive golf course—where politicians, bureaucrats, police, and military officers guarded by scores of armed guards played and socialized on imported American grass—reached out to Dal Lake, the achingly beautiful chameleon changing its shades as light played tricks on its unruffled water. Tourists took photos of the sun rolling toward the quiet, graceful mountains. Near the entrance, two chambers enclosed by granite arches had been converted into barracks and a mess hall. A soldier was busy cooking over a wood fire, and a few others played carom. Behind them in the dome-shaped, dimly lit chamber, automatic rifles rested on cots. A little farther into the palace, on a higher terrace, a sentry with an automatic rifle stood in a sandbagged watchtower. Pari Mahal had become the world's most beautiful paramilitary camp.

I began retracing my visits to the other monuments of Kashmir. I thought of the library of Islamia College, the oldest college in Srinagar, which was burned down in a battle along with many rare manuscripts, including a 1,400-year-old Quran handwritten by Usman, the third caliph of Islam. The 600-year-old shrine of Nooruddin Rishi, the patron Sufi saint of Kashmir, was destroyed in a gun battle between Indian troops and the militants. Hindu temples and Buddhist stupas, circular domed Buddhist shrines, were dying of neglect and misuse, as much a victim of the conflict as people.

The great Indian emperor Ashoka, whose empire covered most of South Asia, founded Srinagari (the City of Wealth) around 250 B.C. on the outskirts of what is modern Srinagar. After one bloody battle, Ashoka renounced violence, became a Buddhist, and dedicated his life to promoting the religion's teachings. It was from the Buddhist seminaries of Kashmir that missionaries spread Buddhism to China and Japan. In 1905 a team of archaeologists led by Daya Ram Sahani, then chief archaeologist of Kashmir, excavated remains of stupas and found Buddhist idols and images of Hindu gods on the mountainside of Pandrethan. Most of those artifacts are stored at the Sri Pratap Singh Museum, named after an eighteenth-century ruler. The only museum in Srinagar is a short walk from the Zero Bridge. Coils of barbed wire lay in front of the tiny gate to the crumbling museum building; soldiers manned a bunker nearby. In the dusty hall, the caretakers gossiped behind a wooden reception counter. They stared at me, the lone visitor, as if I had walked into their living room.

After the awkwardness melted away, I met Mohammed Iqbal, a middle-aged local archaeologist who, despite the conflict, continued to publish booklets about the ancient monuments of Kashmir. The main hall was filled with sculptures from Pandrethan. Iqbal stopped near a glass box containing two free-standing statues. One, a greenish-gray granite idol, portrayed the Buddha after he had renounced the world. His face was broken, but he meditated on. "Look at his half-closed Mongoloid eyes and high eyebrows. That is the Gandharan style, which was highly influenced by the Greek tradition," Iqbal said as he looked at the idol with a smile. He then turned my attention to a black granite statue that depicted the birth of the Buddha as Prince Siddhartha to Queen Maya. Maya, wearing a jeweled crown, two necklaces, and an ornate armband, sat under a tree clutching a branch with one hand and supported by her similarly adorned sister on the other side. "It is not a mere statue, it is a story," explained Iqbal. "Queen Maya, pregnant with Buddha, goes into labor in a forest in Lumbini on the way to her father's house. In her moment of agony, she clutches a branch of a tree and is supported by her sister." The facial features of Maya and her sister are Mongoloid, like those of Buddha. "The ornamentation was the influence of the Maurya and Gupta sculpture of India; the facial features were determined by the Gandharan School. The combination of these two styles was what made the Kashmir school," Iqbal explained.

Farther into the museum, we came across a massive granite sculpture of the Hindu god Shiva, excavated near Pandrethan. It dated to the third century, after Kashmir had reverted to Hinduism. Although the religion had changed, the Buddhist influence was very vivid—the Shiva here looked like Buddha, except with a third eye on the forehead. Many more statues of Buddha, his disciples, and various Hindu gods and goddesses lined the museum hall. Iqbal believed much could be found if the Pandrethan excavations were resumed. But that wasn't likely to happen. "After the monarchy ended and the maharajah acceded to India in 1947," he told me, "the military established their headquarters in the Pandrethan area. After that, because of security reasons, no excavations were allowed there. Things became worse after the conflict, and I haven't been able to visit the Pandrethan archaeological sites that fall under the military camp."

I left the museum to visit the site where some of these statues had been excavated, a mile south of the military headquarters. I walked past the military camp and its propaganda billboards with pictures of smiling, self-conscious soldiers pouring water for old Kashmiri men or showing affection to Kashmiri children. Beneath the pictures were the words: LOVE TRANSCENDS ALL BARRIERS.

A little ahead, I found the village—a small market with signs for soft drinks and potato chips and a cluster of shabby brick-and-cement houses stretching across the plain to the mountains beyond. There were no sites to visit—they still fell under military control—but I was curious whether the villagers knew anything about Ashoka's Srinagar. Two old men vaguely remembered excavations decades ago, but they hadn't heard of Ashoka or his city.

When I was a child, my father told me stories of the Fourth World Buddhist Council, held in Kashmir in the second century under the rule of the learned Gandharan Buddhist king Kanishka. Every now and then someone claimed to have found the true location of the council, but most believed it was held near the ancient Garden of Harwan on the northeastern fringe of Srinagar. On a family excursion to the garden— lined with waterways and shaded by towering chinar trees—my father pointed to the hillock above and told me it was where the council was believed to have gathered.

I went there a few days after visiting the Srinagar museum. A sign, BUDDHIST SITES, guided me to a terraced area where, in 1905, archaeologists found a stupa, a prayer hall, and living quarters. In the center of the site were the remains of the stupa. I stared at its stone base and two concentric squares of roughly polished stones covered with wild grass. It was hard to imagine what it might have looked like. To the left were four fallen stone walls covered with moss. "That was a *vihara*, where the monks met," said Mohammed Khazer, an elderly caretaker who worked for the Archaeological Survey of India, which maintained the site. According to Chinese traveler Hieun Tsang, more than five thousand monks had come together to debate and discuss the faith.

In the museum, I had seen the artifacts from Harwan. They had no relation to the Buddhist council but were fine examples of Gandharan artwork—terra-cotta tiles of floral motifs, an Indo-Greek-looking man running after a deer with a spear, a woman wearing delicate earrings walking with a pitcher on her head, and a husband and wife in conversation on a balcony. The ruins at Harwan hardly seemed a tourist attraction. "Earlier, tourists from Japan and even America would come here," Khazer said, "but nobody came here after the fighting began." Despite the conflict, which devastated Khazer's home village, he continued to spend his days at the site. The task of guarding the monuments was left to watchmen like Khazer after the Archaeological Survey of India moved its office from Srinagar to the southern city of Jammu.

Next to the central ruins, Khazer showed me a recently built wall of polished pebbles interspersed with rough rocks. "The VIHARAS and the stupas were all built like this around the first century. Now some of our archaeologists are trying to create replicas using the same material," he said. There was no other sign of restoration work. The night before, a poet friend wrote to me in an e-mail: "Lovers leave debris like civilizations do." I looked at the debris of the stupa and thought, *Civilizations leave debris like lovers do.*

Back in Srinagar, I visited the Akhund Mullah mosque that the enlightened Mughal prince Dara Shikhoh built for his teacher on the slope of Hari Parbat hill in central Srinagar. I found parts of the complex taken over by squatters. The blue limestone walls of the square edifice were giving way. Its domed roof was falling apart. Some arched windows were gone, replaced by ugly imitations. A Turkish bath next to the mosque had been converted into a gymnasium by the neighborhood youth, and posters of Arnold Schwarzenegger hung from its walls. I read the delicate calligraphy of poetry and Quran verses written on the tiles of the mosque's facade. Hordes of pigeons flew in and out of the holes in the roof; a lonely brass lock hung from the door, which clung to its hinges like a memory of a long-forgotten lover.

Srinagar is a medieval city dying of a modern war. It is empty streets, locked shops, angry soldiers, and boys with stones. It is several thousand military bunkers, four golf courses, and three half-decent bookshops. It is wily politicians repeating their lies about war and peace to television cameras and small crowds gathered by the promise of an elusive job or a daily fee of a few hundred rupees. It is stopping on sidewalks and at traffic lights when the convoys of rulers and their patrons in armored cars secured by machine guns rumble on broken roads. It is staring back or looking away, resigned. Srinagar is never winning and never being defeated.

Srinagar newspapers regularly carry obituaries of dead rebels with young somber faces along with the elegies for the smiling, aging men in expensive suits who guard the gates of privilege. Some print headlines in red, announcing deaths. Some run a box on the front page, giving the daily updated statistics. Srinagar is being in a coffee shop, in an office, outside a college, crossing a bridge, and feeling, touching, breathing history, politics, and war, in unmarked signs and landmarks. Srinagar is seeing a bridge, a clearing, a nondescript building and knowing that men fell here, that a boy was tortured there.

As a reporter, I had the chance to meet Merajuddin, a veteran Kashmiri news photographer, who looked the part in his photographer's jacket. Merajuddin always wore dark sunglasses after he lost his left eye to a splinter from a hand grenade. I once asked him how he had dealt with the violence he encountered as a photographer. He spoke like a man who had seen it all. "I cried like a child when the protesters were massacred at Gawkadal Bridge. Nothing I saw after that made me cry." I remember sitting with my family in my village and hearing the news of the Gawkadal massacre on the BBC World Service; most eyes were moist. The next afternoon I walked with the young and old, men and women, boys and girls of my village shouting slogans in a protest against the massacre. I was too young to understand how brutal brutality could be. But as I grew up and began to understand, the memory haunted me.

Gawkadal was a few hundred yards from Lal Chowk. One afternoon as I was crossing Lal Chowk, a crowd of girls in bright white uniforms emerged from the gates of the nearby women's college, causing a stir amid the clusters of boys loitering around like awkward clones of pop stars. It was the only moment when you saw so many Kashmiri women, who always preferred bright pink, red, blue, and green, wearing white. The boys in a rainbow of T-shirts and regulation denims seemed awestruck. Seeing them reminded me of a recent cartoon in a local newspaper that had depicted a boy holding a begging bowl outside the women's college.

It was a scene that repeated itself every afternoon outside every college and school in Kashmir. Though a largely patriarchal society, Kashmir did put a premium on educating its girls, and they were doing well, winning places in every competitive test—be it the medical colleges, the engineering colleges, the sought-after research degrees in law, journalism, biochemistry, and computer sciences at Kashmir University or elsewhere. On graduating, they were taking their deserved places in the workforce—as teachers, bank managers, doctors, professors, lawyers, journalists, and architects. It was something I always took for granted, growing up surrounded by Mother's five sisters, each of whom got a master's degree in humanities and trained further in teaching before joining various schools and colleges.

Barely a few hundred meters from this lovely chaos was the Maisuma area—a stronghold of the pro-independence Jammu and Kashmir Liberation Front. Newspapers called it the Gaza Strip of Kashmir. Maisuma was a crowded bazaar, and the smell from the cinnamon and cardamom piled on shop fronts in jute sacks wafted across the street. The other smell of Maisuma was that of burning tires and tear gas when the shops were closed and people protested arrests and custodial killings. The Gawkadal Bridge had fallen like the protesters of January 1990. The skeleton remained, two dilapidated pillars standing in a canal full of filth.

On the other side of the bridge was a bunker, and outside the bunker stood two soldiers. A hawker sold bananas from a wooden cart nearby; two men stood next to the cart eating hungrily. I asked them about the massacre. One of them, a man in his mid-thirties whose paunch struggled against his cheap blue sweatshirt, said, "I was in that demonstration." He tossed a banana peel into the muddy canal and told me the place was under curfew for three days; soldiers had cordoned off the massacre site with barbed wire, and armored vehicles were positioned on all lanes. Paramilitaries had offered the residents lentils and bread during the curfew. "But we refused to take their food. Our mothers told us to wear shoes and leave for Pakistan for [arms] training," he said. He picked up another banana and said, "After the massacre, I carried fifteen bodies to the mosque. Their eyes were open; I closed their eyes with my own hands. I will take you to the mosque and show you where we laid the bodies. I will show you the pictures of the bodies, and you can meet the women whose men were killed. But I cannot talk like this. You should bring a television camera, record my interview, and show it on Aaj Tak [an Indian news channel]." I stared at him and protested that I did not have a television camera; he insisted. "Get a camera and come before Monday; I have work on Monday. Ask anyone about Babloo Painter, and they will bring you to me. I am world-famous here."

An hour later, over coffee, I narrated my encounter with the world-famous Babloo Painter to some friends. A friend reminded me of an engineer who had survived the massacre. "I think he was with the waterworks department," he said. Phone calls to the local waterworks department got me nowhere. I was keen to meet the engineer who had survived Gawkadal.

A week later, I got a call from my friend. I was helping my ten-year-old cousin browse the Internet. We had barely managed to open a few pages with the painfully slow dial-up connection when the phone rang. "Basharat, that engineer lives close to your house. His name is Farooq Wani. Take down his number."

Farooq Wani was home when I called. "I live on Green Lane, Rajbagh. Come over, we will have tea," he said. Green Lane was a mile away from my house, an upper-middle-class road lined with a row of redbrick mansions with conical Kashmiri roofs. A girl watered flowers outside the engineer's house. She directed me toward the drawing room. A plump fortysomething man with bluish eyes and light brown hair, wearing a dark blue suit, opened the door. "I am Farooq." He smiled and shook my hand. Walnut wood-carved chairs and tables rested on a carpet. Papier-mâché figures sat lightly on the shelves of the cupboards. Farooq and I sat facing each other.

In January 1990 he was an assistant engineer in the state government responsible for the management of the water supply to various parts of Srinagar. He was on essential services duty on January 19 and left home in the morning with his official curfew pass. Paramilitary Central Reserve Police Force men stopped him a few times on his way to work; he showed his curfew pass, and they let him go. After making water supply arrangements, he walked toward Maisuma to visit an uncle. "We had heard of the house-to-house searches and arrests there. I was worried about my uncle's family and decided to visit them." Near Lal Chowk, he saw a procession marching toward Maisuma. "I followed the procession. We reached Gowkadal. Tense paramilitary men stood along the way, pointing their guns toward the protesters."

Farooq paused, drank some water, and pushed a bell. A servant brought tea, local bread, and *harisa*, a lamb delicacy cooked slowly in copper pots with cardamom, cinnamon, and saffron till it becomes pastelike. "My uncle lived on the other side of the bridge. I planned to leave the procession on reaching his house. The protesters were angry, shouting fiery slogans at the top of their voices," he said. Paramilitary men stood on the bridge. Protesters shouted slogans for freedom. Amid the sloganeering, Farooq heard a burst of gunfire. Bullets tore apart the procession; people shouted, fell, and shouted again. He jumped onto a footpath and lay flat on the ground. "Bullets whizzed past my ears. The bridge was covered with bodies and blood. CRPF men continued firing. I saw more people falling, closed my eyes, and pretended to be dead."

Farooq curled himself up in the chair, leaving his slippers on the carpet. I was not eating anymore; Farooq had left his tea. Memory drowned out the smell of *harisa*; the elegant carpets and ornate furniture faded away. Farooq was not here in his drawing room talking to me. He was on the bridge pretending to be dead. He heard wails and a gunshot every few seconds. Paramilitary men walked around the bridge. He saw an officer going from body to body, checking whether anyone was alive. "I lay still and, from the corner of my eye, saw him firing more bullets every time he found a sign of life in an injured man." Farooq waited for the soldiers to leave. It was getting harder to pretend to be dead. Where he lay, someone had dropped a *kangri*, the fire pot Kashmiris carry around in winter. Embers of charcoal from the *kangri* were scattered on the sidewalk. His cheek was burning from their heat. Slowly, he turned his face to avoid the burn. The murdering officer saw him. "This bastard is alive," Farooq heard him shout. The officer ran toward him, kicked him, and a volley of bullets pierced his body. He lost consciousness.

A police truck came. The bodies were put in the truck; the police put him in, too. The truck moved to the police control room, which was to become the site where Kashmiris would go to collect bodies of their kin in the days to come. Inside the truck, Farooq regained consciousness and lay still. The truck stopped at the police hospital two miles from Gawkadal. As the policemen at the hospital began taking out the bodies, he cried out, "I am alive!" The policemen, all Kashmiris, hugged him. They were carrying him away when a teenager whose clothes and face were drenched in blood jumped out of the pile of bodies. The boy ran his hands over his body and cried, "I got no bullets. I got no bullets. I am alive." He stood still for a moment and then ran out of the building. Farooq was hospitalized. His family heard he was alive a day later. "They thought I was dead."

Months later, he recovered and resumed work as an engineer. "God gave me a new life that day; I thank him and live every moment. I often think of that boy running from the police hospital. Memories like that disturb me. But I was not the only one; there are hundreds like me."

We had another round of *kahwa* and continued talking about Kashmir for a while. He wondered if the conflict would ever be resolved and if there could be a just and lasting peace. It was a question most Kashmiris talked about. None of us knew the answer. Then his phone rang: one of his subordinates. Farooq gave him complicated technical directions. As he spoke with intense focus, it was hard to imagine the same man had survived one of the most appalling massacres in Kashmir. In a corner was a golf bag; now he was a member of Srinagar's posh golf club.

• • •

My ten-year-old cousin, Iffat, was waiting for me at home to help her with a school essay. "Who did you go to meet?" she asked me the moment I walked in.

"A friend of mine," I said.

"What does he do?"

"He is an engineer."

"Why did you go to see him?"

Her questions could be endless, and I suggested that we should work on her essay. Afterward, I sat alone in my room thinking about Farooq, about Babloo Painter and Gawkadal. For me, the massacre of Gawkadal is tied up with the memory of a series of other massacres. In the winter of 1990 Srinagar was the city of massacres. Militants joined the Indian forces in a display of brutality. Mushir-ul-Haq, the vice chancellor of Kashmir University, was kidnapped and killed after the Indian government refused to accept the militant demands for the release of hostages. Prominent Kashmiri Pandits and Muslims seen as siding with India were the next target. On May 21, 1990, militants from Hizbul Mujahideen, a pro-Pakistan militant group, assassinated the head priest of Srinagar, Maulvi Farooq, a controversial politician. A procession of mourners began from his house in the northern part of Srinagar.

Near a hundred-year-old school in central Srinagar established by Maulvi Farooq's father to educate Kashmir's Muslims, paramilitary forces fired at the slain priest's funeral procession. Bullets pierced the coffin; pallbearers and mourners fell. About a hundred men were slain. Their blood-soaked shoes lay on the road after the bodies were carried away. People forgot the head priest's assassination; anger rose against India. His eighteen-year-old son, Omar Farooq, who was sworn in as the head priest, appealed to world leaders to help Kashmir seek self-determination. The images of the massacre found their way into poetry and paintings.

Many of the mourners were buried in a new graveyard that had come up near Eidgah, the traditional Eid prayer ground of Srinagar. For centuries Kashmiris had buried the dead in neighborhood graveyards. Family members gave the dead person a bath, clothed him/her in a white cotton shroud, and took the body to the graveyard for funeral prayers. But the men who had been killed by the Indian forces since the rebellion were no ordinary dead. They were seen as martyrs for the cause of freedom. They were not given a bath or white cotton shrouds. "Martyrs do not need baths and shrouds." I had heard this saying often since the winter of 1990. The men were buried mostly at the newly built graveyard on the western edge of Srinagar, known to Kashmiris as Martyrs' Graveyard. I had been there as a reporter after every newsworthy assassination or on the anniversary of the day when the mourners and the head priest were slain. But I had been there first in the mid-nineties with my friend Shan, who lived nearby.

Bordering Shan's crowded neighborhood of old balconied multistory timber-and-brick houses was a wide grassy playground where local boys played cricket and horses and stray cows grazed. I revisited the place with Shan. In a corner, the graveyard was a neatly walled square with an arched entrance announcing: KASHMIR MARTYRS' GRAVEYARD. Inscribed on the gate are the words: LEST YOU FORGET WE HAVE GIVEN OUR TODAY FOR TOMORROW OF YOURS. In his adolescence, Shan sat at the nearby shop fronts and watched bodies being brought to the graveyard and journalists running around with notebooks and cameras.

We passed through the iron-grille graveyard gate and walked on the cobbled footpaths running between the graves and the defiant reds and violets of roses and irises. Hundreds lay buried in neat rows, each grave marked with a rectangular white marble tombstone with a green border engraved with the name of the dead and the exhortation: ONLY GOD REMAINS! Many of the names were familiar to me: Maulvi Farooq, the head priest, and Ishfaq Majeed, the commander of JKLF, to whose name was added the prefix "His Excellency." There was a grave for Maqbool Bhat, the founder of JKLF, who was hanged and buried in Delhi's Tihar jail in the early eighties. On his tombstone were the words: THE GRAVE WAITS FOR HIM. And there were unknown men and women from all parts of Kashmir. In one grave two children—four and five years old—were buried together. Most graves named the killers: police, army, security forces, as if they, too, were to be immortalized.

In a corner were a few empty graves. Hasan, the old keeper of the graveyard, told us they had been dug in anticipation of the brisk death toll in the early nineties. Hasan lived nearby and used to run a small business. His sons took over after he developed a cardiac problem. Then the fighting began; he visited the graveyard often to pray for the dead. "I found peace sitting among the martyrs. Some years later, I volunteered to look after their graves. Now this is my life." Hasan believed, like most traditional Muslims, that martyrs live after their death and their graves are scented gardens. "Once it rained hard, and some graves were damaged," he said. "Nothing remains in an ordinary grave after a month but earth. But not with the martyrs; their bodies do not decompose. In a grave I saw the hair of a martyr. It was as if he was sleeping. From every grave I repaired, there rose a heavenly scent, the scent of the martyrs." I must have had a skeptical look on my face, because he said, "Son, you are too young to understand this, but I have experienced it."

The tale of Kashmiri rebellions, their brutal suppression by the rulers and honoring the dead as martyrs, is an old one. In Srinagar people still visit the graves of men who stood up to rulers and were killed for their defiance centuries ago. There is another Martyrs' Graveyard, where the men who were killed in 1931 by the forces of the Dogra ruler of Kashmir, Hari Singh, are buried. Kashmir had various foreign rulers after losing independence to the Mughal emperors of Delhi in the late sixteenth century. In the mid-eighteenth century, the Mughals lost Kashmir to the armies of the Afghan warrior Ahmad Shah Abdali. And in the early nineteenth century, the Sikhs led by Ranjit Singh defeated the Afghans and took Kashmir. The Sikh rule was as oppressive as the Afghan rule. Sikh governors closed down mosques and banned the Muslim call for prayer. Heavy taxes were levied; peasants were forced into hard labor. But by the 1840s the Sikh empire was crumbling.

The British declared war on the Sikhs in 1846. Many Sikh commanders crossed over to the British. But the defection that was to have consequences for Kashmir was that of Gulab Singh, a Hindu chieftain of the hill state of Jammu, which is a neighbor of the valley of Kashmir. He had worked his way up to be a general in Ranjit Singh's army. Gulab Singh promised to help the British and stayed away from battle in 1846. The Sikhs lost. Gulab Singh got his reward. The British sold Kashmir to him for seventy-five lakhs of rupees. To recover the price he'd paid the British, Gulab Singh pounced on every penny he found and promoted *begaar* (forced labor).

A few voices were heard against the sale of Kashmir and the plight of its people under the rule of Gulab Singh and his descendants. Some years ago in a library in Delhi, I came across a tiny book printed in London, titled *Cashmeer Misgovernment*, by Robert Thorpe, but his book told me nothing about his own life. On a visit home I found in my father's library an edition of Thorpe's book, edited by a Srinagar-based historian. The historian had added some details. The story began when R. Thorpe, a lieutenant colonel in the British army, was traveling through Kashmir in the early nineteenth century. While staying with a local landlord, he met the man's daughter Amiran. Thorpe and Amiran fell in love, were married, and left for England. Robert Thorpe was born to them in the year 1833.

In his early youth, Thorpe left England to visit his mother's birthplace; he found Kashmiris living like slaves under Gulab Singh's son Pratap Singh. He gathered firsthand accounts of the ruthless taxation and the death of forced laborers due to starvation, exertion, and cold, and he published his accounts as *Cashmeer Misgovernment*. Thorpe described the condition of men taken for forced labor: "None save those who have seen such can fully realise those horrors. Patiently the Kashmiris toil onwards through the drifting snow. Many encourage each other with words of hope. They might reach the other side in safety. But strength departs and the wind paralyses the sinews. Slowly the conviction fastens upon them that they shall never quit those frightful solitudes, never see again their homes or those who dwelt there waiting for their return, far off in the sunny vale of Kashmir." Pratap Singh planned to silence Thorpe. One winter morning in 1868, Thorpe was walking toward the Shankaracharya hill in Srinagar. Singh's men attacked him with daggers.

The brave writer fell and died there. He was buried in a Christian cemetery behind Lal Chowk.

Young boys and girls from two convent schools made a racket in the street leading to the cemetery. Tibetans who sought refuge in Kashmir in the 1960s sold shoes and clothes on the sidewalks. I saw the inscription CHRISTIAN CEMETERY on a small iron gate. Inside, three men sat on the pavement. I asked them about Robert Thorpe's grave; they had never heard of him. "The graves here are of local converts," a thickset man said. Then he pointed at the far end of the cemetery. "You will see graves of important British sahibs and memsahibs there." Weeds grew around the limestone and marble stones on the graves; majestic chinar and pine trees shaded the terraced cemetery. The thickset man joined me and asked me to translate the epitaphs in English. Every time he realized a grave was a hundred years old, he cried out loud, "Nothing lasts! We all have to return to Him! He was and only He will be! We all have to return to Him!" I could not find Thorpe anywhere.

I was reading an epitaph when the man shook me by my shoulder and asked me for fifty rupees. "I will show you a very important grave. Many people come to see that and take pictures." He ushered me toward an old tomb; time had turned the limestone black. Weeds, wild grass, and twigs covered the slab. "Do you know anything about him?" I asked the man. He smiled an obsequious smile. "No! But he is a very important man." I removed the twigs and the grass and scrubbed the mud off the slab. The modest carving on the stone read:

ROBERT THORPE

AGED 30 YEARS

22 NOVEMBER 1868

VERITAS

HE GAVE HIS LIFE FOR KASHMIR

Srinagar is a city of bunkers. Of the world's cities, it has the greatest military presence. But Srinagar is also a city of absences. It has lost its nights to a decade and a half of curfews and de facto curfews. It has lost its theaters: Regal, Shiraz, Neelam, Broadway—magical names I had longed for throughout my childhood. They were closed before I had grown up enough to walk to a ticket counter and watch a bad Bolly-wood movie.

Srinagar has also lost its multireligious character with the migration of the Kashmiri Pandits in the early nineties. I remembered my Pandit landlady in Delhi; she always talked about visiting her old home in Sri-nagar. I did not know where her house was, but I could visit the area where she had lived: Habbakadal, central Srinagar. One afternoon I walked into a coffee shop near the dilapidated Habbakadal Bridge, the third bridge on the Jhelum River as it moves through Srinagar. A teen-ager in an Adidas T-shirt manned the sales counter. His father owned the shop. I asked him about places of interest in Habbakadal. "There is noth-ing to see here. It is a ruin. Go down the road, and you will see some burned houses." He shrugged.

I was about to leave when an elderly man came in. The boy swiftly threw his cigarette away. "He is my father." He jumped off his chair. The father sat behind the sales counter and watched people pass by. I asked him about the area. "Turn left, and the second building from my shop is an ancient Hindu temple," he said.

I left, walked up to the temple door, and stopped. The temple com-plex now housed a paramilitary camp. Fortified bunkers along the wall hid the temple from sight; I saw the tin roof of the temple and a brass spire. A gray-painted iron sheet was attached to a sandbag bunker. On it, bold black graffiti read: INDIA IS GREAT! An Indian flag hung from a mast tied to a bunker.

On the bridge, used only by pedestrians, a group of old men sat in the pleasant afternoon sun. I sat near them looking at the old wooden houses along the riverbank. On a *ghat*, or river bank, women washed clothes, and children ran up and down the stairs leading to the *ghat*. One of the old men, Abdul Razaq, pointed to the crumbling old houses along the riverbank and said, "Most of them are Pandit houses. Pandits left, and now they are abandoned." His eyes wandered over their decaying wooden windows and shingle roofs covered in neglect and dust. Mrs. Kaul, my landlady, would have lived in one such house not very far from where I stood. On the left bank, the brass-plate roof of an ancient temple reflected the mild sun. "It is the Raghunath temple, one of the best here," the old man told me.

I walked through a stone-paved street sneaking between rows of new concrete buildings and old wood houses. The ground floors of the houses had been converted into shops, and the shopkeepers sat lazily behind their wooden counters. In a crumbling building with a burned top floor and roof, a shop announced: NEW GENERATION CHOICE—LATEST BOLLYWOOD AND HOLLYWOOD VCDS AND DVDS. The street turned into a narrow alley. I asked a ponytailed little girl where the Raghunath temple was. She ran ahead, beckoning me to follow her, and stopped near a broken wall.

I climbed over the broken wall and jumped onto a garbage dump inside the temple courtyard. Stray dogs camping inside the temple barked at me. The brass plates of the roof had fallen apart and exposed the baked bricks of the temple. Reeds and wild bushes had invaded the courtyard and the stairs leading into the prayer room. After walking through a triple-arched gallery, I entered the prayer room. It was filled with cobwebs, pigeon droppings, and a gloomy silence. Naked bricks stared at me; I walked over pieces of their plaster scattered on the floor. The Hindu deity's idol had gone missing from the podium, like the Pandits. A horde of pigeons flew into the prayer hall, fluttered around, and flew out into the dusk over the River Jhelum and the city.

Two shabbily dressed young men stood in the courtyard. They were startled to see me; they were smoking pot. Refugees from sanity had found shelter in the abandoned temple. After introductions, they warmed up and offered me a drag. I refused. "Okay. But tell me, why did you come here?" one asked.

"I saw the temple roof from a distance and was curious to take a look."

He took a drag from the joint and looked at the temple. "When I was a child, it used to be crowded with people. The Pandits sang *bhajans* all evening. Then they left. Now only *djinns* live here." The setting sun shone meekly in the darkening waters of the Jhelum. On the way back, I passed through Lal Chowk and crossed the Jhelum again. The dark roads and the gloomy river seemed to be mourning the lost gods and worshippers.

I found myself thinking of Hari Parbat, a hill that towers over central Srinagar and is associated with the legend of the creation of Kashmir. In prehistoric times there was a vast lake known as Satisar, after the Hindu god Shiva's wife, Parvati, also called Sati. In the lake lived a demon who laid waste to the whole country around Satisar. Kashyapa the sage witnessed this destruction and prayed to the Hindu trinity of Brahma, Vishnu, and Shiva to rid the place of the demon. The demon escaped underwater each time the gods attacked him. Then Vishnu assumed the form of a boar and struck the mountains surrounding the lake. Where he struck, a pass opened and water drained out. (The present northern Kashmir town of Baramulla is believed to be the place where Vishnu struck the mountains.) The demon escaped to lower ground near central Srinagar; Parvati assumed the form of a mynah and dropped a pebble on him. The pebble became a mountain and killed the demon. Kashmiris believe that mountain is Hari Parbat.

A steep, narrow alley leads up to Hari Parbat from a market in central Srinagar. Midway stands a famed Sufi shrine. Hari Parbat rises above the shrine in its solid barrenness, crowned by the massive beige walls of a fort built by a medieval Afghan ruler. One afternoon I climbed higher toward the fort; a temple dedicated to Parvati stands there. Two old men chatted beside the track I followed. I asked them about the gate of the fort. "The gate is there. But where are you going?" one asked. "To the fort. I want to see the temple," I replied. He looked at the other man, and they sighed. "Don't you know? It is a camp." I looked at the fort walls and saw the barrel of a gun pointing from an opening in the fort wall. "There used to be a temple, a mosque, a pond, and a few apricot trees there," he added. "Now it is all military."

Srinagar is also about being hidden from view, disappearing. Absences and their reminders stand on every other street. Every now and then I would be walking past a small park shaded by thick chinars

and notice a circle of women and men with white headbands and placards. I would stop at times; other times I would walk past with an air
of resignation. Between four and eight thousand men have disappeared
after being arrested by the military, paramilitary, and police. Newspapers routinely referred to the missing men as "disappeared persons"
and their waiting wives as the "half-widows." The government has
refused to set up an inquiry into the disappearances, saying the missing
citizens of Kashmir have joined militant groups and crossed into Pakistan for arms training. Many Kashmiris believe the disappeared men
were killed in custody and cremated in mass graves. Wives of many
such men have given up hope and tried to move on. Others are obsessively fighting for justice, hoping their loved ones will return. The men
and women in the park were the parents and wives of the missing men.
Dirty wars seem to have a way of bringing mothers to city squares.

Several years ago I happened to meet Noora, a seventy-year-old
woman, in her rundown house near Lal Chowk. Her shopkeeper son
had stepped out to join his cricket team at the Polo Ground. Her neighbors saw a few Border Security Force jeeps stop outside their house, near
Ghanta Ghar, an old watchtower whose clock had stopped working. The
paramilitaries grabbed him, pushed him into the back of a jeep, and drove
away. He had been missing for eight years when I met her in her dimly lit
kitchen. "For a few years, my daughters and I went to every police station, every military camp, every politician we could. Everybody had a
no for us. And then I had to marry off my two daughters. I couldn't keep
dragging them to camps and police stations with me. People talk." Her
wrinkled face showed little emotion; she seemed tired of repeating her
story and getting nowhere. "Many journalists came and interviewed me.
Even some *angrez* came and promised they will write about my son. But
my son has not come back."

Neither has the son of Parveena Ahanger, a sixteen-year-old speech-
impaired boy, Javed, who was taken away from their house in 1990 during a raid by the army. Parveena is a chubby housewife in her forties
who, along with a lawyer, Pervez Imroz, formed the Association of Parents of Disappeared Persons to campaign and fight cases in the courts.

One day she is consoling and strategizing with relatives of other disap-peared youths, helping them with legal advice and charity schools for children; another day she is at the Srinagar airport, catching a flight to talk at a seminar; and yet another day she repeats her story elsewhere, and her sad brown eyes hold back tears. Each time I have seen her, she is with a new woman whose husband or son has gone missing. She is a mother to them all, holding them, consoling them, scolding, egging them on. Old bearded men talk to her with reverence, as if she is a saint. Young rakish men sit on bare ground, their heads lowered, and listen to her. Reporters stop to greet her and ask if there is something that needs to be written about.

I remember sitting on that rug in her house, barely a year-old reporter, taking notes, asking earnest questions, and naively believing that telling her story well might bring her son back. The government had offered her monetary compensation (around $2,500) if she accepted that her son was killed in unknown circumstances in the conflict. "I will not sell my son for any amount," she told me. The numbers of the missing have come down since Parveena began her battle, but the dis-appearances have not stopped. Every time the police and the military announce that an unidentified body has been found, Parveena gets ner-vous phone calls from the relatives of other missing men. "You never know who it will be. One can hope as long as you have not seen the body or the grave."

That pain and longing often remind Kashmiris of an old story of pain and longing—again inflicted by imperial Delhi. On the Srinagar-Jammu highway, about six miles outside the city, a sign reads: WORLD'S BEST SAF-FRON GROWS HERE. Past the beds of violet saffron flowers, a dirt path leads to the village of Chandhara, the village of Zoon, or Habba Khatoon, a sixteenth-century poetess and singer. Despite her talents and refine-ment, Zoon was married off to a peasant who insisted that she devote herself to her household chores and working in the fields. Zoon sang her songs as she tilled and planted.

The ruler of Kashmir at the time was Yusuf Shah Chak, a prince fond of poetry and music. One day he was passing by the fields near Chandhara when he saw Zoon singing. Yusuf Shah fell for her. Historians have competing claims about their romance and marriage, but in Kashmiri folklore, the peasant girl became Queen Habba Khatoon, spent joyous days and nights with her husband in pleasure gardens, wrote poetry, refined her singing, and composed classical music inspired by Yusuf Shah's court full of musicians and singers.

However, they were caught in the whirligig of imperial politics. Akbar, the Mughal emperor of Delhi, invaded Kashmir in December 1585. Yusuf considered resistance futile, but his army fought and stopped the Mughal march. Fearing an eventual defeat, Yusuf agreed to visit the court of the Mughal emperor for peace talks, where he accepted Mughal sovereignty. Kashmir lost its independence. Akbar imprisoned Yusuf and a year later sent him to Bihar as a petty Mughal official; he died in anonymity a few years later. Habba Khatoon roamed the villages of Kashmir, singing songs of separation, yearning to be reunited with her beloved. Yusuf died alone in faraway Bihar.

Despite his cowardice, Yusuf Shah's imprisonment and betrayal by Akbar has become a metaphor for the relationship between Delhi and Srinagar. In a literary history of Kashmir, I found a picture of Yusuf Shah's grave in the village of Biswak in the Nalanda district of Bihar. Mohammed Yusuf Taing, a Kashmiri writer and cultural critic, had been there in the early 1980s with Kashmir's most respected leader and head of the government, Sheikh Mohammed Abdullah. I met him in Srinagar in his study lined with books. "A generation has passed since someone visited his grave." His voice quivered with emotion. A week later, I called the old writer and sought directions for the Bihar village where Yusuf Shah was buried.

Some time after meeting Taing, I left Srinagar for Delhi and from there boarded a night train for Patna. In the morning I took a taxi from Patna and drove into the countryside. We passed tiny mud houses with hay roofs scattered amid vast stretches of fields and obstinate bullock carts unimpressed by cars; we overtook buses with commuters sitting gaily on their roofs. I dozed off till the driver woke me up in a tiny market in the small town of Islampur. A group of men in checked sarongs and *kurtas* drank *lassi* on wooden benches outside a sweets shop. A young man named Hari volunteered to accompany me. "The Kashmiri saint's tomb is near Biswak, where I live," he explained. "It used to be a Muslim village called Kashmiri Chak, but after Partition, the people migrated to Pakistan." We followed a dirt track into sugarcane fields. A few miles on, Hari asked the driver to stop. A banyan tree towered over a mound of bricks, partly covered with vegetation. We were there. On a raised piece of land with a fallen brick boundary was a tomb. It had no plaques, no inscriptions, and no names. Wind rustled the sugarcane; an old man passed by, wearily pedaling a bicycle. I sat there for a while, looking at the featureless grave of Yusuf Shah Chak, after whom Kashmir was never free.

11 ∾ Papa-2

Prague had protested and won; Berlin had protested and won; Kashmiris too had believed that their protests would win Kashmir its freedom. The early nineties were a naive, heady time. But Kashmiri demonstrations faded out after the massacres. The conflict might not have turned so fatal if India had allowed those peaceful demonstrations, mostly throughout 1990 and 1991, and then every now and then through 1993 and 1994, and even later but not on the same scale. Maybe those demonstrations would have become the dominant force of politics in Kashmir; Indians and Kashmiris could have talked, and thousands of deaths might have been avoided.

But that did not happen. Instead, firing on protesters, arrests, disappearances, custodial killings, kidnappings, assassinations, and torture dominated Kashmir. In a prose poem, Agha Shahid Ali wrote:

> *The doctor who treated a sixteen-year-old boy*
> *Recently released from an interrogation centre asked,*
> *"Why didn't the fortune tellers predict*
> *The lines in his palms would be cut by a knife?"*

One November afternoon, I crossed the Zero Bridge and continued past the old Radio Kashmir building on a rather quiet road. Old buses waited outside the elite Burn Hall boys' school; supplicants with applications hung around the gates of government ministers' heavily guarded mansions; the leafless chinar branches hung over empty stands of the cricket stadium. I crossed another road and found myself facing a colonial mansion painted blue and white. A plaque on its gate read: UNITED NATIONS MILITARY OBSERVER GROUP FOR INDIA AND PAKISTAN. The old mansion and the UN mission both seemed hapless reminders of a lost time. The architecture of the mansion was a dying style that blended the Kashmiri use of woodwork with British sensibilities; the United Nations resolutions on Kashmir, recommending a plebiscite, lived as hollow quotations in books and journals. A short walk from the UN office, Gupkar Road was a well-bunkered and -patroled neighborhood. Senior politicians, bureaucrats, and intelligence operatives lived here in lovely houses with high, ugly walls and stern guards. Gupkar was our Green Zone. The road turned toward the Grand Palace, the palace of Hari Singh, the last monarch of Kashmir. During the nineties, most people dreaded Gupkar Road. It was the road to Papa-2.

Papa-2 was the most infamous torture center run by the Indian forces in Kashmir. Originally, it was a large mansion built by Hari Singh, later converted into a guesthouse and known as the Fairview Guest House. Hundreds who were taken to Papa-2 did not return. Those who did return were wrecks. The center was closed down in 1998. A top government official renovated the Papa-2 building and turned it into his residence. Before moving in, the Oxford-educated officer called priests of all religions to pray there and exorcise the ghosts.

A friend got me permission to visit. I was supposed to be interested in architecture. After an identity check, I walked past well-tended flower beds leading up to the porch. Apple and apricot trees grew in a corner of the lawn. The pine-clad ridge of the Zabarvan hill rose gently behind the mansion with its white facade and a red roof. The politician was not home. One of his men welcomed me into a wood-paneled reception room with three phones, a fax machine, and a desktop computer. We began our tour of the house. My guide, a local young man my age, walked in silence through the rooms. I looked at the chairs, the tables, the ceilings, and the whitewashed walls. Soft honey-hued curtains hung on the windows of the politician's bedroom on the first floor. A brown bedspread covered his bed; paperbacks and hardbacks on law and literature filled the bookshelves. My guide removed the curtains from the windows, and clear, bright light fell on the mementos and awards resting on the shelves. A carpet with verses from the Quran woven into it hung from one wall, and a painting by the famous Indian painter Raja Ravi Verma adorned the other wall. My guide was silent. Finally, he spoke: "This was Papa-2, brother! This was Papa-2."

An hour later, I was in Lal Chowk, talking to two friends about my visit. I told them I had to meet people who had survived Papa-2. At the same time I dreaded the idea. "Where can I find them?" I asked my friend. "Ask anyone on the street," he told me. "Half of Kashmir has been there. Or just walk up to Maisuma, and you will find ten guys on the street."

Later in the day, I walked past the soldiers and policemen toward the J&K Liberation Front office in the nearby separatist neighborhood. A group of young men stood outside the nondescript building. "Papa-2?" I asked. A brief silence followed. They asked one another: "Were you there?" "No. I was in Rajasthan." "No. I was at Kot Balwal." "No. I was at Gogoland." "No. I was in Ranchi." Names formed a whole geography of Indian prisons. "Sayeed was at Papa-2." "Irfan was there." "And Irshad was at Papa-2." "Shafi was there, too." In under five minutes I had six names. "Shafi will be home now," said Abid, one of the men. "Let us go." We walked through narrow, musty lanes past old, modest houses whose roofs seemed to lean into an embrace to keep the weak winter sun out. Old men stared blank stares from shop fronts; younger men stood in twos and threes, lazily shuffling a bit to make room for a cyclist or a rickshaw.

Abid stopped to greet a few men on the way. He asked them whether they had been at Papa-2. Some talked about their friends who had been in Papa-2; others talked about different jails and torture chambers. Finally, Abid stopped near a rather decrepit two-story house. He knocked. A woman's voice asked, "Who is it?"

"Abid here. Is Shafi around?"

"He is at the mosque," the voice shouted back. "Wait there; he shall be back any moment."

A few minutes later, we saw a tall, frail, bespectacled man in his early thirties limping toward us with the help of a wooden staff. He shouted a happy greeting to Abid. They talked for a while, then Abid introduced me and left. Shafi shook open the door and led me in. We climbed old wooden stairs and entered a neat room with a layer of cheap green paint on its mud walls. The floral designs on the floor rug were worn out. In a corner a bedspread covered a stack of bedding; there were no closets. Shafi pulled two pillows from the stack, adjusted them as cushions against the wall, and asked me to sit. In another corner a short, plump, dark woman sat near a kerosene stove. On the wooden shelves on the wall facing her were a few cups, plates, and utensils. "She is my wife," Shafi said. I greeted her; she muttered a welcome and pulled down a curtain partitioning the makeshift kitchen from the drawing-room part of the room. Shafi asked her for tea, adding, "Do not add sugar. He will take as much he likes." His eyes seemed to disappear behind the thick glasses. His cheeks were deeply hollowed, but his hair was still brown and curly. Shafi lit a cigarette, bent toward me, and said, "I was at Papa-2 for seven months."

In 1990, like most other boys, Shafi, who was nineteen, had decided to join a militant group. JKLF was the most influential and charismatic group in his part of Srinagar, so he joined its student wing. His war with India began: Attacking patrols of Indian soldiers, moving with guns from one hideout to the next, and evading arrest in crackdowns became his routine. "We thought Kashmir would be free in a year or two," he recalled. Instead, he was arrested by a paramilitary patrol. After initial interrogation at a camp in Srinagar, he was sent to the Kot Balwal and Talab Tilloo jails in the Jammu province. Two years later, he was released. Back home, he met his comrades-in-arms. "I began working for the movement again."

One day in the autumn of 1992, he was spotted by a local boy collaborating with the paramilitary Border Security Force. "I knew him. He had become a BSF informer and pointed me out. I was not carrying any weapons and was arrested."

Shafi's wife called from behind the yellow curtain. "The tea is ready," he said. He rose, brought a tray full of biscuits, two cups, and a flask. He began pouring tea but fumbled with the cups, squinting. I volunteered to help, and he let me. I kept his cup next to him, and he again touched it slowly, as if assuring himself of its presence. "They kept me in the local BSF camp for a week before shifting me to Papa-2." At the BSF camp, he was interrogated, beaten with fists, feet, batons, guns. They wanted information about his group; they wanted his weapons. He did not tell me whether he gave the information and the weapons. It is hard to ask that question if you are a Kashmiri.

Shafi was moved to Papa-2. "It was hell," he said, fumbling to find the cigarette burning on the ashtray. He was thrown into a room crowded with twenty men. The floor was bare. Smears of blood blemished the whitewashed walls. Every man had a coarse black blanket for bedding. The blankets were full of lice. "We called them lice blankets." He laughed. A corner of the room was their toilet. The prisoners defecated and urinated into polythene bags in that corner; they then threw the bags into a dustbin. Every time a man had to go to the bathroom, two others held a blanket like a curtain to give him some privacy. Others stared at the floor. Shafi and his fellow prisoners slept laid out like rows of corpses. Throughout the night, people woke up shouting, cursing the lice, trying to sleep again, only to be woken up by the next man battling the vermin. Some managed to sleep, though the lights were never switched off. "During the interrogation, I was made to stare at very bright bulbs. Even in our room the light burned my eyes. I craved darkness." Darkness came. "I began losing my eyesight there. I can barely see now, despite my glasses."

After his release from prison, doctors prescribed an operation to restore his sight. "Why didn't you have the surgery?" I asked. Shafi smiled. "I cannot afford the cost." He could not find work anywhere. In the summer he sold secondhand garments on a wooden cart in Lal Chowk; in the winter he followed his brother to Calcutta, hawking Kashmiri shawls on commission. His family wanted him to get married and begin a new life. They went around looking for a girl for him. Nobody would marry Shafi, a man shattered by his militant days, prison, and nonexistent job prospects. His brother knew a Muslim family in a Calcutta slum. They had a squint-eyed girl whom nobody would marry. Her family was happy to marry her off to Shafi. Now she was there behind the curtain, asking whether we wanted more tea. "She is pregnant, and I have to take her to Calcutta for the birth." He sounded tense.

Shafi lived off a thousand rupees that Yasin Malik, the JKLF chief, gave him every month. "I did ask other leaders for help. I said that I am here because I spent my youth for the movement, but I was disappointed." Some separatist leaders asked him for proof of his being a militant, of his jail days. "They live in big houses and drive big cars bought from the money that came for the movement. But they are not willing to help those who destroyed their lives for the cause." His face contorted with anger; he took long, hard puffs from his cigarette. "I never went to them after that. None of the leaders except Yasin Malik had to go through what the boys [arrested militants] endured. They cannot even imagine what being tortured is like."

He drank the last gulp of tea and lit another cigarette. I thought of the separatist leaders giving statements to crowds of journalists in their mansions; I thought of the security guards from Indian paramilitary and the J&K police guarding them; I thought of their white Ambassador cars making them look like mirror images of their ideological rivals in the state. They spoke of the sacrifices of the people of Kashmir; they spoke of the struggle for freedom. Shafi had believed in them and felt let down by them. The contrast between his and their lives was stark. He held my hand and said again, "They cannot even imagine what being tortured is like."

He wanted me to know. "They made you sit on a chair, tied you with ropes. One soldier held your neck, two others pulled your legs in different directions, and three more rolled a heavy concrete roller over your legs. They asked questions, and if you didn't answer, they burned you with the cigarettes." He paused and then, as if suddenly remembering something, said, "The worst part was the psychological torture. They would make us say 'Jai Hind' [Victory to India] every morning and every evening. They beat you if you refused. It was very hard, but everyone said it except Master Ahsan Dar [a top commander of Hizbul Mujahideen]." He stopped abruptly. "I cannot talk about it. It makes me crazy."

He said I should meet Ansar, another former militant who had been in Papa-2, who would be willing to talk about torture. I was unsure whether I should. Was I scared of facing it, of having to write about it later? I spent the next few days arguing with myself before meeting Ansar.

I met him at his brother's grocery shop near the grand mosque in downtown Srinagar. We sat in a small, poorly lit room in his house behind the roadside shop. Ansar was a robust, mustached man in a beige *shalwar kameez*. He had joined a separatist organization called People's League in the mid-eighties and become one of the earlier members of its militant wing. One day he was visiting his parents when the BSF raided his house and arrested him. "They had information that I was here. Someone in my neighborhood was the informer." He talked about various prisons he had been in.

"And Papa-2?" I asked.

"How can I forget it? Not even stray cows would eat the food they threw at us there." He passed a plate of plum cake to me. "That place destroyed most people who were there. You do not live a normal life after that torture. It scars you forever." He lit a cigarette. "They beat us up with guns, staffs, hands. But that was nothing." He talked as if he were reading from a manual. "They took you out to the lawn outside the building. You were asked to remove all your clothes, even your underwear. They tied you to a long wooden ladder and placed it near a ditch filled with kerosene oil and red chili powder. They raised the ladder like a seesaw and pushed your head into the ditch. It could go on for an hour, half an hour, depending on their mood.

"It was the beginning. At times they would not undress you but would tie you to the ladder. You almost felt relieved until they tied your pants near the ankles and put mice inside." He paused, poured more tea, and said, "Or they burned your arms and legs with cigarette butts and kerosene stoves used for welding. They burned your flesh till you spoke." He rolled up his right sleeve and pushed it a little beyond the elbow. An uneven dark brown patch of flesh sat in ugly contrast to his pale skin. "They tied copper wire around your arms and gave high-voltage shocks. Every hair on your body stood up. But the worst was when they inserted the copper wire into my penis and gave electric shocks. They did it with most boys. It destroyed many lives. Many could not marry after that."

After his release, Ansar was treated for urinary tract infections and some other disorders he did not mention. "I was not ready to marry. But my family supported me in a big way. I agreed to marry only after I was treated for a year and a half. Thank God, now I have a daughter and run my small business."

After leaving Ansar, I kept thinking about the attacks on the boys' masculinity, which had left them vulnerable even after the prison sentence was over. I tried to write about Papa-2 but failed. I stared at my computer screen, typed and deleted a few words, and switched it off.

A forgotten memory returned. A few years ago I had met with a teacher from my middle school. His family name was Khatana, and he taught us Urdu poetry. I was passionate about Urdu poetry, attended all his classes, and was his favorite student. But I left that school, left Kashmir, and forgot all about him. Meeting him after almost a decade, I had asked him about his family, his work. He was teaching in a different school and had not married. During a raid on his village, he had been arrested and tortured. "The bastards destroyed me. I have had three unsuccessful operations on my testicles. So no chance of a marriage, really," he told me. Later I wondered why, at that moment, I failed to understand the import of what he had told me. I wanted to meet him again and called friends to ask about him. Nobody seemed to know where he was.

A few days later, I called Shahid, a doctor friend at Srinagar's premier medical institute, Sher-e-Kashmir Institute of Medical Sciences, and talked to him about Ansar. "We have had hundreds of cases here. Those electric shocks led to impotence in many, and many lost their kidneys," he said. Shahid, a short, jolly man, grew up in a South Kashmir village. On weekends he drove up to his ancestral village and spent his Sundays treating the villagers for a nominal fee. "I am going home on Sunday. If you can come along, I will introduce you to someone with the same problem."

On Sunday morning I set out with Shahid to his village to meet his cousin Hussein, who, after being tortured in detention, thought he was impotent and refused to marry. "The problem is that he is not ready to meet a doctor. He does not even talk to me," Shahid told me as we drove from Srinagar toward the South Kashmir town of Bijbehara. We turned onto a dirt track near the town and for half an hour passed through clusters of mud-and-brick houses, groves of walnut and willow trees, and fields. Vapor rose from the frost-covered fields warmed by the bright morning sun. "The sun is so rejuvenating," Shahid said in his physician's manner.

A hand-painted Red Cross sign hanging from a roadside shack with his name misspelled announced Shahid's clinic. It was barely nine in the morning, and a crowd of patients was already waiting for him. Hussein, his cousin, was there. Hussein had gentle eyes and a subdued manner. We sat at an empty shop front in the sun. I offered him a cigarette, which he reluctantly accepted.

Hussein seemed to have surrendered to his fate. I struggled to find the right words. Sexuality was almost never discussed in our culture, and impotence was even harder to talk about. I began telling him about Shafi, Ansar, Papa-2, and the medical correction of torture-imposed disorders. He listened in silence, for the most part expressionless. Finally, he began to talk about his experience.

He was in the first year of college when the armed militancy began in 1990. He was the eldest son of a teacher and had four siblings. One day he left home with a group of thirteen other young men. After spending three days in the North Kashmir town of Baramulla, they boarded a truck and drove toward the town of Kupwara, near the Line of Control. Halfway from Kupwara, the Border Security Force stopped them. Their guide sat with the driver on the front seat; Hussein and his friends sat on the bare floor in the back. They had agreed to pose as construction laborers, but they were arrested and taken to a nearby paramilitary camp.

In the morning Hussein and his group were taken into tiny tin sheds lit by bright electric lamps for interrogation. "I was asked to undress, be naked. The first time I resisted, was beaten, undressed forcibly, and tied to a chair. Then they tied copper wire to my arms and gave me electric shocks. I could not even scream. They had stuffed my mouth with a ball of cloth. I thought I would die. They would suddenly stop, take the cloth out, and ask questions. I fainted a few times. They brought me back to my senses and inserted a copper wire into my penis. Then they switched on the electricity." Most of them broke after two days of torture. "You cannot bear pain beyond a point. Everybody talks," Hussein said. "We admitted we were going for arms training and were shifted to jails in Srinagar after two weeks." He added as an afterthought, "Maybe I should have admitted straightaway. Life could have been different."

I closed my eyes and then opened them and looked away, out at the road and the patients awaiting their turn at Shahid's clinic. An old man walked up to us and asked whether I was a doctor. "No, sir. I am only the doctor's friend." The old man told me about his high blood pressure because of "the situation" and left.

Hussein and I walked down the road leading out of the village through the fields. There was no traffic. Hussein walked slowly, lost in thought. We sat on a parapet by the road. Hussein lit a cigarette and resumed his story. "I can't tell you about the pain one feels when they gave the electric shocks. I thought I would die. At times I think every shock lasted a minute or two; at times it seemed an hour," he said.

After his interrogators threw him back in his cell, Hussein kept losing consciousness. "At least during the blackouts, I felt no pain." He was bleeding when he urinated, his penis had swollen, and pain crawled up it like a leech. When he was moved to the detention center at Srinagar, an infection had set in, and he saw pus and blood in his urine. There was no medical aid for weeks. "Then a Sikh paramilitary officer asked me about my condition. I told him what had happened. He was an angel; he got me

some medicine, cotton, and Dettol antiseptic lotion. That helped a lot."
It made me think of what Ansar and Shafi had told me about different
interrogators: "Some were sadists and some were decent men." Hussein
was silent again. I asked him whether he knew the Sikh officer's name
or had been able to maintain contact. "Unfortunately, I do not know his
name. I did not see him after a few weeks. I think he was transferred."

Hussein was released from jail after two years. A year afterward he
began running a small business dealing in carpets and shawls. One day
he decided to tell his family about his impotence. He had not spoken
about it to anyone. That night he did not sleep till he heard the morning call to prayer. "I went to the mosque, prayed, and broke down while
asking God for help. Only He knew what I had been through." Walking
back home from the mosque, he felt stronger and decided to talk to
his brother-in-law, a schoolteacher. His brother-in-law advised him to
see a doctor. "For a year I went to various doctors at the Anantnag district hospital; they wrote a long list of medicines, but they did not help
much." Shahid wanted to take him to the Medical Institute at Srinagar.
Hussein was not comfortable talking to Shahid. He refused to meet any
more doctors and spent his days running a small grocery and praying at
the village mosque.

His family gave up till another crisis arrived—his younger brothers
were getting married. In Kashmiri tradition, a younger brother does
not get married before the elder. Hussein's father, brother-in-law, and
uncles tried to convince him again. The village was talking about it:
"Why isn't their elder son getting married when the younger ones are?
Is something wrong with him? They say something happened to him in
the jail." Hussein insisted his younger siblings go ahead with their lives.
They did. Hussein played with their kids. "It is hard at times. But I simply
do not think of a life with someone." Hussein's voice could not hide his
longing.

We walked back to the clinic. I turned to him and said, "Hussein,
you will be all right. Your condition is curable." I told Hussein about
Ansar's marriage and his three-year-old daughter; I told him about the
urological surgeries I had read about, about the drugs, about psychiatric

counseling, about him being a brave man, about faith, about Prophet Muhammad saying that hopelessness is a crime. We reached the clinic and entered Shahid's mud-walled, bare-floored clinic. We waited till the patient he was examining left. I turned to Hussein and urged him to talk to his doctor cousin. He looked into my eyes and smiled. "I will. Thanks." We shook hands, and I walked out of the clinic.

12 ⌒ Heroes

Winter was setting in. The last leaf had fallen from the mulberry tree outside my window, and the clouds were a dull, wintry gray. Srinagar seemed to have shrunk, turned more introspective, like a middling man noticing yet another shock of gray hair in the morning mirror. The desolation outside mirrored my desolation inside. I spent my afternoons reading and tried to write in the evenings. But I had no distance from the experiences I was trying to process and shape into words. I sulked, turned irritable, and had pointless arguments with friends. I called Shahid. We met in our favorite café near the city center. "It is common among people who come into contact with trauma victims," Shahid said, and suggested I should try not to write for a few weeks.

"That won't help. I have to finally get back to writing it down."

"Then remember that people like you and me are a privileged minority in Kashmir. Our backgrounds have shielded us from a lot. We have been able to get an education and build a career. We can get out of here whenever we want to." He paused and said, "Didn't you leave?" Shahid had never left Kashmir. He had studied at the medical college in Srinagar. His remark felt like an allegation.

"I came back, Shahid. I did not forget anything when I was away. I came back to write about Kashmir," I shouted.

"Then face it! Don't run away every time you hear stories that depress you," he retorted. We smoked our cigarettes and drank our coffee without any words. After a few minutes, he stamped out his cigarette and said, "I am sorry. I know it is hard. I couldn't even get Hussein to speak to me about his problems. I am the doctor here. But I was talking as a friend."

We ordered more coffee, and Shahid continued to talk. "It happens to everyone who had strong attachments to this place. When I was posted in the emergency ward, they used to bring scores of injured every day. At times we were able to save them. At times they died on the operating table. I used to cry in my room after every such death. It affected my work. I wanted to be transferred and talked to a senior doctor about it. He told me that we must know that we can't save everyone, and yet we must try to be better doctors." Shahid had faced his fear and continued to work in the emergency ward. I had to confront my own ghosts.

I walked back to my parents' house, thinking once again about people I had failed to write about, places I had postponed visiting because I feared it would be painful. I thought of Mubeena Ghani, a woman from a South Kashmir village an hour away from my ancestral home whom I had heard about while I was in school. In May 1990, a few hours after her marriage, she was raped by a group of Indian paramilitary soldiers.

Later, in college, I read the short stories of Saadat Hussein Manto, the greatest chronicler of violence on the subcontinent. Manto wrote a series of very powerful sketches about the sectarian violence that followed the partition of British India into India and Pakistan. In one story, "Khol Do" (Open Up), he talks about a father finding his daughter in a hospital ward a few days after she's gone missing during the sectarian violence. The doctor in the ward asks the father to open a window for his daughter. When she hears the doctor's phrase *khol do*, the daughter drops her pants. She had been repeatedly raped and associated the phrase *khol do* with the rapist's command to undress.

In the spring of 2002, I had traveled to Kashmir on a reporting trip from Delhi. One day after I had filed my news reports, I went in search of Mubeena. I found out that she and her husband, Rashid Malik, lived in the village of Chawalgam, an hour away from my village. The next morning I took a taxi to Chawalgam. In the village market, shops hung placards advertising Coke and Parle biscuits. A shopkeeper directed me up a narrow alley that ended with a bakery. The baker was kneading dough in a wide wooden tub. "Where does Rashid Malik live?" I asked.

The baker stopped and said without taking his hands off the dough, "Do you mean the one whose bride was raped? Are you from the press?" He pointed to a hutlike house of unbaked bricks and wood. Rusted barbed wire nailed to poles of willow branches formed its boundary. Polythene sheets took the place of window glass, and haystacks placed on rough timber lofts formed the roof. A brown cow was tied in the courtyard corner, and a child played with twigs on the stairs. I stood outside the house; I felt like a trespasser and wondered whether I should leave them undisturbed. I was debating the thought when a haggard-looking man appeared.

Shadows circled his sunken eyes, stubble with dashes of white covered his sallow cheeks, and his shirt hung loose on his bony shoulders. "I am Rashid. The shopkeepers told me a journalist was looking for me. Please come home."

He led me to his house. The mud walls of the house were cracked and the bare bricks exposed. A patchwork blanket covered the floor in the drawing room, which didn't have any furniture. His son left to call Mubeena from the fields where she was working. I talked to Rashid till Mubeena came. Her pale skin seemed to hang lifelessly on her oval face; the skin on her hands was cracked, and her brown eyes were reluctant and apprehensive. She wore a battered *pheran* and brought tea and biscuits for me. Rashid was apologetic for not being able to offer me anything better. Mubeena poured tea for me in a cracked porcelain cup, and they told me their story.

On the evening of May 16, 1990, Rashid Malik got a haircut and dressed in a white suit and an embroidered turban. The village girls sang marriage songs. In their songs, the groom was a prince and his bride a princess prettier than the moon. His family hired a photographer to take pictures of the marriage ceremony. One of those pictures shows Rashid leaving for his bride's house. His dark brown eyes gleam in his ruddy face. His wide shoulders and muscular chest fill the jacket. His teeth shine beneath his thick black mustache. Another picture shows him sitting on the front seat of the bus hired to take him, his friends, and relatives to Mubeena's house in Hiller village, five miles away. The bus left at nine in the evening. Half an hour later, Rashid sat on a velvet-covered seat in his bride's house. A mullah arrived, and the Muslim marriage ritual, the *nikah*, was performed. Three times the mullah asked Rashid if he was willing to marry Mubeena of his free will, and three times he asked Mubeena if she was willing to marry Rashid of her free will. Both agreed and became husband and wife. The families celebrated, and the feast was served. An hour later, Rashid prepared to leave with his bride. More songs were sung. Then they heard gunfire.

Rashid's in-laws believed it was the militants firing in the air. In those days militants would order people not to sing marriage songs or have lavish feasts in a time of sacrifice. Rashid and his relatives insisted on leaving. The bride's family was worried and asked them to stay put. They argued about the wisdom of traveling five miles at that time of night. The groom's side prevailed, boarded the bus, and left with the bride. Rashid's elder brother, who worked for the Indian Railway Police Force, sat next to him, carefully holding a travel permission slip acquired from an army colonel posted nearby. Those were the days of night curfews in Kashmir. Every man moving around after dusk needed a curfew pass. The bus moved slowly on the dirt track that led to the groom's village.

Two kilometers on, Rashid, who sat in the front seat next to the driver, saw a Central Reserve Police Force vehicle. The bus stopped, and his brother showed the CRPF men the permission slip. They let the marriage party proceed. A few miles ahead, at a crossing in Hakoorah village, Rashid and his companions saw soldiers from the Border Security Force, who an hour ago had come across a patrol party of the CRPF. The paramilitary groups had mistaken each other for militants and exchanged fire. The bus stopped again. The BSF personnel ran toward it. A BSF man shouted at the driver to switch off the headlights. Darkness fell on the road, and a few miniature decorative bulbs lighted the bus. Rashid, his companions, and his bride shivered in their seats. His brother rose, permission slip in hand, and opened the door. He moved toward a BSF officer to show him the piece of paper. The BSF men did not even look at the slip. Rashid saw two of them grab his brother by the neck and drag him to the roadside, where they began beating him. Rashid wanted to protest or beg for mercy, but his feet failed him. He saw the BSF men circle the bus; he looked over his shoulder at his bride. She huddled in her seat with the bridesmaid; he wanted to rush to her. But then there was gunfire.

The BSF men poured bullets into the bus. Rashid threw off his turban and ducked under his seat like all the others. The next moment he felt something grazing his shoulder, and a cry rose from the next seat. The bullet grazing his shoulder had hit his cousin Sabzaar in the arm. Another volley of bullets pierced the tin body of the bus and his cousin Asadullah's chest, killing him. Rashid was yet to realize what had happened to his cousin when he was hit in the back; doctors later found five bullets. Three bullets hit Mubeena in her shoulder, back, and hips. The BSF officer ordered the passengers off the bus; a round of mass beatings followed. Rashid fell on the road and lost consciousness. Mubeena stood along with her bridesmaid and others by the roadside, bleeding. A group of soldiers dragged her and the bridesmaid to the mustard fields beside the road. An unknown number of BSF men raped the two injured women. "I could not even remember how many there were. I had lost my senses," Mubeena said.

Another group of BSF personnel led by a senior officer reached the place. They took the injured men and women to a hospital in Anantnag. The next morning the state government officials reached the hospital and took the statements of Rashid, Mubeena, and the other injured. The district administration head awarded them state relief of three thousand rupees each. They refused. Separatist leaders visited them in the hospital and later in their village, where they addressed the villagers and urged them to stand by the couple.

Rashid was shifted to a better hospital in Srinagar. The doctors gave him a choice: Live with the five bullets in your body or risk a surgery that can take your mobility. He decided against the surgery and returned home, determined to begin his life anew. A hostile silence greeted Rashid and Mubeena on their return. For Rashid's family and the villagers, Mubeena was a bad omen: the cause of a misfortune that had taken one life and injured ten. Her in-laws rejected her. Mubeena's parents and some friends stood by the couple. Rashid could not work for a year; the couple lived on help provided by Mubeena's parents. He wanted to sell his share in the family property. His family denied him even that.

A year later, Mubeena gave birth to a son; the child died in a few weeks. She was suicidal. Rashid begged her to live, to be stronger. Leaving his trauma behind, he took up work as a carpenter when there was work. On other days Rashid was a manual laborer, carrying bricks, plowing fields, harvesting crops. Mubeena pitched in; she stitched, tailored, and worked at the village farms, braving taunts thrown by her in-laws, neighbors, and village folk. At the village tap, waiting in the queue for water, she lowered her head. On the streets of the village, she moved like smoke, trying to be invisible. The smallest altercation would become a reminder of her trauma. "Aren't you the bride who was raped? Aren't you the one who brought ill luck?" The village had nicknames for them. "They call us 'Crossfire Bride' and 'Crossfire Groom,'" Mubeena told me.

An inquiry was ordered; some paramilitary soldiers were suspended. New personnel took their place: soldiers who did not recognize Rashid and Mubeena. But she still shivered at the sight of a uniform.

That night lingered like a ghost, refusing to be exorcised. Mubeena poured tea for me and wiped her tears with her scarf. Rashid was silent. I stared at a faded design of flowers on the patchwork blanket we sat on. Their daughter came in and relieved us of that difficult silence. She wore a white-and-blue uniform and carried a satchel. She rushed to Mubeena and sat on her lap. The girl was a fourth-grader at a local school. She showed me her notebooks. In her English notebook, she had written about her aim in life: to be a doctor. Rashid and Mubeena looked at her with pride. I looked out the window; a wind rustled the willows behind the house and flapped the polythene sheet nailed to the bare window panels. Rashid and Mubeena walked me to the door. Rashid held his daughter's hand, and their son clung to Mubeena. They waved and smiled.

Sometime after meeting them, I came across a poem by a Kashmiri poet, Farooq Nazki:

Mothers wash the bloodstained apparel of grooms
On stream banks,
Bridal wear burns to ash,
Bridesmaids cry
And the Jhelum flows.

But I failed to get myself to write about Mubeena and Rashid. I had failed also to visit Kunan Poshpora, the village in the northern Kupwara district where the Indian army raped more than twenty women in 1990. Kunan Poshpora had become a symbol, a metaphor, a memory like Srebrenica.

In early December I arrived in Kupwara, three hours from Srinagar. Kunan Poshpora was minutes away, and I planned to catch a bus to finally visit it. Majestic mountains and miles of lush green paddy fields surrounded Kupwara. Its beautiful surroundings heightened the squalor of the town. The shared taxi I boarded in Srinagar stopped in a vast, unpaved bus yard that marked the beginnings of the town. Two rows of cramped and ugly blocks of shops formed the main market. Eateries displaying potato chip packets and bottles of Pepsi stood next to mechanic shops smelling of petrol. I saw an army check post and the barrel of a machine gun poking out of it. A sign hanging on the check post read: TOWN COMMANDER KUPWARA. The military presence around the town justified the title.

Then I heard a boy in clothes blackened with grease shout, "Kunan Poshpora." A green-and-yellow-painted bus revved its engine. An old man with a scraggly beard, wearing a peasant's embroidered cap, tied two long iron pipes used for water supply to the roof of the bus. Three women sat on the seat behind the driver. A plump girl in a yellow dress and green bangles jumped restlessly in the aisle, chewed gum, and blew bubbles. A couple cuddled on a seat. The conductor shouted, "Kunan Poshpora." The driver revved the engine again. The couple continued their whispers. Two schoolboys in white shirts and black trousers jumped onto the bus, and it began to leave. I watched it go and thought of Rashid, Mubeena, and their daughter who wanted to be a doctor.

I sat in a run-down tea shop, smoking, thinking. But I couldn't be alone for too long. Shabir, an effeminate young man who said he was a poet, introduced himself and asked what I was doing in Kupwara. I told him I found escape in journalism. "I thought so. I could tell from your bag, your notebooks. Most journalists dress like you do," said Shabir. He loved watching television news and had ideas for me. "I can take you to some places you might like to write about," he said. "The first news I can give you is about a graveyard here. Most people buried there are the boys who were killed in encounters with the army on the border."

The Line of Control ran through many mountains towering over the villages bordering Kupwara. Shabir told me that after every encounter, the bodies of the youths trying to cross over to Pakistan for arms training or returning from there were handed over by the Indian army to the local police and then buried in the graveyard. "Because nobody knows the names of the dead, the locals who manage the graveyard have marked them with numbers."

"What was the latest number you saw there?" I asked him.

"I think it was two hundred something."

"I will go there soon," I lied. I thanked Shabir and left the café. I was tired and boarded a taxi headed for Srinagar. I wanted to be home. I wanted to be in my room.

13 ∽ Price of Life

Mubeena and Rashid had lived through brutality and ostracism, yet they had made a home and were bringing up their children. Parveena had moved on from being an anonymous housewife to a celebrated crusader for justice. Tortured, broken men like Ansar had built new lives. Hussein had begun the process of discussing his problems with Shahid, and I had finally been able to write about people, places, and subjects I had run away from. In those tales shadowed by death and loss, there were also feats of resilience and fortitude. Despite everything, people survived. Yet how many could really move on?

It was early February. Winter was refusing to wear out; the mountains were still frozen ash. My shoulders no longer felt the weight of multiple layers of sweaters and a thick wool *pheran*. The beige weed frames of the *kangris* we carried all winter, even to our beds, had turned a dark brown from long hours of intimacy with our hands. The soles of my shoes had taken the color of mud despite the daily violence of a shoe brush. And morning breath still imitated my cigarettes. Father wore his black Jinnah cap and brown overcoat to work; Mother was mostly home, her school closed for a two-and-a-half-month-long winter break. She suggested that we visit a cousin of my father who was back from his pilgrimage to Mecca.

Most Kashmiri Muslims looked forward to the pilgrimage to Mecca for years. People went to work, built houses, educated their children, married them off, and when their worldly duties were taken care of, they took their savings, walked to the government office that issued Hajj forms, and bought a ticket for Mecca. Traveling to Mecca is the only traveling most Kashmiri Muslims do. The pilgrimage is mandatory for every Muslim when he or she can afford to make it. My uncle was done with his worldly duties when he and his wife left for Mecca. Now they were back, and their journey had accorded them a new status: Hajjis. Kashmiri tradition required friends and relatives to visit newly returned Hajjis. The conflict, however, had limited mobility, and extended families met only on major social occasions like engagements, weddings, hospital visits, or funerals. "Your father can't come, so you have to come with me to Uncle Rahman's house," my mother said.

Father used to visit my uncle and his family regularly despite the strong presence of Indian troops and militants around my uncle's village. But he had stopped after the mine attack. My parents still lived with fear.

Some time ago we had been in his car when the driver drove over an empty tetra packet of a mango drink lying on the road. As children, we used to jump on those empty packets to make them burst like crackers. My father had ducked under the seat, his hand covering his head. "Daddy, it is a Frooti case," I said slowly. He'd eased back in his seat and was silent. "You know, after that mine blast . . ."

I had seen my father's helplessness another day when we heard the news of the death of his aunt. She lived in a village close to my uncle's, and Father had not been able to visit her during the last phase of her illness. "She was very kind to me when I was a child. She always took care of me, more than any relative I had," Father told me. "But I couldn't even visit her when she was dying."

Mother and I boarded a local bus to visit my uncle's village. I was excited to meet many of my relatives whom I hadn't seen in years. The bus ambled along the slope of our mountains and stopped a mile ahead for an identity check at one of the two military camps bordering our village. Two very young soldiers in flak jackets stood at the checkpoint, daintily dangling their Kalashnikovs. They asked us to walk. We walked a hundred meters and a soldier shouted, "Stop." We stopped. Nobody was frisked. No bags were searched. We boarded the bus and moved toward the village. I wondered at the absurdity of these instructions. They served no purpose, even when I looked at things from a soldier's perspective. It felt like a video game. The soldier moves his finger; buses stop; people form queues, walk, stop, board, and leave. Another vehicle reaches the checkpoint, and the game repeats itself.

The absurd exercise reminded me of "The New Disease," a short story by Kashmiri writer Akhter Mohiuddin, who died in 2001. His son-in-law was killed in a militant attack on a bank in a hospital complex where he worked. His younger son, returning home from work, was killed in retaliatory firing by the military after it came under militant attack. In protest against the excesses, Akhter had returned the Padam Shri, one of the highest civilian awards, which the Indian government had given him for his services to literature. He wrote like Isaac Babel, had similar intimacy with war, power, and fear, and had dedicated his last book to "young men who were murdered at unknown places." Like Babel was.

In "The New Disease," a man waits for a long time, as if in a queue, before entering his own house—and then turns away and leaves in another direction. His family takes him to a doctor. The doctor says, "Ever since frisking has been introduced, a new disease has come up. Some people need to be frisked every time they see a gate; others frisk themselves." He prescribes a body search every time the man reaches a gate. The family follows the prescription, and the man's condition improves.

An elderly man in a blue suit sat on the bus seat in front of me. He turned around and said, "What was the point of that? They just want to assert their presence, tell us they rule this place." The bus moved toward my uncle's village. There were no more check posts on the way, but we were traveling on the road where my parents were almost killed. I could see Mother turning stiff. We remained silent and kept looking out the bus window. A few minutes later, the bus crossed the water pipe in the road where the mine had been planted. Ordinary Kashmiri brick houses flanked the road, and groups of villagers sat lazily outside their homes, staring at the passengers. I saw those people, but Mother seemed to see the man pressing the remote control of the mine. She pointed at a group of villagers and said, "That was where they [the militants] sat with the remote control." I bit my lip and shook my head. We made the rest of our journey in silence.

Narrow lanes ran between mud-and-brick houses circled by leafless walnut trees in the village of Panzmulla, where my uncle lived. On the way to his house, we exchanged greetings with acquaintances and relatives returning from the customary visit. My uncle, a tall, tanned man, sat on a carpet surrounded by men and women listening to his stories of Mecca. Young girls and boys served *kahwa* in tin-plated samovars. The visitors sipped the *kahwa* and heard the tales of faith. Uncle ordinarily would have been offended if my father hadn't visited him after his return from the pilgrimage. Instead, the moment my mother and I walked into his house, he hugged me and said, "How unfortunate are these times that Ghulam Ahmad can't even come to see me today."

Groups of visitors arrived; Uncle rose from his seat to greet each one. Every visitor was offered a glass of Aab-e-Zam Zam, the water from Mecca's spring of Zam Zam, believed to have healing powers. They all asked the same questions. Yes, the traffic moves on the right side of the road there; yes, there are people of every color and country wearing the same white cotton robes. Yes, the shops are very big and full of all kinds of expensive things. Yes, you are mesmerized when you first see the Qaaba. Uncle seemed to be getting tired of repeating himself. The *muezzin*'s call for prayer rescued him, and he left for the mosque. Mother joined a group of relatives and was soon engrossed in conversation. She was talking spiritedly and laughing at the jokes. I watched her from a distance and was glad to see her happy.

I obsessed about the attack on my parents in the months following it. Lying sleepless at night, I would fantasize about avenging them. Then I would return to the real world and think of my grandparents, my aunts, my cousins who still lived in and near my village. I thought of the shelves full of my father's books and my own aspirations of writing. Most families accepted the killings of their kin with resignation and struggled to continue with their lives. Under the Kashmir government rules, a family member of any innocent person killed in the conflict in Kashmir was given a low-level government job and the family was paid a hundred thousand rupees as compensation. In the early years of the conflict, most people refused to accept such compensation, deeming it unethical. But life was harsher and more complex than ideas of resistance. With time, people opened old files and began thinking of making their lives a little easier, even if that had to be done by accepting the official price of life. Maybe I would have applied for the monetary compensation and the job. I had seen that happen in my own extended family while I was still at college.

One afternoon while I sat in our kitchen and talked to my mother, there was a knock on the door. Bashir, her cousin who lived in a village an hour away, stood there, looking distraught and holding the door for support. Between sobs, he said slowly, "They killed Gulzar. The army killed him last night, blew him up with a mine." We stepped back in shock. Gulzar was a cousin to both my mother and Bashir. Two of my cousins, an aunt, and my grandparents rushed into the kitchen. Grandfather held Bashir in his arms and stoically said the prayers Muslims say when someone dies: *Ina Lilahi Wa Ina Ilahi Rajioon* (Whatever comes from God, returns to Him.) Grandfather's wrinkled face hardened with pain, and tears filled his blue eyes. An image of Gulzar flashed in front of my eyes: a frail boy of fifteen years standing in the courtyard of his house, the beginnings of a mustache turning his upper lip a shade darker than his pink face. His hair was short and spiky, and he held a cricket bat.

Half an hour later, my family left for his funeral in his village. I stayed behind. Somebody had to remain at home, for it was unsafe to leave your house unattended.

Gulzar's village had grown distant because it was located close to a massive army camp, and the area was more volatile than our own. I could not help thinking of the endless frisking and identification parades my family would have to go through. I was thankful they had a car. Visiting the place on a local bus was a nightmare. A mini-stampede would follow after you crossed the check posts. People would run toward the bus in a frenzy, pushing, elbowing to grab a seat on the overcrowded vehicle. Bitter arguments followed as the earlier occupant of a particular seat would try to regain it after the check post.

The next morning they returned, worn out and grieving. Gulzar had been a twelfth-grade student at the local high school. The new academic session had just begun, and the senior students were expected to rag the newcomers. One day Gulzar and his friends ragged a newcomer to walk up to a girl and propose to her. "Propose" is the word Kashmiri boys use for asking someone out for a date. The newcomer, a shy boy, reluctantly walked up to the girl and did what he had been told to do. The girl retorted sarcastically and humiliated him.

The boy turned out to be the son of an army officer. The following evening an army patrol surrounded Gulzar's house. They asked for him, searched the house, and found nothing. Then they took him to the cowshed used to store firewood, plows, shovels, and sickles. Ten minutes later, his parents and brothers heard a blast. The cowshed fell apart. The soldiers had detonated a mine that killed Gulzar. They claimed he was a militant and had mistakenly blasted the mine after identifying it.

Gulzar's death changed our relationship with his family. My parents, grandparents, aunts, and cousins visited them every other day. Mother enrolled his younger sister in a school near our home, and she stayed with our family till recently, when she graduated from the local women's college.

After Gulzar's death, nobody talked about fighting in a court to punish the soldiers who had killed him. Those things happen elsewhere, in countries where the law is implemented; in Kashmir you try to save the living from further trouble. The extended family talked about getting compensation and finding his unemployed elder brother, Ayub, a job. For months we could not get a certificate from the army attesting that Gulzar was not a militant. We petitioned India's National Human Rights Commission, and after some time, the No Objection Certificate was received. The fact that our family had connections in the local government expedited the process. Ayub got a job in the rural development department and was married a year later. Daily life went on. Gulzar was rarely mentioned at home in conversation. But he remained an invisible presence.

The schools opened after the winter break. March mornings were filled with the shouts of children marching past our house. The soldiers at our neighborhood bunkers seemed to smile a little. The newspapers would soon carry the standard annual story about snow melting on the Line of Control and the increase in militants trying to cross over. I stepped out to buy coffee when the dreaded neighborhood barber standing outside Bombay Hair Dresser shouted, "Your hair is all haywire." He took at least two hours to give me a haircut, yet I was a regular because he had a lush imagination and told stories in the long cigarette breaks during a hair-cutting session. I couldn't forget a story he told me earlier in winter, after militants detonated a land mine targeting Indian soldiers patrolling our area. "The glass panes shattered, and it was very, very loud. I thought I was dead. And then in a fleeting moment I saw the Angel of Death holding a notebook. It had names of the dead in it. My name wasn't there! And then I lit a cigarette. I knew I would be fine."

I shook my head and praised God and Prophet Muhammad. After a while I asked him, "Was the death register in English or Urdu?"

"Urdu, of course! You know I can't read English."

Stories! There are no good stories in Kashmir. There are only difficult, ambiguous, and unresolved stories. I often heard stories about what happened to families whose kin died in the conflict and who did not have the relative financial comfort and connections that made moving on easier for people like Gulzar's family. I had heard many stories about families seeking compensation for their dead children, visiting government offices for months, and being entangled for years in red tape. One of those stories was about Shameema, a woman in a village not very far from my own. "You must meet her," said the friend who told me about her.

Shameema lived in the village of Larkipora, around thirty kilometers south of my village. Larkipora was a huddle of houses and serene fields, its tragedies hidden from the casual visitor. I walked up a lane that led to a gate of corrugated iron sheets nailed over rough timber lofts. Beyond the gate, a thin, sharp-nosed woman in a faded orange *pheran* sat on the cobbled veranda of the house. She was bent over a wicker basket full of *haakh*, a spinachlike local leafy vegetable. She kept the vegetable basket aside and rose from her seat. She looked at me for a long time before saying, "Sit here, son. I am Shameema."

I sat facing her. Her younger son, a thirteen-year-old, sat in the other corner of the rectangular veranda next to a hookah. Shameema's sister-in-law joined us. The women sat behind baskets full of vegetables. Shameema held a long leaf of *haakh*, tore a portion, and said, "It was May eleventh, 2001." I was struck how most people remembered the exact dates of the most horrifying events in their lives. She continued, "I had cooked tomatoes and rice and was waiting for Shafi for lunch."

Shafi, her seventeen-year-old son, was a tenth-grade student at the government school at Qabamarg, a nearby village famous for a Sufi saint's shrine. Her other son, Bilal, was in ninth grade and her husband, Majid, worked as a farmer and sold cheap dried fruit at a bus stop in Anantnag. On the morning of May 11, Shafi went for lessons in physics and chemistry to two different teachers in neighboring villages despite his father wanting help at the Anantnag stall. He returned around noon. "I asked him to have lunch. He asked me to wait till he had brought firewood for the nearby sawmill." Twenty minutes later, Shafi was back with a cart of firewood. Shameema pointed at a patch of ground near the stairs where a child stood eating a banana and said, "That was where he kept the firewood." She sighed. "Then he left for the mosque for the Friday prayers."

"I met him near the roadside mosque," a male voice said. I had failed to notice a young man in a brown shirt and loose jeans sitting on the edge of the veranda. He turned out to be Shafi's friend Mushtaq. "We were five of us, including his brother, when Shafi joined us. We did not pray, we sat under a chinar tree by the road and talked." A gunfight had started between the militants and the Indian army at Qabamarg. "We talked about the encounter and thought the school could be burned.

Then we saw some army trucks come from far off in the distance." The boys left and walked quickly to the lane leading toward their houses. The army trucks stopped and the soldiers ran after the boys. Mushtaq and another boy escaped; the four other boys were caught and taken away. Villagers saw the soldiers throw the boys into the trucks and head back toward Qabamarg.

Shameema's neighbors came running and told her the army had taken Shafi and Bilal. In a matter of minutes, the mothers and sisters of the boys gathered near her house. They began running toward Qabamarg along a track that connected the two villages through mustard fields. Soldiers circled the fields outside the village. They tried stopping the women, who pushed and shouted back. Shameema raised her head and looked at the distant sky and said, "God gave me courage that day. I fought with every soldier who tried to stop me. Normally, you are scared of soldiers, but I did not stop that day till I reached the house where the encounter was going on." She saw soldiers and Ikhwanis (renegade militants working for the Indian forces) all around. They were firing at a single-story house. In the courtyard of the building next to it, she saw the arrested boys. "I saw Bilal from a distance, but Shafi was missing." She paused. Then she sighed and asked her younger son to bring her some water. He ran inside and came out after a moment with a copper tumbler. Shameema drank, put down the glass, and pushed the vegetable basket away as if preparing for a battle. "I ran toward Bilal, grabbed him by an arm, and began walking away with him." Bilal hugged her and said that the soldiers had sent Shafi inside the militants' house with a mine in his hands.

A soldier hit Shameema on the arm with the butt of his gun and pulled Bilal toward him. She shouted at the soldier and grabbed Bilal's hand. He said, "Let me go, Mother. They must have already killed Shafi; let me die, too." The soldier pulled harder and began walking away with Bilal. Shameema stood frozen, watching. The soldier thrust a mine in Bilal's hands and pushed him toward the house. The gunfire was still going on. "Something seized my heart as I saw Bilal's shivering hands holding the mine. His legs were giving way, and he was falling to the ground." Shameema took another gulp from the copper tumbler, wiped sweat from her forehead, and said, "I lunged ahead and threw myself on Bilal." She took the mine from her son's hands and held him in her arms. Three soldiers and an officer circled them, asking her to leave her son. She told the officer to leave her son and let her take the mine into the house. "I held on to the mine and asked the officer to blow me up." He remained silent; she shouted again. "Then he ordered the soldiers to let us go. I held Bilal. As we walked away I saw them push an old man toward the house with the mine in his hands."

That night they did not sleep. She held Bilal in her arms, and they cried for Shafi. Her husband, who had stayed in Anantnag, reached home in the morning. Neighbors told him that his son had been killed. Three days after Shafi was buried, they held the final mourning ceremony. For three days, as was the custom, no food was cooked in their house; their neighbors cooked for them. On the fourth day, they cooked for their neighbors and invited the village mullah to offer prayers for Shafi's salvation. "We cooked the meal on the firewood Shafi had bought the last time he came home," Shameema said, wiping her tears.

Her thirteen-year-old son was crying, too. She hugged and patted and consoled him, saying I was there to help with Bilal's job. Then she lit the hookah and gave it to him as if it were a glass of juice. He puffed violently and stared at me. Shameema told me he was psychologically disturbed. He had been in the same school as Shafi and would run from his classroom to cry outside the house where Shafi was killed. His condition had worsened, and he refused to go to school. Then he began smoking. "I took him to Aishmuqam, to the shrine of Zain Shah Sahib [a revered local Sufi saint]. He has been better since I prayed there. But every time Shafi is mentioned, he is agitated. Which mother would pass a hookah to her son? But I have to; it calms him down."

After the mourning period, Shameema and her family began fighting the wars of daily life. Bilal resumed school, Shameema did the household chores, and Majid, her husband, took a bus every morning to sell sweets in town. A month later, one of their educated neighbors told them about compensation. Majid and Bilal made the required applications and ran between the police station and the office of the district administrative head, the deputy commissioner, where the case for compensation was processed. Since June 2001 Bilal and Majid have become weekly presences at the deputy commissioner's office. The clerks processing the compassionate-appointments cases have the standard answer: "Come next week. Your turn has not come yet." The next week they hear about a nonexistent ban on such compensatory jobs. "Last month the clerk told Majid our serial number is four hundred; this week he said it is six hundred," Shameema told me. "Why don't you meet Majid? He will be on the pavement at the Achabal bus stop in Anantnag near a fruit shop. You can ask any shopkeeper there, and they will tell you where he is. He knows more about the case."

I promised to meet him and began to take my leave. She walked with me till we crossed the wood-and-tin gate opening onto the lane. She stopped and stared at me with blank, teary eyes. "Throughout our conversation, I have wanted to tell you something," she said. I hoped there was not some other horror that had befallen her family. She held my hands and said, "You don't know my son. But you look exactly like my Shafi. If he was alive today you would pass off for twins." I did not know how to respond and hugged her. I dragged my feet till I reached the main road. On the other side of the road, I saw a tall chinar tree swaying in the mild wind. Under its shade, Shafi had chatted with his friends for the last time.

I saw a bus approaching and waved it down. I got on and rested my head against the backseat and closed my eyes. Around an hour later, we reached the Anantnag bus yard, where Majid sold sweets. Dust blew around; buses and cars honked. Hawkers shouted the prices of their wares; villagers carrying groceries in colored polythene bags ran around looking for the buses leaving for their spacious, beautiful villages; and a group of bored-looking paramilitary men in bulletproof jackets stood on the pavement holding their assault rifles. A shopkeeper selling fruits from a shop jutting onto a pavement knew Majid. "Where is his shop?" I asked. He smiled and pointed to a tiny corner of the pavement between his and the next shop. I saw a wicker basket full of *seemnih*, a pink sweet I had loved as a child, raised on a pile of bricks. The gray-haired man with sunken cheeks wearing a beige *pheran* was almost invisible behind it. I walked up to him and said, "Are you Majid?" He rose from his jute mat and said, "How many grams, sir?"

I could not muster the courage to disturb his world again. I walked toward the deputy commissioner's office to meet a man who once was in charge of cases relating to compensation death. A short walk bought me to the gates of the office complex in Lal Chowk, an unimaginative imitation of the Srinagar city center. This was the heart of Anantnag town—a jumble of houses and shops, open sewers full of filth, noisy hawkers, honking buses, and whistling policemen. It was somewhat like the sad small towns of northern India. Past the check posts and metal detectors, the office complex was a set of barracklike buildings with windows painted in a dull blue used only on government buildings. It was the local seat of power, the administrative unit inherited from the colonial civil service. Groups of impatient supplicants, small-time lawyers, village politicians, and elders hovered around for audiences and favors, and the carnivorous foot soldiers of bureaucracy searching for prey to bolster their meager official salaries spilled over the lawns. The hurried, hectic sound of hustle and barter filled the place.

Inside, liveried peons shouted the names of supplicants who had been granted an audience with various officers. I walked through a dark corridor to meet the man who might know about Shameema's relief case. I had known him for many years. Piles of tattered cardboard cover files lay on his decrepit wooden table. Similar files covered with dust were stacked away on shelves behind his chair. Four more people sat behind similar tables covered with stacks of files, typing on antique Remington typewriters. He smiled as he saw me looking at the typewriters and files. He had seen me as a kid and was both amused and disappointed to see me not as a bureaucrat, like my father, but as a writer interested in "random, unimportant people."

"What happens is that first they have to get a first information report lodged in a police station and get certificates from the police saying that the person killed was not a militant. So they pay anything from five thousand to ten thousand rupees to the policemen who would not otherwise give the report. Then the cases come here to the relief section in the D.C. office. We have to make the file move." He paused to smoke. "The file does not move by itself from one table to another. Nor does the typist type an order for free. The senior officers are to be convinced and given their share, too. All this takes time and money. Out of the relief money of one *lakh*, the applicant has to spend twenty-five to thirty thousand rupees. Otherwise he will waste years visiting offices. And once he pays that, we ensure that his name in the compensation job list goes up and things move fast." He sounded like an automaton.

14 ⌒ In the Courtyards of Faith

Shameema and Majid, who had lost a son, were wading through the painfully slow bureaucratic procedures to find a job for their other son, and they didn't have enough resources to pay for treatment of their younger son with psychological disorders. All they seemed to have was each other and faith. Hussein, who refused to marry after he was tortured, prayed regularly to find the strength to deal with his predicament. I had seen my own parents credit God for saving their lives and increase their prayers after they survived the mine blast. Shahid told me that even the doctors at the crowded psychiatric hospitals recommended a reliance on faith. God and his saints seemed to have become the psychiatrists with the largest practice in Kashmir; faith was essentially a support system.

That was how it had always been. In my childhood and adolescence, I had no self-consciousness about Islam—it was just there, a part of our life, like my village, my neighborhood, my family, and the books on my father's shelves. Our neighborhood mosque was a place I visited with most of my friends on Fridays and occasionally in the evening for prayer. There was a sense of community, a joyous banter, and an ease with which religion was practiced. We were all neighbors who went to the same baker, the same doctor, and the same grocer. Our mosque was a modest two-floor building a few hundred yards from my house, on the bank of a small stream that went through the village. Children would swim in the stream for hours; village women would wash clothes and utensils on the bank, or *yaarehbal* (literally, the place where friends meet), and gossip. When the *muezzin* gave the call for prayer, the women would look for their head scarves and wear them till the prayer was over, then return to their talk.

Handwoven grass mats softened by years of use covered the mosque floor, and a few dim electric bulbs cast a pale light on the walls covered by a fading green paint. An arch-shaped recess in the prayer hall marked the space for the imam to lead the prayers, facing west toward Mecca. Next to the prayer hall was the *hamaam*, a small room with a limestone floor heated by burning a few logs of wood in the basement. Gul Khan, the tiny baby-faced farmer who lived next to the mosque and gave the call for prayer, often went door-to-door soliciting contributions for the upkeep of the mosque. In the winter, men sat in the *hamaam* and discussed village affairs, religion, and politics. It was the warmest place in the village.

The imam read the same sermon in Arabic every Friday. I knew where the names of the prophets Muhammad, Eesa (Jesus), Moosa (Moses), and Ibrahim (Abraham) appeared, though I never understood what the sermon meant. We always walked back home from the mosque with relatives and friends. After the Friday prayers, it was customary to prepare a big samovar of tea and gather around it for hours. In those conversations, we would often retell a joke about a Kashmiri villager who went to Mecca for the Hajj. He stayed in a hotel, and the hotel manager got irritated with him at some point and began shouting at him in Arabic. The villager knew Arabic as the language of prayer and responded, "Aameen."

I could put many faces to that hypothetical villager. A group of old men would sit in the warm *hamaam*, half asleep. I often suppressed laughter on seeing them jolt out of their reveries as Gul Khan shouted the call for prayer. After the prayers, they would settle into a quasi-musical recital of *darood*, the praises of the Prophet and saints in Persian and Kashmiri, rocking back and forth as they spoke the revered words. My friends and I never really remembered the *darood*, but we would pray along, sit cross-legged, rock our bodies, and call out *"Ya Allah"* in chorus, after the old men. Everyone in the mosque smiled when Saifuddin, my mother's grand-uncle, would stand in the mosque after Eid prayers and say, "Oh God! Please bless those who fasted for you throughout the month of Ramadan. Oh Merciful God! Please forgive and bless those, too, who ignored your orders and did not fast in the month of the Ramadan." We knew that Saifuddin never fasted and would slip behind a curtain in his shop for lunch every afternoon during Ramadan.

In the late eighties, a college teacher leading a Salafist group became active in my village, and they set up a separate mosque. Most of the members of the group were lower middle class, with college degrees and low-rung government jobs. They revolted against the way Islam had been practiced over centuries in Kashmir—a mixture of text and tradition. None of them was a trained Islamic scholar, but they were enthusiastic readers of various Urdu commentaries on the Quran and Hadith. They wanted to shear the local traditions created in the long process of conversion from a Hindu past to Islam. They even introduced differences in appearance: They folded their trousers an inch above the ankles, grew their beards long, and prayed at slightly different times of the day. They saw themselves as social reformers, saving the peasants from the mumbo-jumbo and exploitation of the priestly class—the *moulvis* and the *pirs*, the Muslim Brahmans. A friend described it: "The *moulvi's* son's motorcycle does not run on petrol. It runs on the blood of the villagers." Grandfather, who was always critical of the *moulvis* and *pirs*, left our neighborhood mosque and began praying at the new revivalist mosque three houses from ours.

I went to the Salafist mosque for Friday prayers a few times, but I found them dry and strict. I was not comfortable with their intense, self-conscious piety and certainty about being on the right path. They were dismissive and contemptuous of the not-so-faithful. They endlessly debated correct Arabic pronunciation and the sin of mispronouncing the verses of the Quran and Hadith. Another of their obsessions was the right length of beard: three inches or four inches, one fistful or two fistfuls. The village children called the leader of the revivalists the Goat.

Fortunately, Grandfather never let his affiliation with the revivalists affect his friendships. He maintained his relations with both the Muslim villagers who opposed the revivalists and his Hindu friends. His visits to Somnath's grocery store continued, and so did his friendship with Bhaskarnath, with whom he taught for many years. Unlike many parts of India, where violence between Hindus and Muslims had killed hundreds of people and pushed Indian Muslims into slumlike ghettoes, relations between the Hindus and the Muslims in Kashmir had been peaceful. There was a consciousness of religious identities and differences in political opinion. Many Muslims and Hindus would keep separate cups and plates in their homes for visitors of the other faith.

In our house, there were no separate cups or plates. We ate together. I was about ten when I attended the Hindu marriage of Bhaskarnath's younger brother. I wore black trousers and a black-and-white-checked shirt and tamed my hair with mustard oil. Grandfather dressed in his favorite tweed jacket, shaved carefully, and applied liberal doses of Old Spice aftershave. We sat in a carpeted room full of guests. Lunch, a mixture of vegetables and lamb dishes, was served on small steel plates. It was different from the Muslim wedding feasts, where four people eat together from a tin-plated copper plate; the vegetables are minimal, and the lamb dishes are spicier and numerous. Somebody who sat next to me asked, "So you eat at Hindu homes?" Somebody else took pictures and later gave us copies. I have one of those in my album: Grandfather is talking to Bhaskarnath; I am holding a morsel of food in my right hand and staring at the camera.

After the rebellion against India, along with the stories from the political history of Kashmir, militant groups used Islam for mobilization. Images from Islamic history had been borrowed, and words like "martyrdom" and "jihad" were thrown around. By 1993–94 the Islamist militant groups had gained the upper hand in the separatist militancy, and the Kashmiri nationalist groups like the pro-independence Jammu and Kashmir Liberation Front had surrendered and adopted the politics of nonviolent protest. Pakistan was key to that, being as resolutely against the idea of an independent Kashmir as was India.

Pakistan turned toward its old-time supporter in Kashmir: the Jamaat-e-Islami Jammu and Kashmir, a right-wing politico-religious organization that had been a very small presence in Kashmir since the early 1950s. Maulana Sayid Abu Ala Mawdudi, a journalist, founded the Jamaat in Lahore in 1941; he hoped to establish an Islamic state by reforming individuals, being morally upright, and adhering strictly to Islamic convictions.

Jamaat reached Kashmir a decade later and tried to expand its influence by running schools, holding regular cadre meetings, and extensively distributing pamphlets and cheaply printed books written by Mawdudi. It remained close-knit, cadre-based, and grew in the self-righteousness and political ambition common to such groups. It contested state elections in the late 1960s, hoping that its continuous criticism of the National Conference's failure to get a plebiscite held in Kashmir would convert into votes. But it never got more than three or four seats out of seventy in the Kashmir assembly. Though most Kashmiri Muslims were disillusioned with India and had sympathies for Pakistan, they did not take very kindly to Jamaat. In 1979, when Pakistani dictator Zia-ul-Haq hanged the socialist prime minister of Pakistan, Zulfikar Ali Bhutto—who was liked by Kashmiri Muslims—Jamaat supporters were attacked by mobs in Kashmir and their houses burned. Grandfather saw the angry villagers throwing copies of the Quran into a bonfire in the road near our house. "I tried to stop them but they wouldn't listen and said that it was a Jamaat-e-Islami Quran."

But in the early nineties, Jamaat reasserted itself after its militant wing, Hizbul Mujahideen, was founded. Jamaat men became all-powerful because of their influence in the militant group, which had immense support from Pakistan and sought Kashmir's accession to the country. I remember a Jamaat man from my village who ran a drugstore. He used to be a polite, quiet man, but something changed around 1992. He did not walk; he swaggered. You can tell a Jamaat member from his self-assured bearing, his eyes blazing with certainty, his air of some hidden, conspiratorial knowledge, and his short regulation beard. There is also the cultlike devotion to the ideas of Mawdudi. People from all shades of the political spectrum had used Islam in Kashmir for political gains, but nobody emphasized its place in the Kashmiri polity as much as the Jamaat. In the early nineties, they had regular meetings called *ijtimas*, where their workers would try to convince young men to join Hizbul Mujahideen.

I remember sitting at a shop front outside my house one day. The Jamaat chemist from my village was walking by. I said the customary greeting, and he leaped to attention, addressing me in an elaborate, earnest litany, asking about my family, my studies, talking about his hopes that I would be engrossed in the study of *deen*, or religion. His tone turned conspiratorial, as if he were sharing the best-kept secret with me. He threw a brotherly arm around my shoulder and urged me to walk a little away from the crowd near the shop front. He said, "We need boys like you. You should come to our *ijtima.*" But he never brought it up again after I replied, "I will come with your son."

Many Kashmiris credit the 1990s rise of the brutal counterinsurgent group Ikhwan-ul-Muslimoon (the Muslim Brotherhood) to the excesses of Jamaat men and Hizbul Mujahideen. Commonly known as Ikhwanis, these men were armed by the Indian government and given a free hand—immunity from prosecution for their crimes. The Ikhwanis knew both the separatist militant groups and the Kashmiri society, and that knowledge made them ruthlessly effective counterinsurgents. They tortured and killed like modern-day Mongols. Ikhwan was armed and funded by the Indian army and went on a rampage, killing, maiming, and harassing anyone they thought to be sympathetic to the Jamaat or the separatists.

I once met the son of Kuka Parrey, the ruthless founder of Ikhwan. Parrey used to operate mostly in Baramulla; by the time I met his son, separatist militants had already killed Parrey. His son told me that Parrey, who used to be a small-time folksinger, had been a supporter of the separatist movement and celebrated the young Kashmiris crossing the

Line of Control for arms training by writing and singing a song: *"Shahzaad Lukh Draayih Azad Kashmir!"* (The Princes Are Marching to Free Kashmir!). Parrey's son told me that his father had collaborated with the Indian army only after a Jamaat member insulted and slapped him. Parrey and his counterinsurgent group were so despised by Kashmiris that when the militants killed him, his family did not have the nerve to bury him in the village graveyard. Leaving Parrey's fortresslike house, guarded by scores of armed paramilitaries, I saw a grilled enclosure in a far corner of the grassy lawn—it was Parrey's grave. His son told me that the Jamaat man who had led his father to become a counterinsurgent had changed sides and worked now as an informer with a paramilitary force.

After the late nineties, Jamaat tried to distance itself from the militant groups, partly because hundreds of its members were arrested and killed by the Indian troops and many more during the campaign by Ikhwan counterinsurgents. Jamaat continues to be a minority in Kashmir. If it ever goes to the polls again in Kashmir, I suspect it won't find any support beyond its traditional supporters or manage to gain more than the three seats it won in the 1960s.

The majority of Kashmiri Muslims continue to follow an unorthodox Islam. In fact, Kashmiri society has opened up in the last decade and a half. Thousands of Kashmiri boys and girls left in the early nineties to study in Indian cities and towns or universities in North America, Europe, and Russia. I was one of them; my friends, too, were part of that wave. Most of us returned to Kashmir as educated professionals, and our long journeys did change us. While we were gone, another revolution was taking place all over South Asia, including Kashmir: cable television. Throughout the conflict, as the Kashmiris' mobility was reduced and they stayed indoors, they watched thousands of hours of television—mostly Bollywood movies, song-and-dance shows, and news. The spread of the Internet and cybercafés also opened up society.

There have been fringe efforts to impose a Saudi-style Islamic code in Kashmir, although they invariably fail. In the mostly agrarian society of Kashmir, men and women have worked together in fields and orchards, and though women wore head scarves, the idea of veils never really took off. Even in nonagricultural and urban settings like schools, offices, and universities, only a small number of Kashmiri women chose to wear veils. There were a few failed attempts at imposing veils on women, especially by a puritanical Islamist women's group, Dukhtaran-e-Millat (Daughters of the Muslim Community), headed by Asiya Andrabi, who is not known for much else. I had not heard about her for over a decade. Then one summer day in 2004 she resurfaced in the public sphere. I had gone to my preferred cybercafé in Lal Chowk. The manager seemed distraught and resigned; the doors of most wooden cubicles had been pulled off the hinges. "Asiya Andrabi and her women were here," he said.

She and her activists had begun harassing young couples catching a few moments of intimacy in Internet cafés or sharing lunch in dimly lit restaurants. In newspaper photographs, Andrabi looked like a female Zorro, a veiled woman raising fists covered in white gloves. Much later, I managed to meet her in her Srinagar house; she was barely four and a half feet tall and covered from head to toe in her signature veil. She told me she had become a born-again Muslim in 1986, a time when she had been feeling depressed and thwarted because her family forbade her from pursuing postgraduate studies in biochemistry in Pune. Frustrated ambition is a dangerous thing.

She had begun her activism soon after college in 1987 by painting out the actresses in Bollywood film posters that were put up every week in Srinagar and elsewhere in the valley. She also agitated for separate seats for women on crowded buses. Later, she joined an Arabic and Islamic studies program at Kashmir University. She talked about her well-educated and upper-middle-class family; indeed, I had been struck by hundreds of books, including books by Noam Chomsky, Edward Said, and a copy of the *Bhagavad Gita*, on the multiple bookshelves in her drawing room. In the early nineties, Andrabi married a commander of Hizbul Mujahideen who had been in prison for years. She considered it an honor to be married to a militant despite the accompanying hardships, and named her son Mohammed bin Qasim, after the medieval Arab general who conquered India. As we spoke that afternoon,

Andrabi lamented the spread of cable television and conceded that very few Kashmiri women had followed her.

Puritanical interpretations of Islam continued to fail in Kashmir. On a visit to my family home in the village, one of my cousins told me about the eldest son of the teacher who had been the leader of the Salafist group in our village since my childhood. The boy, in his teens, had studied with my cousin. It was common knowledge that the man brought up his children in an ultra-puritanical manner. They had obeyed for years, but the boys had grown up and were rebelling. "He is a joke in the school. He runs after girls, speeds his car, and we call him Rainbow," said my cousin. I was struck by the nickname and asked what it meant. "He colors his hair in different colors every week. One day he has black hair; another day it is red or green."

I remembered how, in my childhood, this boy's father and his group campaigned against prayers at shrines, as they believed that making the saint an intermediary between the creator and the creation was un-Islamic. They had been so fiercely opposed by the rest of the village that they'd hidden in friends' houses lest a mob set upon them. What the Salafi teacher and his cohorts didn't seem to understand was the social and cultural significance of the shrine in Kashmiri life. It wasn't merely a spiritual center but a club, a space for social gatherings, festivities, and business.

The shrine closest to my house was in the village of Aishmuqam, near my old boarding school. One early April afternoon I took a bus to Aishmuqam. A family friend, Kallu, ran a textile shop in the small bazaar near the bus yard. A road climbed from the bazaar through the village spread out on clearings on the slope to the shrine cresting the hill.

Before I could begin my trek, I saw Kallu sitting on a wooden platform in his shop in an elegant Nehru jacket and a Jinnah cap. "Where have you been all this time?" he asked. His familiar high-pitched voice was reassuring. His two front teeth were missing; his face had wrinkled. I narrated the highlights of my absent years: college, university, and journalism. "And what about marriage?" Everyone always asks you that—family, relatives, acquaintances. Razia, his daughter, and Altaf, his son, were married and ran a school. His own business had been bad since the fighting began. "But thank God everyone in the family is safe. In these times every day is a gift." Two men sat beside me in the shop on wooden chairs. They nodded in agreement. "There are no guarantees," one said.

"This morning the troops killed a boy from Pulwama; his body is lying in the police station," Kallu said. "A policeman came to buy cloth for his shroud. The army said he was a militant. But who knows?" He turned to the shrine atop the hill and lifted his hands in prayer. "Oh! Saint Zainuddin! Be our mediator with the Almighty! Ask Him to take pity on these people! Ask Him to forgive our sins! You are among His dear ones!"

Wanting to lighten the atmosphere, I reminded him of an old story that made him laugh. One of the names Muslims use for God is Noor (the divine light). A white-bearded, pink-faced old mullah from the Aishmuqam mosque was also known as Noor. As a child, I once accompanied my grandfather and Kallu to the grand mosque for Friday prayers. My little bit of religious education had taught me that a mosque was the house of God. Noor was delivering a sermon. I thought he must be God. After the prayers, I saw Noor walking the same road; I was surprised and asked Kallu, "Why is God walking the same road as us?"

"You were all of six then. Those were very happy days. Your grandfather and I told the story to our friends, and poor Noor was embarrassed." He smiled and said, "That 'God' of yours is dead."

Allah-o-Akbar! Ashadu An La Ilaha Illalah! (God is great! There is no God but God!)

The words calling Muslims for afternoon prayers descended mistlike from the shrine over the tin rooftops dotting the hill. The smell of fresh bread in the wicker baskets of bakeries and sacks of spices on the shop fronts surrounded me as I climbed the steep rocky stairway to the shrine. Every spring people gathered here for an annual fair celebrating the end of winter and the beginning of the sowing season. Hundreds of men, women, and children would light torches (twigs of pine tied to a willow staff) and stand humbly near the fortresslike perimeter and in the cobbled courtyard of the shrine. The arched wooden gate of the shrine inlaid with calligraphy, the latticed windows, and the pagoda-shaped green roof supported by ornate pillars and crowned by a brass spire would glow in the bright yellow of the torches.

Years later, devotees still packed the cobbled courtyard. I leaned for a while over the low boundary wall, taking in the rushing Lidder stream, the yellow miles of mustard flowers, the roofs and villages miniaturized by distance and the dark brown arc of the Himalayas. Buddha thought Kashmir was an ideal location for meditation. Every hillock had a shrine, and every spring had a temple. It seemed easy to be a believer here. I turned back toward the courtyard and watched a scraggy-bearded barber sharpen his razor on a stone. A young couple and an older woman holding a baby also watched him. The old woman helped the barber tie a white cotton sheet around the baby's neck. A child's first haircut, according to Kashmiri Muslim tradition, is performed at a shrine. The barber massaged the light brown wisps with warm water from an aluminum bowl. The baby cried, the old woman lulled him into silence, and the young parents fidgeted. The barber shaved off the baby's hair. The father gathered the wisps of hair in a handkerchief. The mother took a bowl full of *tehr*—turmeric-colored spiced rice—and distributed it among the devotees, who blessed the child.

I followed the family inside the shrine. The keepers of the shrine, the *babas*, sat on wooden platforms behind brass trays full of coins. The family donated generously, placing a note or two for each *baba*, all of whom blessed the child. The interior of the shrine was an ancient cave with modern modifications. Women in bright floral prints prayed on one side of a greenish marble platform, and more *babas* sought donations on the other. A strong stone pillar supported the cave roof. The *baba* sitting there shouted, "It is Mehboob-e-Alam's pillar. Those who lean against it are relieved of their problems. Make a donation here and lean on the pillar, young man. Your worries will go away."

I walked toward the end of the cave, where a low, narrow opening led to a tiny chamber in which the saint used to pray. An elderly man came out of the opening; two young girls followed him. They bent their backs and walked backward. The devout do not turn their backs to the saint's place. An earthen lamp was lit near the opening. Devotees dipped their fingers into an oil-filled palm-shaped hole in the rock and rubbed their foreheads. "It will heal your diseases and solve your problems," an old turbaned *baba* sang. I crawled into the saint's chamber. A green silk sheet covered his grave. Eight devotees stood in two rows facing the tomb. A *baba* prayed for a while and moved from devotee to devotee with his brass tray. "Leave big notes on the tray; the saint will take care of you." I left a little dejected about the domination of commerce over solitude and gravitas.

As I walked down the stairs to the bus stop, I heard someone calling me. The short, wiry young man's face seemed familiar. "We were in the same school. I am Mubashir." He ran a drugstore nearby. I sat on a rough wooden bench facing the bare wooden desk where he sat on a plastic chair. Second-rate antacid and cough syrup and paper bags of tablets for sundry ailments sat on the rough timber shelves along the mud walls. Floral paper covered the ceiling of wooden beams, and a dim bulb gave the shop a jaundiced look. Mubashir left to fetch tea. I watched him cross the street; he limped. When he returned, we talked about our lives after school, and Mubashir told me that he never finished college.

Mubashir's father was sick in the winter of 1997. The local hospital was closed. The nineteen-year-old ran to a chemist near Kallu's shop. He was waiting for his turn when he saw an Ikhwani counterinsurgent walk toward the shop. Mubashir felt uneasy as he watched the Ikhwani loiter. "I wondered who was going to get into trouble." Separatist militants hated the Ikhwanis, and there was bound to be a skirmish. Mubashir wanted to get the medicine for his father and leave.

The queue moved slowly. The Ikhwani stood near Mubashir, looked around, made small talk, and juggled a hand grenade like a cricket ball. Mubashir shouted at the chemist to move faster. Nothing happened. He waited. Then he heard an explosion, and everything went dark. Six hours later, he regained his senses on a hospital bed in Srinagar. The grenade had slipped from the renegade's hand, fallen on the metallic road, and exploded. The renegade had died there. Scores of splinters had pierced Mubashir's legs. For three months doctors operated on and nursed him. He returned home in a wheelchair and left it after two years with a limp. His treatment cost the family a fortune. His father retired from his low-rung government job. Mubashir had to support the family. His degree did not guarantee a job, and he knew no influential men. He dropped out of college and set up his drugstore, which fetched a little money. Every day he sat on the blue plastic chair behind the bare wooden desk, waiting for patients to buy medicines and dreaming of what could have been possible.

I left his shop and began my descent to the bus yard. He joined me, dragging his legs from one cobbled step to another. I dissuaded him. He paused, turned back, and said, "Basharat! It is hard to say, but can you help me find a job? Help me out of this hell." It was difficult to answer that question. Yet if I saw hope, it was in education. "I will talk to my friends," I told him, "but you will have to complete your degree. Without your degree, there is no hope."

He agreed. "I will call you once I finish my degree. With Zain Shah's blessings, something might work out." His eyes had a faint glimmer of hope. We parted. His words accompanied me home. I thought of his hopelessness, his clinging to straws of faith.

People seemed to need faith, to need miracles. A week later, I was at my Srinagar house, talking about it with a poet friend who made his money by producing unwatchable programs for state television. He said, "In these times, faith has become the support system for the rich, the famous, and the unknown poor. People have no hopes from the government or any other politicians. They turn to the shrines, to the Prophet, and to God." He told me about one of the most distinguished poets of Kashmir, Professor Rashid Nazki, who had immersed himself in faith after a personal tragedy during the mid-nineties. "He left public life and lives a retired life in his ancestral village in Bandipora," my friend said.

The small town of Bandipora is around a hundred kilometers from

Srinagar, in the North Kashmir district of Baramulla, close to the Line of Control. One morning I took a shared taxi from Srinagar to Bandipora. Half an hour outside Srinagar, the road to Bandipora runs along the Jhelum for miles as the river goes north to cross over to Pakistan and then the Arabian Sea. Canopies of willow branches shade the road till it rises onto a plateau occupied by a military camp.

Gazing through the taxi window on my right, I was entranced by the sight of a lake. "It is the Manasbal Lake," a fellow passenger told me. On the clear blue water, two yellow *shikaras* moved gracefully. The road rose toward the hills in the distance. We rushed past apple and almond orchards and glittering tin roofs. In a village, a hand-painted billboard announced: MUSKAAN BEAUTY PARLOUR, FECIAL, MASAJ AND HEAR-CUTTING.

On the seat behind me was a family with two energetic children. Their mother prodded them to behave properly. Excited by the breeze blowing in through the lowered windows, the boys launched into a nursery rhyme about the light and the cold breeze.

A check post announced Bandipora. An armored car was parked nearby, and columns of soldiers stood along the road. The taxi stopped. The boys in the backseat shouted, "Dishkiaon, Dishkiaon," in their shrill voices. They used their curled hands as imaginary guns. They were imitating the sound effects that accompany gunfire in most Hindi movies. The central market in the town was crowded, though not dirty, like most other small town markets in Kashmir. The Indian soldiers were the only outsiders one could see. Until the 1930s, if you had walked around the same market, every fourth person would have been from one or another great medieval city of central Asia. The journey from Bandipora to the cities of Central Asia, even by medieval modes of horse and mule, took a few weeks. Kashmir's cultural interaction with the cities of Samarkand, Bokhara, and Kashgar was rich and intense.

Rashid Nazki, the poet, lived in a single-story house with a cedar tree outside. A boy led me in. The poet huddled under a shawl in a small room. He had deep black eyes shining out of his sculpted, sunken face.

"You must be the one coming from Srinagar," he said, pushing a cushion toward me. Offering a guest a cushion to lean against instead of a bare wall is a local gesture of respect. He stretched out his legs and, leaning back on a cushion, puffed at his cigarette with shivering, fragile fingers. "I am an old man living away from the world. What brings you here?" My friend had introduced me as a journalist, and the poet expected an interview about his thoughts on the conflict in Kashmir.

He was both surprised and relieved that I had no such questions for him. "These are difficult times, and journalists ask questions that one can answer but cannot afford to," he said, a little irritated. "I just wanted to meet you," I said. A boy in his early teens walked in and asked whether he would have lunch. "You are joining me for lunch," the poet commanded. He took a hundred-rupee note from his pocket and handed it to the boy. "Get some lamb and tell your mother to fry it. The guest will eat with me." He told me, "He is my grandson." He asked me to tell him stories about my travels. I told stories; he commented and smoked and commented and smoked. Food arrived: rice, lamb, and beans. The poet piled my plate with pieces of lamb. "I would eat that for two days," I protested. "You are a young man, and you need to eat," he insisted.

After lunch we talked about poetry. "What do you think of the poetry written in Kashmiri after the conflict?" I asked. "A lot has been written. The younger generation talks about the conflict directly. Some fine poems have been written. In English, there is Agha Shahid Ali's work."

"Yes. I love his work," I agreed.

Professor Nazki was silent again. "He was a very fine boy. We were at his house, and Shahid used to walk like a drunken man. His father is my friend, and I told him once Shahid was not well. But he believed it was just a poet's way of being. Soon after that, they detected his tumor. His death was a great loss. Kashmir needs poets like him, but who can evade death?" The old poet moved himself to a more erect posture. "Shahid wrote political poetry, but he did not compromise on technique. Most political poetry is like blank verse. The polemics remain, and the poetry dies."

I asked about his own poetry. His poems were in a mystical vein and had won various awards. I asked him whether there were any English translations. "Yes, they have been translated into Urdu. Someone from Delhi has translated my poems into English. The translator never sought my permission; he did not even send me a copy." He had not written much since 1990. "I lost half of my family in a grenade blast and stopped writing after that." I dreaded this moment and bowed my head in silence. The poet narrated his story in a calm voice.

One afternoon in 1990, when he was teaching at the University of Kashmir, news came that a bomb had exploded near his house. He rushed from the university to Bandipora. That morning a militant was loitering on the lane beside the poet's house, planning to throw a grenade at a column of soldiers passing by. Afraid of retaliation from the soldiers, the poet's two sons went out to persuade the militant to throw it away from the residential area. He was adamant; so were they. Their mother joined them. Sometime during the argument, which might have seen much swaying of arms and pointing of fingers to make a point in Kashmiri fashion, the militant accidentally pressed the pin that sets off the hand grenade. When the poet reached home, the grenade blast had killed the militant, his sons, and his wife. "I was in a coma of sorts for the next eight years. I did not write a single poem. Every time I picked up a pen, my fingers trembled." He had no courts to turn to for his loss. "I complained to Prophet Muhammad. I sent my prayers and plaints to his court." He overcame his loss with his love for the Prophet. "I devoted my time to translating a biography." He was alive again; his eyes sparkled as he talked of his work. "You will feel the Prophet's breath when you read the book. I have used the stream of consciousness." I remembered one of his lines:

> *I asked the dervish sitting on the pavement*
> *How far is the world from here?*

Nooruddin Rishi is the patron saint of Kashmir. He was mentored by Lalleshwari, a Brahmin woman who, after much suffering at the hands of her in-laws, rebelled and became a mystic, preaching oneness of God and arguing against the ancient Hindu caste system. As a child, Nooruddin had been sent to a local mullah, but he refused to read beyond the first Arabic alphabet, Alif (One). His teacher asked why; he answered, "There is one God, and I need not know beyond Alif." In his youth, he renounced the world and prayed in a cave for twelve years. Sometime after his cave worship, Nooruddin met Mir Mohammed Hamdani, an Iranian Sufi. Mohammed was the son of the great Sufi scholar Syed Mir Ali, who arrived in Kashmir in the fourteenth century and attracted Kashmiris to Islam, and is popularly known as Shah-e-Hamadan (the King of Hamadan). Before his return and death in the central Asian town of Khatlan, Shah Hamadan had willed his infant son, Mohammed, to travel throughout the world in search of learning. After many journeys, the young man arrived in Kashmir and resumed the missionary and scholarly work of his father.

Mohammed Hamdani taught Nooruddin Rishi the intricacies of Islam and the life of the Prophet Muhammad. The discussions of the two men convinced Nooruddin to focus on social reform rather than renunciation. He traveled throughout Kashmir, talking to people in their own language. His interpretation of Islam was rooted in the local traditions and culture; the masses understood him better than the Iranian and central Asian Sufis who had brought Islam to Kashmir. He was critical of the orthodox Muslim priests and the Brahmins for reducing religion to empty rituals, turning it into a means of self-promotion, and fueling hatred among the followers of Hinduism and Islam:

Poring over books they become strangers to their own selves.
Like donkeys whose backs are laden with books.

The Mullah is happy with gifts and feasts,
The old Pandit searches for a young virgin wife.

Under his influence, the majority of Kashmiris became Muslims, although the conversion to Islam had begun in the early fourteenth century after Rinchana, a Tibetan prince, became the ruler of Kashmir. To consolidate his position, Rinchana decided to convert to Hinduism. But the Brahmin priests refused to convert him, unsure which caste Rinchana would have. His Muslim friend and adviser Shah Mir told him about Islam. Rinchana went to sleep in his palace on the banks of the River Jhelum and woke up to hear the Muslim call for prayer. On the riverbank facing the palace, a Persian Sufi, Bulbul Shah, was offering morning prayers. Rinchana rode across the river to meet Bulbul Shah, who answered his questions. Islam had no caste; men were equal. Conversion was simply saying: "There is no god but God and Muhammad is His messenger." Rinchana converted to Islam, patronized the saint, and ruled generously for three years.

Shah Mir won the battle for succession after Rinchana's death. Among the successors of Shah Mir, two men are remembered the most: Sikander, a fanatic, and Zainulabideen, a liberal. Sikander banned music, wine, and dancing, and is accused of destroying many Hindu temples in Kashmir near the end of the fourteenth century. Kashmiris remember the reign of the liberal king Zainulabideen, from 1420 to 1470, as the golden age. People still refer to him as Bud Shah (the Great King). He built colleges and offered generous grants to students and scholars of logic and grammar. He invited master craftsmen and artisans from central Asian cities, who taught Kashmiris the fine arts of papier-mâché and carpet weaving. He ended the persecution of Hindus and revived theater and music. Bud Shah was one of the pallbearers in the funeral procession of Nooruddin Rishi, who was buried at the town of Chrar, an hour's drive west of Srinagar, where he had spent the last years of his life. A shrine built there in his memory became one of the holiest places in Kashmir.

In May 1995 the Indian army besieged the township of Chrar. Militants led by a Pakistani, Mast Gul, were hiding in Chrar, since snow had made their mountainous hideouts uninhabitable. A battle raged in the town, and soon it was on fire. Twenty-five hundred houses were burned; scores of civilians were killed. The army took the battle to the shrine complex where the militants were hiding. The fighting burned down the shrine:

six hundred years of history destroyed in a day. Kashmiris mourned and marched toward the gutted shrine. Soldiers arrested them, firing on the protesters. Mast Gul and his men broke the army cordon and escaped. Kashmiris blamed the Indian army for destroying the shrine; the army and the Indian government blamed the Pakistani militants, arguing that they had destroyed the shrine to save themselves.

On a bright May afternoon I was on my way from Srinagar to the shrine at Chrar. Half an hour later, the taxi left the city and the denser villages beyond it. We drove through fields, climbed a plateau, and passed some checkpoints. Nine years later, Chrar seemed like a newly built town. The jeep stopped outside the new government-built shrine. It was a white cement building. Its varnished wooden window frames were shaped in clumsy arches in a halfhearted imitation of the originals. The galvanized tin sheets mocked the memory of the old shingles. I stood in the taxi stand, staring at the new shrine. An aged couple walked out backward in reverence. They stopped near me, their lips moving in loud prayer: "Oh Sultan of saints! Be kind to us, be kind to our children. Save them from storms and fires, save them as you have saved them till now." They had tears in their eyes.

15 ⮑ The Missing Shiva

The practice of Islam in Kashmir borrowed elements from the Hindu and the Buddhist past; the Hindus in turn were influenced by Muslim practices. In my childhood, nobody raised an eyebrow if a Hindu woman went to a Muslim shrine to seek the blessings of a saint. The religious divide was visible only on the days India and Pakistan played cricket. Muslims supported the Pakistani cricket team; Pandits were for India. Yet the tensions, which were partly class-based, never simmered into sectarian violence. Nobody was surprised if a Hindu and a Muslim were friends. My father's best friend was and remains a Pandit; my mother had long friendships with Pandit women who taught in the same school.

Things fell apart after the eruption of the armed conflict. The separatist militants had no tolerance for dissent. Along with killing hundreds of Muslim pro-India political activists and suspected informers for Indian intelligence, they killed a few hundred Pandits on similar grounds or without any reason at all. The murders sent a wave of fear through the community, and more than a hundred thousand Pandits left Kashmir after March 1990. The affluent moved to houses in Jammu, Delhi, and various Indian cities. But a vast majority could find shelter only in the squalor of refugee camps and rented rooms in Jammu and Delhi.

Despite the ensuing bitterness, both Muslims and Pandits tried to maintain their personal relationships. My father stayed in touch with his Pandit friends and visited them in Jammu and Delhi whenever he was there. Mrs. Kaul, my landlady in Delhi, often talked about her memories of Kashmir. She recounted tying threads at the shrine of Sheikh Nooruddin or visiting the shrines close to her ancestral house in central Srinagar. Living in various cities of India, the Pandits hoped to return home someday. Even those who were too old to begin life anew pined for the homes they had left behind. Most Pandit houses were abandoned or burned during the conflict and the temple complexes taken over by the Indian military.

In my childhood, I visited the local temples with my Hindu friends, mostly the ancient Martand sun temple near my village. I remembered a visit to the Martand temple, when my Pandit friend Vinod told me authoritatively about the temple being built by the Pandavas, the five heroes of *The Mahabharata*. The five brothers had defeated their hundred villainous cousins, the Kaurvas, with help from Krishna. Vinod told me that the massive boulders of the temple were lifted to their position by the giant Pandava brother, Bhima. Our school principal corrected us: "Lalitaditya, one of the greatest kings of Kashmir, built the temple." Muktapida Lalitaditya had ruled Kashmir from the end of the seventh century to the mid-eighth century and is believed to have conquered a lot of India, Iran, and Central Asia.

Would the Martand sun temple, too, be a garrison? I wondered. Or would some teacher still be telling his students about its place in the history of Kashmir? I left Srinagar for my ancestral village, spent a day with my grandparents, then headed for Martand. I took a bus from the busy town square in Mattan, three miles from my village and the site of my first school, the Lyceum, for the Martand temple. The bus followed the same winding road up a plateau that I had taken years ago on school excursions. The barren mountains, the bad roads, the muddy lanes of the villages surrounding Martand hadn't changed in twenty years. The bluish limestone temple stood like a wrinkled patriarch. Most of the colonnaded wall stretching from the entrance to form a square around the temple had collapsed. Inside the temple chamber, wild grass and weeds grew. The memory of my school excursion with Vinod was still vivid.

The temple complex had seemed colossal to our eyes then. It felt diminished now.

I walked back and waited by the desolate roadside for a bus. I missed Vinod. I had not seen him since the conflict erupted. I was twelve when I left the Lyceum for a boarding school; his family had migrated to the southern province of Jammu.

Vinod was a plump boy with cheeks so red that I thought he wore makeup. After school, we would usually rush to bathe in a temple complex spring nearby. We would try to scare each other by shouting "Snake" from the bank of the spring. We also loved to explore a nearby cluster of caves cut into a limestone cliff. He believed that if we kept going in the dark tunnel, we would reach China. Scared by the darkness, we never ventured beyond a few feet. I learned to ride a bicycle on his red Atlas on the road leading to the caves.

There were no signs of the bus on the road outside Martand temple. I walked the few kilometers to Mattan. Vinod used to live in the adjoining village. From a roundabout, I saw people walking down the lane leading to his village. I could not hold myself back and followed the road. A mile ahead, a dirt track ran across paddy fields to a grove of walnut trees near his house. Men and women worked in the fields, and children rode down the dirt lane on bicycles. The Pandit houses stood apart in their desolation. I remembered the way to his two-story house, and in a few minutes, I was there. An old brass lock stared from the wooden door, and cobwebs decorated the closed windows. Vinod's family seemed to have left in a hurry; he did not even come to say good-bye or leave an address.

The next morning I visited our old school, hoping to meet our lovable principal, Kantroo. A freshly painted sign hanging on the school read: LYCEUM PUBLIC SCHOOL. The building looked the same. There were new faces in the same gray shorts and white shirts. I knocked on the principal's door. A middle-aged man in a casual shirt and jeans opened the door. I introduced myself and asked for Kantroo. He offered me a seat and said, "I am the principal." He sat in my old teacher's chair. "Mr.

Kantroo migrated to Jammu in 2002." The new principal knew where in Jammu my teacher lived but did not have his phone number. I left knowing I had to visit my teacher and find Vinod.

Jammu, a small city with brutal summers, had become the refuge for most Kashmiri Pandits. I was nervous at the prospect of seeing my teacher and my childhood friend as refugees. Some years ago I had been in Jammu as a reporter, visiting the migrant camps. On the outskirts of the city, surrounded by desolate land full of wild bushes, I reached a cluster of one-room brick huts stacked together in long claustrophobic rows. "Nobody cares about us," a teenager told me. He did not speak like a Kashmiri. And he hated Muslims. I could not muster the courage to tell him I was one. I told him I was a Punjabi from Delhi. I walked around, trying to locate the people from my part of Kashmir. A fiftysomething man in white *kurta* pajamas appeared out of a narrow lane. I asked him if he knew anyone from Anantnag. He looked at me carefully. "Are you from there?"

"Yes," I replied.

"Where in Anantnag?"

"Seer," I said.

"You are from Seer! Whose son are you?"

I gave my father's and my grandfather's name. In my part of the world, you are always your father's son and your grandfather's grandson. His eyes lit up. He laughed, swore at me fondly, and hugged me. Before I could ask him who he was, he grabbed my arm and told me to keep my mouth shut and follow him. We walked through the dirty, cramped lanes running between rows of camp houses. He stopped outside a shabby hut where a frail woman was washing clothes. "Get up, Gowri!" he said. "Hug him! He is your son!"

She didn't recognize me, and we reluctantly hugged. "She is your father's sister," Avatar told me. I stood there completely perplexed. My father never had a sister. I was stunned when the woman said, "Is he

Ammul's son?" Ammul was my father's childhood nickname, which hardly anyone outside the family knew. She looked at me again, held me in her arms, and cried. Her husband sat on the ground and broke down. My eyes were wet. Gowri abandoned her half-washed clothes in a bucket near the communal tap. We walked into their one-room hut. A bed took up most of the space in the room. In a corner was a tiny kitchenette. Gowri moved a few utensils and made room to squat before a small gas stove and brew tea.

We talked for two hours about Kashmir and our lives there before the armed conflict. They lived in a neighboring village near my uncle's house, where my father spent his childhood and adolescence. In his early twenties, he worked as a teacher in Pulwama. Gowri also had a job in the village. Her parents worried about her traveling back and forth alone every day. "They allowed me to join there only after they knew your father would take me along," she said.

On the walls hung clothes and pictures of Shiva, Rama, Krishna, and Saraswati. I was about to leave when a young girl walked in almost unnoticed. She had Gowri's face and Avatar's black eyes minus the wrinkles and the grief. We were introduced. I made small talk about her school. She sat on the edge of the bed uneasily, her school bag on her lap. Sweat rolled from her forehead like teardrops.

August is a time of miserable heat in Jammu. I had become oblivious to the heat on meeting Gowri and Avatar. I felt my shirt sticking to my back despite the whining ceiling fan. The girl turned to her mother with a pleading glance. Gowri asked Avatar and me to take a walk outside. The girl had to change. She was thirteen. There was no other room. There were no prospects of a bigger house in sight for them. And the girl was growing up. How long could she sleep on a mattress on the floor beside the bed her parents occupied? What meaning would words like "drawing room," "study," "bedroom," or "balcony" have for her? How would she relate to stories of people living in houses? Maybe her parents would try to explain. They once lived in a house that had rooms.

In the evening I called my father and told him about the meeting. He was silent for a long time. I thought I heard him crying. As if talking to himself, he said, "Those were great days, son. Her family was like my own. I did all the chores when she and Avatar were getting married. I have not seen her for years. Tell her I will."

Finally, one morning I boarded a jeep in Anantnag and, after eight hours on a mountainous highway, reached Jammu.

The next morning I called a few acquaintances from my hotel room, inquiring about my teacher. They could not help. The government lists phone numbers, but they rarely work. I called; no response. Another call; no response. On the fifth call, the recording said, "We are pleased to receive your call. Your call is very important to us. Our operators will soon assist you." "Soon" meant five long minutes before the phone disconnected. I was used to it.

I paced around the room and called again. The phone beeped, and I heard a man's voice, a real operator. "Can I have Chaman Lal Kantroo's number? He lives in Amphalla." I heard typing. "Take down the number," he told me. I stared at the phone number on my pad, pulled myself together, and punched in the number. His wife answered the phone. She remembered me; I could talk to my teacher if I called after ten minutes. I did, and he picked up the phone. His voice was hoarse, tired. He did not seem well. "Can I come to see you, sir?" "Get here before ten," he said. "I have an appointment with my doctor at ten-thirty." He coughed and gave me directions. It was nine-thirty.

I rushed to the road and grabbed a rickshaw. The driver sped through bazaars, crossed a few flyovers, shot up a slope, turned onto a lane, and stopped. We were at the landmark, a jail, in fifteen minutes. I sought directions for a local writer's white bungalow. A narrow, empty lane took me there. A vegetable seller pointed out the house. From the writer's house, I had to take the first lane on the left; my teacher lived in the first house. It was a run-down yellow-painted brick house. The doorbell did not work. I knocked. A girl opened the door. "I do not know any Kantroos. There is a Kashmiri Pandit family living on the top floor. That might be them." She disappeared behind a curtain on the ground floor.

A steep stair led to the rooftop. Behind a curtain of clothes hanging on a nylon rope was a garret. "Come in, Basharat," Mr. Kantroo called out. He sat on a bed by the lone window of the room. We shook hands, and he asked me to sit with him on the bed. I looked at him; he had aged. His cheeks had sunk deep, his hair was almost white, and his black mustache was missing. His eyebrows were still bushy and black; his eyes were still deep brown but seemed to have lost their verve. I saw in them resignation and fatigue. He broke the silence to ask me about my life and work, about the other students in my class.

I answered while running my gaze over a blue plastic bowl, a razor, and a cup of shaving cream lying on a newspaper in front of him. Some of my fellow students were doctors, some were biochemists, some were lawyers, some were engineers, and some were dead. Paint was flaking from the walls, and the fan overhead moved noisily. I wanted to ask him what had forced him to leave Kashmir twelve years after the conflict started. I remember the new school principal talking about a "problem" he had. I could not ask.

His wife, who had helped him run the school, joined us. We talked about Kashmir. I had forgotten my teacher was a poet, too. When I was about to leave, I asked about his writing. "I am not writing much nowadays. I did write when I was in Kashmir. A collection of poems was published in 2002." His eyes sparkled again. "But the collection is not with the booksellers. I could not accept their terms. Mostly, friends and acquaintances come and take a copy."

"But we need to read your poems," I protested. "You cannot hide them from the world."

He smiled, indifferent to publishing advances. "Turn around and pick a copy from the shelf." I held a lean hardbound monograph in my hands. The cover read: *Eternal Sin.* I left my poet-teacher.

Near the jail, I noticed an empty tea stall and found a seat in a corner. I opened the book dedicated to the "non-beings of the world." I turned a page; the tea-stall owner brought me a glass full of tea. I read the poem "Innocuous Innocent," describing a dying man:

A bloodstained label
Stuck to his lapel

Reads: In . . .
Does it mean "Indian, Informer, Intruder, Insurgent"?
It bewilders to make it read "Innocuous Innocent."

I saw the dead: Prem Nath Bhat, my father's friend and a bright Pandit lawyer of Anantnag, shot by militants; Abdul Sattar Ranjoor, a leftist poet from Kulgam, slain before he could write a dissenting poem; Zahoor Dalal, a shopkeeper on an evening walk, thrust into a police van, shot, and dressed in the camouflage of an intruder/insurgent. Journalists rushing back and forth in taxis, typing on their battered computer terminals the words: INNOCUOUS INNOCENT.

Another poem was titled "Handcuffed Wishes." I remembered our last conversation in Kantroo's office in Kashmir. "People talk about nothing but death. Talk about life, talk about books." I had found my answers in his verse. I left the tea stall and walked amid heavy traffic, indifferent to the world, holding the book in a close grip.

Kantroo had told me Vinod's family lived in a place called Palora. I called information again. I asked for his father and got the number. His mother told me he worked in Delhi. Vinod had trained as an engineer and worked for an air-conditioning company. His mother barely knew the name; she did not have his number or office address. She told me he was planning to join another company. I left my phone number with her; she promised to pass it on to Vinod.

After all these years of going separate ways and failing to keep in touch, I was impatient. I searched the company name on the Internet, which gave me an address. I looked at the computer screen in disbelief. It was a block away from my office in Delhi. We had worked a block away from each other and never met. Maybe we had and did not recognize our adult faces. I wondered how many times we had passed each other, along with a thousand other office workers. I loved Delhi for the anonymity it provided; I also hated it for that very quality. I rushed back to the phone booth and called the engineering company in Vasant Vihar. The receptionist's cordial voice said, "I am sorry, sir. He does not work with us anymore. He has taken up another job."

I returned to Srinagar, having lost the trail. One afternoon I walked into my usual cybercafé. I waited on a gaudy sofa for my turn. A remixed version of the latest Bollywood hit blared from an invisible speaker. I tried reading a few days' old newspaper lying on a table. A young man with black hair parted sideways over his narrow forehead walked in. He seemed vaguely familiar. We looked at each other in a moment of knowing and not knowing.

"Vikas!"

"Basharat!"

"God! It is you!"

I had last seen him as a small boy standing next to Vinod in an old school photograph. Vikas and I had competed for the attentions of a classmate in a childhood romance that never was. Vikas, too, had migrated with his family to Jammu in the early nineties. We had lost touch. He was now a sales manager for a pharmaceutical company, in Srinagar to make an assessment of their sales. He was staying in a hotel on the Dal Lake. I said, "You have to come home, Vicky! To hell with the hotel!"

"I would love to, but I am leaving in two hours. Have an afternoon flight to catch, just dropped in to shoot an e-mail to my office."

We talked about our families. Neither of us mentioned anything about the conflict; it seemed remote from a chance meeting of two friends after fifteen years. He asked about our Muslim friends and class-mates; I asked about our Pandit friends. He had lost touch with most. We shared a cigarette and laughed about things from our childhood.

An hour later, I walked past Polo View toward the Zero Bridge, beyond which I was staying in a southern area of Srinagar. Strains of a song playing on a radio escaped from a solitary bunker near the bridge. A lonely-looking soldier stood behind a machine gun. The setting sun shone in the green water of the Jhelum; its last rays reddened the horizon. I thought of my grandmother telling me as a child, "When an innocent man is killed, the sky turns red." An innocent man had died in Kashmir almost every day after the winter of 1990.

16 ⮑ The Black Blanket

Two words had remained omnipresent in my journeys. Whether it was at a feast or a funeral, a visit to a destroyed shrine or a redeemed torture chamber, a story about a stranger or about my own life, a poem or a painting, two words always made their presence felt: militants and soldiers. They had shadowed every life I wrote about, including my own. Yet they remained ghostlike presences. My friends in Delhi often asked me who they were, what they were like. I asked myself the same question. I, too, had wanted to carry a gun, fight, kill, and die. Some people I knew had crossed the line, carried a gun, fought a battle, killed, and died. Some had survived.

I had recently visited the family of my cousin Tariq and met with his younger brother, Shabnam. Twelve years after Tariq's death, I had walked with Shabnam to the playground where we had last seen Tariq. It was empty. The cheering crowds of August 1992 had melted away; the militants were dead. Shabnam talked about his career, and there was a girl. He wanted to marry her; their parents opposed the relationship. Things had turned bitter after he dropped her off outside her college on his bike. One of her relatives saw them and complained to their parents about their waywardness. Now they met clandestinely at a friend's place. He had spoken to his father about marrying her and wanted him to take a proposal to her parents. His father had talked about family honor, about marrying his children into respectable families, about the girl's family being newly rich. Shabnam had asked friends and relatives to convince his father, but the old man was rigid, unshakable.

Shabnam broke the unwritten rule with his father: He talked about his dead brother. Families who had lost someone in the conflict rarely talked about the dead. He confronted his father and said the most painful words: "Tariq would not have turned to guns if you had allowed him to marry the girl he liked." Now he regretted his words. His father had wrapped himself in a brooding silence ever since. "What should I do? I feel terrible for mentioning Tariq, and yet I cannot leave her. Should I elope and marry in a civil court, or should I give up?" The wars of nations and the wars of the heart mean pain, longing, and tears.

Before Tariq joined the militants, he was an ordinary student. I remember him as being respectful to my father; whenever I visited their house, he would be either working on his bicycle or playing cricket on the nearby playground. I had heard about his hurried, nervous homecomings but knew barely anything about his life as a militant. I couldn't bring myself to talk to his brothers or his father about it. I thought of various youngsters I had known during my adolescence who had joined such groups. But I had to be careful. *The conflict is not over yet,* I reminded myself.

Then I remembered Asif, a friend from school who had joined the militants for a few years and returned to a civilian life. I had not seen him since our school days in the early nineties. I leafed through my album and found a photograph from our school days: I was fifteen and standing with Asif in a garden in front of our boarding school. We lived in the same hostel and played for the same volleyball team.

Asif was a dandy. I envied him the female attention and the accessories such as Kamachi shoes. Kamachis were Russian sports shoes that the militants made fashionable. To the teenagers of Kashmir's early nineties, Che Guevara and Malcolm X were unheard of; militants walking the ramp of war determined the fashion trends. Militants replaced the stones in their rings with bullets, and boys replaced the stones in their rings with bullets. A range of militaristic jewelry became fashionable. The Sufi tradition of wearing an amulet was improvised upon: To the string was added a Kalashnikov cartridge. Asif had his Kamachi shoes, his bullet ring, and his cartridge amulet. He was cool.

I left Srinagar in early August for Anantnag, where I boarded a bus for Asif's village farther south. I wasn't sure whether he would be there; I didn't even have his phone number. The bus passed through scores of Kashmiri villages and stopped an hour later at a military check post near Asif's village. The frisking, the proof of identity, and the rude questions that had seemed humiliating earlier were routine now, like brushing your teeth. The soldiers let us pass; the bus moved on and stopped in the village square. I walked through the bus yard to a grocery displaying a Coke billboard with a life-size picture of Bollywood actress Aishwarya Rai.

Two boys idling at the shop front volunteered to show me Asif's house. We jostled along a labyrinth of lanes and reached the entrance of a mansion with two wooden balconies. One of the boys rushed in and returned with Asif's father, a lean, fiftysomething, balding man wearing a Nehru-style jacket popular with politicians.

"Is Asif around?" I asked.

"Who are you?" he asked, surveying me keenly.

I introduced myself. He warmed up and welcomed me into the house. "I am sorry, I was not sure who it was," he said. "One has to be careful." We sat in a carpeted drawing room. A picture of Mecca and a cheap print of wild horses hung on a wall. Asif was visiting an uncle at the other end of the village. There were no phones in the village. His father sent the two boys to call him. "We got a phone booth for the whole village last year," he said with a sigh, "but that does not work anymore."

"What happened?"

"The militants thought it could be used to inform the army about their whereabouts, so they blasted the house where it was installed. The house was damaged, and half the family was killed. Nobody even thought about a phone after that." His village and the adjoining village were known to have a strong military and militant presence; people lived there obeying either the soldiers or the militants.

Asif's sister bought tea. She was at the university studying literature, and Asif was getting a master's degree in history. I remembered his father was a lawyer, and to keep up the conversation, I asked him about his practice. "Well! I visit the court occasionally. My heart was never in law. I make my money from my apple orchards." He paused and then added wearily, "I always dreamed of politics. I wanted to contest elections, be a politician. That remains my sole ambition."

"Have you joined any political party?"

"You think I want to die?" He laughed. He was in the ruling political party, National Conference, until 1989. After the militancy began, he published his resignation in local newspapers, like most other activists of pro-India political parties. Militant groups were as intolerant of dissent as the Indian state, and killed many activists. Public resignations saved many lives. Asif's father gave up his political ambitions and stuck to apple farming.

"Basharat," said an eager voice from the door. I turned around to find a sturdy young man with short hair and big black eyes set in a chiseled face. "Where have you been all these years?" Asif cried. We hugged. I was always struck by the beauty of the friendships I had made during my childhood. I would meet these boys after a decade and feel I had never been away. His father left us alone to talk. Asif spoke slowly, carefully, and seemed to forget his sentences halfway. He lived in the university hostel in Srinagar, and visited his parents once a month. He attended classes and read his textbooks. "There is not much to do after classes," he said. "I generally sit by the lake or stay in my room."

He drank his tea and looked at me as if debating whether to tell me something. I was there to ask him about his militant life. But I couldn't ask that question; it felt wrong to be even meeting an old friend because I was keen to understand his militant experience.

After a while he began to talk about his life after school. He had gone back to his village and joined a local college. Surrounded by barren brown mountains, his village had become a militant stronghold. They would parade in the open, slinging assault rifles from their shoulders, hanging hand grenades from their belts. Indian troops stayed away most of the time. There was no television, no telephones, not even a hospital or proper municipal services. Militants stayed with the locals and ate at their houses.

Asif got to know some militant commanders. He was impressed and increasingly influenced by them. One day he left home and joined his militant friends. At various hideouts, he learned to use an assault rifle, throw a hand grenade, blast a land mine, and plan a guerrilla operation. He roamed from one village to the other with his comrades-in-arms. I tried hard to picture Asif in fatigues, carrying deadly weapons—and using them. He had been a militant for two years.

"What was it like?" I finally asked him.

"Scary," he replied. "My battalion treated me very well. We moved around together and were generally quite happy being the way we were. But it hurt me when we had to move from village to village, seeking shelter and food. People welcomed us in their houses. But at times I felt that people hosted and fed us because they were scared. I felt unwelcome, almost like an armed beggar. I had grown up in luxury, and my parents bought me everything I asked them for. And then I was a militant sleeping in a house whose owner was scared that the army might come there, who smiled at me and wished we would leave. I could not sleep, and I missed my family."

Asif found it hard to talk about those days. I had an urge to ask him if he had killed anyone. Instead, I asked him about his departure from the militant group. "One day our commander told us that we had to attack an army convoy," he told me. "I picked up my Kalashnikov. We were about to leave, and I began shivering. I was too scared, and death seemed so real. I left soon after that. My commanders were kind enough to let me go."

We left his house, walked to the bus yard, and bought two Cokes from the shop with the Aishwarya Rai poster. Asif loved Aishwarya and watched all her films. I found her mechanical and told him so. That talk lightened the atmosphere. We were boys again. Asif talked about graduating from the local university and trying for a Ph.D. in Delhi or some other Indian city. I voted for Delhi. "It is the best Indian city for a student. You find good teachers and wonderful libraries. You must try Delhi University and Jawaharlal Nehru University."

He agreed. "It must be fun being there."

"It can be great."

He had a mischievous smile on his face. "Tell me something?"

"What?" I was curious.

"Did you go to a discotheque in Delhi? Did you dance with the girls?"

I told him about my awkward attempts; we laughed.

We shook hands. I hopped onto a bus gliding out of the yard. Asif turned onto the lane leading to his house. I watched him from the bus window. I was happy for Asif, happy that he had survived and returned home.

I reached Anantnag after sunset. The town was deserted, the shops were closed, and groups of commuters huddled together in the bus yard. I decided against heading for Srinagar and waited for a bus to my village. After a few long minutes, a rickshaw stopped, and the driver yelled the name of an area near my village. In half an hour, I was knocking at the iron gate of my house. There was silence for the next few minutes. Then my grandfather asked, "Who is it?" "It is Basharat, Baba!" The door opened. I shook hands with Grandfather and two of my cousins standing behind him like bodyguards.

After dinner I sat on a small balcony of the house overlooking the road, beyond which paddy fields spread for miles to reach the arc of mountains. A half-moon cast a faint white light on the village. In the distance I heard the murmurs of the stream passing by. I sat on a chair, plunked my feet on another, and stretched myself a bit. My thoughts drifted to Asif and his militant days. He had talked about missing the comforts of home as a militant. I understood. He couldn't have argued with his fourteen-year-old cousin about changing the television channel and resisted his grandmother's attempts to feed him food enough for three people. Being a militant wasn't only about getting arms training and fighting; it was also about being excluded from the simplest joys of life.

Some of the militants became mythical figures, but they were dead.

And so were the men they had killed. People went home after the funerals and the slogans and continued their lives till the next funeral and the next round of slogans. I had witnessed that in the early nineties and saw it again in the spring of 2004 on a visit to my old friend Hilal's house.

Hilal lived in a village south of Anantnag along the highway leading from Srinagar to the Indian plains. We were in the same class at college, had lived in the same dorm, and misspent our early youth together. We had stayed in touch. He was a tall, lean youth with curly hair and restless blue eyes. His usual dress was a T-shirt and jeans, and he almost always walked hurriedly, carrying some novel or another in his hand. He had worked as a journalist for some time after college but had given it up after things turned a little nasty. Lately he had returned to study sociology at the university in Srinagar. Now he looked like a slightly grown-up version of himself from our college days, and he walked around with a bag full of books. He was infamous for not returning the books he borrowed.

The next morning I left to visit Hilal. At a bus stop in Anantnag, a bunch of office workers waited along with me. For around half an hour, there was no sign of a bus. We speculated about the reasons for the delay and hoped it was not a general strike. Beside the highway, a row of motels came to life, a regiment of soldiers patrolled, students walked to a college nearby, and a policeman stood on a roundabout with no traffic to redirect.

Then a truck screeched its brakes near the bus stop. Twenty or so shabbily dressed men jumped out and stood near the roundabout. I heard the battle cry *Allah-o-Akbar* and turned around. The defiant posturing against an unseen adversary seemed the beginning of a protest. The men persisted in shouting. The workers at the motels, the shopkeepers, the office goers, and the students eyed them in anticipation. The policeman was nervous, and my comrades-in-waiting whispered: "Has someone been arrested?"

A wiry youth carrying a bunch of sticks soaked them in petrol and lit them with a match. He passed a burning stick to each of his fellow sloganeers. They held the burning sticks like Olympic torches and moved in a circle, chanting, "It is darkness everywhere." The policeman tried to stop them; they continued. The soldiers returned, and the torchbearers froze. The policeman talked to the soldiers, grabbed a baton, and joined the determined soldiers in a baton charge. The protesters ran where their feet took them. The burning sticks fell around the roundabout. The policeman and the soldiers crushed the feeble fire with their heavy leather boots. Bystanders watched; some smiled.

Later, I asked the policeman about the protesters. "They are from some backward village and have no electricity," he told me. "So they have come to disrupt traffic on the highway to force the government to consider their demands."

I called Hilal; he told me the buses were off the roads because the army had killed a militant commander in a nearby village. A strike had been called to show solidarity. Hilal came to pick me up on his motorcycle. We turned onto a dirt track meandering away from the highway through fields. For miles there was no other vehicle on the road; the villages seemed asleep. The dirt track entered Hilal's village, and we overtook a row of trucks full of agitated men, women, and children. Hilal told me the slain militant commander belonged to a village two miles from his. The trucks were ferrying mourners to his funeral procession. We parked the motorcycle and were watching the mourners when some local boys walked up to Hilal and asked whether he wanted to go to the funeral. "The trucks are going there. You can get on board."

We were unsure how safe this would be but decided to go for it, and soon we were on the road. As we approached the village, we began to see an unending stream of trucks and cars heading for the funeral. Men, women, and children, old and young, were moving at a frenzied pace toward the slain commander's home. We covered the four miles in half an hour. We parked the motorcycle and followed a growing crowd. I saw a wave of heads form the crests and troughs of hurrying humanity. People stood on the mud walls bordering the lane, on the verandas of houses, on the wooden rice barns, and on cowsheds. Some youngsters watched the scene from tree branches. We heard pro-freedom slogans in Urdu: *Hum Kya Chahte? Aazadi!* (We want? Freedom!)

The commander's home was a bare house with maroon-painted brick walls. His body was being taken to the graveyard. I jumped onto a mud wall and saw a body covered with a green silk shawl lying on a cot: Arif Khan, the South Kashmir commander for Hizbul Mujahideen. The cot floated over heads; bodies jostled and hands stretched to carry it. The wave moved like a flood, as if invigorated by the sight of the dead man. I lost Hilal in the crowd. I looked at the faces around me. They were unlike the hired protesters ferried in buses from villages by the political parties to impress the television crews in Srinagar parks. Some cried, some held back tears, and some burned with anger. Many brushed their hands over the shroud and then rubbed their palms over their foreheads and chests. It was a ritual Kashmiris followed at Sufi shrines, where people rubbed their hands over the stairs leading to the saint's grave or the cloth covering the saint's grave. The procession moved forward with more slogans:

Arif, Tere Khoon Se Inquilab Aayega!
(Arif, your blood will bring revolution!)

Ae Zaalimo, Ae Jaabiro Kashmir Hamara Chorr Do!
(Oh tyrants! Oh tormentors! Quit our Kashmir!)

Arif Se Poocho! Arif Kahta hai! Aazadi!
(Ask Arif? And he will tell you: freedom!)

The pallbearers passed by where I stood on the mud wall. I peered hard to catch a glimpse of the slain militant. Khan had been in his early thirties, a short, lean man whose baldness gave an elongated look to his face. I saw his lifeless, half-open black eyes and an unwashed mark of clotted blood on his forehead. I saw the gray shirt he was wearing when he died. The procession moved on. A young man climbed onto the wall holding a black leather shoe and shouted, "Whose shoe is it?" A boy who had lost his shoes turned around to look and said it was not his.

I joined the funeral procession. A little ahead, I heard singing. It sounded like a chorus of female voices singing traditional marriage songs, and it was rising above the fervor of the men's slogans. The tune reminded me of a song girls sang in my village on the eve of Eid. A group of around fifty girls and women followed the procession. I waited for the women and walked behind them. Some adjusted their head scarves, and others let the scarves slip as they swept through the street and sang: "*Shaheedo Mubarak! Shaheedo Mubarak!*" (Congratulations! Oh Martyr! You have earned the martyrdom.)

Outside the graveyard, comrades of the slain commander were affirming the longevity of their organization after his death. A group of militants in their early twenties raised their Kalashnikovs and black Chinese pistols in the air and saluted the dead man with intermittent volleys piercing the azure sky. A mustached man with a pistol shouted a Kashmiri militant version of "The king is dead; long live the king": "*Zinda Hai HM*" (Hizbul Mujahideen lives). Militants and the mourners shouted back in chorus, "*Zinda Hai*" (He lives).

A group of men circled the grave dug out for Khan. Fresh, moist soil piled around the pit. Pallbearers laid the cot near the grave. More people had arrived; they wanted to see Khan's face before he was buried. Mourners argued, and the burial was delayed. The wooden graveyard gate creaked against the mass of people trying to push it open. Men and women were pulling and pushing the fence.

I barely managed to jump over the fence and was pushing my way out when a tiny, middle-aged woman caught me by the collar and shouted, "Listen to me." Her face, shining with sweat, almost matched the shade of her bright pink *pheran*. "He was born here, but he grew up, he fought, and he died in my village. I have walked ten miles with a hundred people to get here. Tell them they cannot bury him till we see his face." I told her the burial was delayed. She hugged me and charged at the graveyard fence, which was giving way.

I pushed my way out of the procession. I took off my jacket, washed my face, and drank from a roadside tap. I rested for a while at a shop front. It seemed like a day borrowed from the early nineties, when such funerals were held almost everywhere, almost every day.

An old man standing by the shop front scanned me; I could see his eyes registering my denim jacket, my corduroy trousers, my satchel, and my notebook. "You are not from these parts?" he asked. I gave him the name of my village. He could see I was not a mourner. "What brought you here?" I said, "I am a journalist." The old man blurted the word with disdain and shouted, "Where are the TV people? Go back and tell them what happened here! Tell them this is what they should show live."

Hilal waited beyond the mile-long row of vehicles. He seemed exhausted by the experience; I was. We left for his village. Reclining on cushions in his room, boosted by a good cup of coffee, we slowly recovered from the dizzying fervor of the funeral. Hilal saw the world like a student of sociology. He talked about the class composition of the funeral gathering: lower-middle classes and peasantry. Fascinated by the role that myths and legends played in a society like Kashmir, he narrated the myths he'd heard about Arif Khan at the funeral. "Some people said he would change costumes and escape detection by the army. One day he was a shepherd herding cattle on the highway; another day he was a Gujar nomad, dressed in a waistcoat and turban, riding a horse past an army patrol in a village."

The nature of the separatist militancy in Kashmir had changed. The pro-independence JKLF had been dominated by the pro-Pakistan Hizbul Mujahideen by 1994; by the mid-nineties, the Pakistani pan-Islamist militants from Lashkar-e-Taiba and, later, Jaish-e-Mohammed had become a significant presence. The Pakistani Islamist militants mostly kept to themselves and did not mingle with the population, like the Kashmiri militants. Lashkar and Jaish believed in suicide bombings, which the Kashmiri militants—including the Islamist Hizbul Mujahideen—had avoided. I had never met or interviewed a Lashkar or Jaish man except on television or in newspaper pictures, which showed the dead men being dragged by Indian soldiers after a suicide attack on a military camp. Much of the reportage described them as either the poor or the orphans of the Afghan war, raised in madrasas and then pushed into Kashmir by their handlers in the Pakistani army and intelligence.

I had a sense of Kashmiri militants; I knew their context, could place them somewhere on a social map. A lot of them had been killed, like my cousin Tariq and my friend Pervez; a lot of them put down their arms and returned to quiet civilian lives, like my school friend Asif; and a lot of them had played all sides, trying to make what they could out of the chaos and the confusion of the conflict, like Yusuf did.

I knew Yusuf from my childhood. He had many lives since then. In 1987 Yusuf was a constable in the local police. In his free time, he hovered around Heavan, the only theater in Anantnag, getting a bunch of tickets and selling them for a quick profit to the hordes thronging for matinee shows. In 1991 Yusuf returned to Kashmir after four months in a militant training camp in Pakistan. I saw him on the road outside my house. He wore an expensive leather jacket over blue jeans and a white shirt, with a shining silver pistol jutting out of his trousers. "Is masterji home?" he said, asking about my grandfather, who had at some point taught him, like thousands of others. Yusuf sat on a sofa in our drawing room and, putting on an air of gravity, told Grandfather, "Masterji, you are like a father to me. If anyone gives you any trouble, tell him you are Azad Khan's [Yusuf's new name] teacher." He put the pistol on the table and had some tea and biscuits. Grandfather made some small talk and then reluctantly asked, "You were in the police and already knew how to use guns. Then why did you go to Pakistan?"

Yusuf laughed. "Just to see Pakistan! And then it is like a certificate, a degree, that you are a real militant! Otherwise people wouldn't take me seriously."

In 1995 I saw Yusuf again, in Anantnag, outside a counterinsurgent camp. He said that being a separatist militant was too dangerous. Death seemed close, so he had changed sides, living under the protection and patronage of the Indian army.

In 1996, after six years of direct rule from Delhi, India decided to hold local elections in Kashmir. The election was a joke. Almost nobody voted. The counterinsurgents contested; the few people who were dragged by the soldiers to polling booths voted against them. Yusuf had sensed the mood and left the counterinsurgents. Militants had issued threats against electoral candidates. The Indian government promised them official housing, bulletproof cars, and armed police constables and paramilitary soldiers as bodyguards. Yusuf seized the moment and joined a small-time political party that never won a seat. I was home for the holidays from college. My father was posted in Anantnag as the additional deputy commissioner, the second most senior administrator of the district. Father stayed in his official residence, a housing complex where only senior government officers and politicians lived. I saw Yusuf leaning against a bulletproof jeep a few houses from my father's residence. He seemed healthier and more prosperous.

In 2003, whatever happened in Kashmir, people like Yusuf—and there were a lot of them—found ways of "doing well." I had flown from Delhi to report on a massacre of Kashmiri Hindus in the village of Nadimarg. The place was reeling with pain; the wails of survivors and the traces of the massacre brought tears to every eye. All major Indian politicians, including then deputy prime minister L. K. Advani and the Congress party president, Sonia Gandhi, and her charismatic daughter, Priyanka, were there. Sonia Gandhi was talking to a few survivors. Priyanka stood beside her, stately and composed in a sari. Commandos guarding them formed a circle around the mother and daughter. A tall man in a politician's regulation white *kurta* pajamas and Nehru jacket walked up to Priyanka Gandhi. It was Yusuf. They spoke for a bit, the princess speaking slowly; the sycophant, at his obsequious best, listening. Then Yusuf turned around; his face was glowing with that brief moment of intimacy with the most powerful daughter in Asia, a woman whose word could take him far in politics.

In June 2004 I was walking in Srinagar city center. A fancy car stopped next to me, and Yusuf called out my name. He stepped out of the car and hugged me. "I hear you have become a big journalist. But you shall not forget me! Write something about me, too." One day, I promised. I had to rush somewhere and couldn't take him up on his offer for coffee.

In September 2004 I was home reading a local newspaper. The headline read:

MILITANTS' BROAD DAYLIGHT STRIKE IN ANANTNAG
CONG LEADER, PSO GUNNED DOWN

On the morning of September 29, 2004, Yusuf, now the vice president for the Congress Party in Anantnag, had stopped his SUV in an Anantnag market. He asked his bodyguard to stay in the car and walked toward a shop. A few militants came out of an alley and fired at him. Yusuf and his bodyguard were rushed to a hospital. The doctors couldn't help; they were dead.

Even Yusuf did not get out alive. I had come to believe he could play his cards, that he would survive, that we would meet again.

The Pakistani militants operating in Kashmir were very different from the Kashmiri separatist guerrillas who started the anti-India rebellion in 1990. I was curious about them and wanted to meet some. Friends suggested visiting Shopian, a small town in South Kashmir.

Bill Clinton called Kashmir the most dangerous place on earth. Those who lived in Kashmir called Shopian the most dangerous place in Kashmir. The town had a heavy presence of Indian troops and Pakistani and Kashmiri militants fighting them. Some years back, at my university in Delhi, I had met Ahmed, an engineering student from Shopian. We became friends and spent many nights in my hostel room, smoking, drinking coffee, and talking about literature—Orwell and Steinbeck and Ayn Rand, Ahmed's goddess.

He seemed to fancy himself Howard Roark, Rand's protagonist from *The Fountainhead*. He repeated Rand's theme throughout the night. "Ego! Basharat, Ego is the fountainhead of man's progress. A man should be like Howard Roark, committed to excellence and undeterred by circumstances." His deep brown eyes shone, and his voice quivered with excitement every time he repeated the lines. His hands rose and fell like hammers hitting imaginary nails as he spoke.

I did not have his address now; it seemed unlikely that I would find such an ambitious guy in the drowsy but dangerous town. I called a mutual friend in Srinagar who gave me his home number. He was not sure whether Ahmed was there. A woman received the call and told me he worked in a bank in town.

The road to Shopian ran like a black streak through cone-roofed brick-and-wood houses. The usual Kashmiri landscape of fields, willows and poplars, orchards and military camps separated the villages. Beyond them were mountains, bald and forested. The driver of the taxi I was sharing with five other people from Srinagar was a grim-looking man who drove at a self-destructive speed. A folksinger whined on the car stereo: "Oh magician! Which arrow have you pierced my heart with?"

Two hours after leaving Srinagar, our jeep stopped in the dusty market in Shopian. The market—two opposing rows of garment shops, grocers, booksellers, chemists, and tea stalls—was the typical Kashmiri small-town market. Jeeps and buses waited for passengers; villagers carrying grocery and apple pesticides for their orchards hung around. Soldiers with rifles slung over their shoulders patrolled the road. Drinking tea in a kiosk at the taxi stand, I remembered a winter holiday spent here with my parents in the mid-eighties, when my father worked here. I thought of his copies of *Reader's Digest*, which I read eagerly; a blue lawn tennis ball with which my brother and I used to play cricket; and the legend narrated by my father and his friends: the romance of Prince Nagirai and Princess Heemal, believed to have lived here in ancient times. Two springs on the outskirts of the town were named after them. Nostalgia drew me to look for them.

The driver was still waiting for passengers. I asked him about the springs of Heemal and Nagirai. His grim face lit up. "I have spent many hours by those springs. I will take you there." We headed back on the road out of town. He stopped the car the moment we had left the clutter of the town and entered a grove of willows. He walked off the road and pointed to a chinar tree. "That is the spring of Nagirai." Under a young chinar was a tiny loop-shaped spring covered by crimson leaves. A heap of apple branches lay beside it.

The basin of a vast river, now dried to a trickle, spread beyond the poplars behind the chinar. Beyond the dried-up river rose a hill. "The spring of Heemal lies near that hill," Hasan, the driver, said. We drove farther on the road leading out of the town. "Nagirai's spring is sacred. We still see snakes come and go from it. Last year three soldiers killed a snake at Nagirai's spring. Three days later, those soldiers were killed in a mine blast." The ancient Hindu reverence toward the snake gods seemed to live on despite the conversion of most Kashmiris to Islam.

A few miles ahead, the road turned into a dirt path going up the hill. The hilltop housed a huge army camp. Hasan stopped the car half a mile before the camp and said, "The passengers are supposed to walk." I walked to the gates, where the soldiers frisked me and checked my identity card.

"What business do you have here?" a soldier shouted.

"I want to visit the spring beyond your camp."

"Spring?" His tone was both sarcastic and skeptical.

I guessed he was from Punjab, famous for a similar legend. "The spring here belongs to the memory of the Heer of Kashmir. Her story is to Kashmir what Heer-Ranjha is to Punjab," I replied.

He drew his head back, weighed my words, and smiled. "I have been here for a long time, but I never knew this. Go ahead! Visit your Heer!"

Beyond the last gate of the camp, Hasan had parked the car by a willow grove. He pointed to another chinar tree down the slope. "That is the spring of Heemal."

A rectangular concrete wall shaped the spring. A boy bent over the wall and stirred the moss-covered water with a twig. He looked up and stopped. I asked him about the spring. "It is Heemal's spring. The world knows it; she was the princess of Kashmir in ancient times and loved Nagirai, who was the prince," he said, trying to be authoritative. Then he paused and asked, "Isn't that why you have come here?"

"Yes."

He smiled and stirred the moss-covered water with the twig. The legend lived.

· · ·

On the way back I walked to Ahmed's bank. A blue-and-white sign announced the presence of the bank in the ground floor of a newly built featureless square brick house on a lane bridging out of the market. Howard Roark would not have approved of the architecture. A wooden counter with cheap brown Formica sheets nailed to it stretched like a border between the customers and the employees. Behind the counter, five men sat on wooden chairs, heads bent over thick registers or voucher slips. A short bearded man and a tall veiled woman argued with a clerk. The clerk, a tall man with deep brown eyes and high cheekbones, was waving his hands in the air. I watched him for a long moment.

"Basharat!" Ahmed jumped from his chair. "How the hell did you get here? I cannot believe this!"

He took leave of his office, and we almost ran out onto the street, laughing, backslapping. We headed for his home at the other end of the town. It was a neat brick-and-stone house overlooking a lawn beyond which spread an apple orchard. We sat in Ahmed's room, smoked cigarettes over cups of tea, and exchanged stories. He had returned home two years back for a vacation and found his parents leading a life of loneliness and fear. An only child, he decided to stay. There was no job in the town for a man of his qualifications, but a clerk's job in the local branch of a bank came up six months later. For months he struggled with himself, hoping to return to Delhi and his dreams. They faded. Ahmed fell in love with a local girl who studied literature at the local college. "She is like me. She, too, loved Ayn Rand and dreamed of individual achievement. She too has taken up a job in a local school because of her family."

Ahmed opened a window. Its frame seemed to organize the view of the garden, the apple orchard, and the hump of a hill rising in the distance. We saw his wiry, aging mother and stooping father sitting on the lawn. He looked at them engrossed in their conversation. "This is my truth. Howard Roark was an illusion." His words came slowly, and he closed the window again. We did not talk about the conflict. We were trying to relive the old days. We talked about books and writers. I was carrying a copy of *Homage to Catalonia* and gave it to him. "You will find Kashmir in its pages," I said.

The sound of brisk footsteps made us look out of the window. We saw a group of young men with guns walking down the alley beside the house. Ahmed told me they were Pakistani militants. "They must be going to some hideout," he said. I asked if he had met one. He told me that three of them had knocked on the door one night. He and his parents had to serve them dinner after one of the militants pushed his father in his chest with a gun. Ahmed hadn't gone beyond nervous small talk, and after dinner the militants had left. "They were in their early twenties and carried their guns, sleek satellite phones, and laptops."

I was about to ask Ahmed about the possibility of meeting one of these men when he told me a story that was making the rounds of Shopian. Pirated DVDs of a Bollywood movie starring actor Salman Khan had reached the local video shop. Khan played a roguish small-town college student, and the story of his self-destructive love, titled *Tere Naam* (In Your Name), was one of the biggest hits of the year. Its soundtrack was all the rage. Every other youngster was getting his hair done like Khan; the hairdo became famous as the *Tere Naam* style. In Shopian, a nineteen-year-old Pakistani member of Jaish-e-Mohammed bought a copy of the video. A few days later, he ordered a local barber to shave his beard and cut his hair in the *Tere Naam* style. Over the next few weeks, the new-look militant was seen outside the local women's college staring wistfully at a girl he had fallen for. Ahmed told me, "He wants to marry her and take her back to Pakistan. But her parents are against it. I saw him a few times in the local market; he looks completely lovestruck, and now the entire town calls him *Tere Naam*."

Outside, the day was dying; the lawn, the orchards, and the hill were turning into dark outlines of their former selves. As if suddenly remembering something, Ahmed looked at the intruding darkness and got up. He lit a candle, closed the window, and drew the curtains. He pulled two black blankets from a cupboard, threw them over the curtains, and switched on the light. "Why the blankets?" I asked. "To make it look like a dark room from outside; we do that in every room after dusk," he said. "We have no streetlights and switch on no lights at the entrance or in the courtyard." Bright lights would provoke the soldiers to barge in and check the house for militants, and attract the militants to choose the house as shelter for the night. Hundreds of homes were destroyed in those encounters between soldiers and militants; hundreds of people were arrested, tortured, and jailed by the soldiers for housing militants. People hoped not to hear a knock at the door in the evening. The drone of a passing vehicle or the sound of footsteps outside a home was enough to make a family shiver. How many deep breaths did we breathe after sounds died into the night and nobody knocked?

I had experienced that fear only a few days before I traveled to Ahmed's town. One evening Salaam, our cook, came rushing into the room. He was a thin, balding guy obsessed with the radio. My father was busy with his files in the next room. Salaam was sweating and breathing heavily. He motioned for me to be silent. "Somebody has come into the drawing room." A door opened from our kitchen into the drawing room. Salaam tried opening that door and felt that someone was pushing it back. In the past, if you were superstitious, you blamed it on ghosts, while rational people looked for rational explanations. Today the first thought that came to mind was of unidentified gunmen.

Salaam believed that the person who had entered our drawing room could mean harm. We decided not to disturb my father and to deal with it on our own. We tiptoed into the kitchen. Salaam locked the door leading to the stairs from the ground floor to the first floor. We stood staring at the door that hid the intruder. We pressed our ears to the wood to listen for any signs of movement. We heard silence and stray dogs barking on the road. We moved away from the door and decided in whispers to find a weapon and go into the room. The weapon was a problem, but we managed to find a kitchen knife. Being bigger and older, I grabbed it; Salaam stood behind me, holding a kitchen fork like a dagger. I tried to hide my shivering hand from Salaam, who was trying equally hard to look brave. We were scared but ready to put up a fight.

The moment to charge at an unseen enemy came. We kicked open the door and rushed into the room. A kitchen knife and a fork rose at a murderous angle. We looked around the room. The sofa was empty, the chairs were empty, only the bookshelf was there. The intruder was nowhere. A corner of the carpet had upturned near the door. It had gotten stuck in the door and wedged it. We saw it at the same moment and looked at each other. We threw our weapons on the floor and laughed.

The prospects were not humorous in Ahmed's town, which, like many other places in Kashmir, lived with intense fear. I imagined his aging parents huddled alone in their kitchen all those years when Ahmed was away, and I understood why he had stayed. In that moment I came to respect him more than ever; he had done better than Howard Roark. I turned toward him with a respectful gaze as he silently puffed on his cigarette and stared at the designs of the carpet where we sat. Lighting another cigarette, he looked at me with the expression of an aged, tired man. "It is killing me," Ahmed said.

The fighting had destroyed whatever work culture there was in Kashmir. In his town, there were no libraries and no bookshops. People wanted to be safe and nothing more. Ahmed spoke of the fear of seeing his house in rubble after an encounter. Even if no militants or soldiers barged in, he expected it. Ahmed's family, friends, and townsfolk talked of nothing other than the conflict. "My parents worked all their life to save enough to build this house. An hour-long battle can turn it to charcoal and rubble." I asked, "Why don't you leave? You can go to any big city and make a career. Why don't you return to Delhi?" I had no other words. He wanted to leave but could not leave his parents. And even if he left to seek a better career elsewhere, many Ahmeds would have to stay.

It was close to midnight. Ahmed removed the blankets and the curtains from the windows. "It is safe now. There is no movement at this time." The town was wrapped in darkness; the dark blue sky and the silver stars were quiet.

I couldn't bring myself to ask Ahmed to risk himself by introducing me to some Pakistani militants, but the visit to Shopian had heightened my awareness of life in a heavily militarized society. On my way back to Srinagar, I passed Indian military and paramilitary vehicles and camps every few minutes. India has more than half a million soldiers in Kashmir. Srinagar is a city of bunkers, and the armored cars and soldiers patrolling roads or manning check posts had become a part of the Kashmiri landscape, like the willows, poplars, and pines. I knew soldiers were mostly the rural and urban poor of India, who stood outside the military and paramilitary recruitment centers in long lines with great hopes of getting the dangerous and absurdly low-paying job. I remembered seeing reports of a growing shortage of officers in the army as the Indian economy got better, but I never saw any reports of a shortage of soldiers. The poor were numerous. But beyond the olive or khaki uniforms, stiff faces, curt commands, and threatening guns, I knew nothing about them as people. The only words we had spoken to each other were the litanies of an identity check. Since I was a Kashmiri, it was also unwise to attempt prolonged conversation with a soldier.

Now, with Indian Independence Day on August 15, a few days ahead, the soldiers expected more militant attacks and were more aggressive, and frisking and identity checks had increased. I stayed home in Srinagar and thought about the soldiers I had come across. I thought of the two who had interrogated me in the crackdown on our village.

I remembered another soldier I had a chance meeting with in June. I remembered his face, his name, and his words. In May 2004 India had its parliamentary elections; the results were declared in June. The Bharatiya Janata Party (BJP) was thrown out of power, and the Congress Party came to power, supported by a Communist coalition. The newspapers and television channels screamed the results in shrill voices, and big headlines and hundreds of editorials and opinion pieces analyzing the unexpected change in regime followed.

I was at Lal Chowk to meet a journalist friend, Amir. He was relaxed; the election results would fill the pages of his Delhi-based newspaper for the rest of the week. There would be no space for the news from Kashmir, and he was taking it easy. We had a coffee and talked about whatever we were reading. He had a book I wanted to read, and we left to fetch it. In his office, heaps of newspapers were stacked on dusty tables, and cigarette butts filled an ashtray. Smoke hung in the air. Some journalist friends dropped in and the conversation shifted to news. "It is peaceful today; no news yet," one reporter said.

Suddenly, the door was thrown open. "May I come in?" We turned toward the entrance. A soldier in a bulletproof jacket, slinging an AK-47 over his shoulder, marched in as Amir said, "Yes." A leaner, meeker subordinate followed. "I came to check on you," the first soldier told Amir. He had stopped Amir in the morning on the way to the office. Amir had shown him his identity card. The soldier had talked about the need to check suspicious-looking people and had asked Amir about a nick on his face that came from a shaving razor. Amir had felt insulted and asked the soldier to speak to his officers, who knew him as a journalist with a leading Indian newspaper. The soldier had let him off.

Seeing the soldier walk into his office irritated Amir. "Didn't you see my identity card in the morning?"

"I did. But we still have to check anyone who is suspicious-looking. I am here to confirm whether your identity card was a real one."

"You should know how to spot a suspicious-looking person." Amir raised his voice. "You should know the difference between a grocery and a newspaper office."

It seemed to have no effect on the soldier. He walked around haughtily and, turning to Amir, said, "You should know I can enter any place anytime. It is my job." Amir pulled out his telephone directory, called a senior officer from the soldier's force, and explained the situation. The officer spoke to the soldier on the phone. He kept muttering, "Nothing, sir," and then walked off. Amir told me the senior officer had apologized for the soldier's conduct and had promised to send an officer to look into the matter. Two more reporters from other news organizations dropped in. The seniormost reporter advised Amir not to take words like "esteem" and "dignity" seriously.

Coffee and conversation followed for the next half hour, and then there was another knock on the door. An officer in combat dress walked in, followed by around ten soldiers. The officer asked the soldiers to leave; they stood at the gate. The officer walked briskly to the corner of the room, where we sat. He was a tall, muscular man with small brown eyes shining beneath the visor of his cap. Pointing a finger at each of us, he asked in a single breath, "What is your name? What do you do? Journalist? Which newspaper?" We gave our introductions; he gave none. Someone offered him a chair. He sat and told us that he was there to look into the matter. He seemed angry. "You guys can see my rank and read my name on my uniform. I am an officer and not a civilian who needs an introduction. And still, when I walked in here, you did not show me the respect an officer deserves. Nobody stood up from his chair. Nobody spoke with respect." We looked at one another. He stared at us. An awkward silence fell. One of Amir's colleagues tried to pacify him by offering tea and cigarettes. He refused, saying he did not drink tea and did not smoke.

A series of explanations began. "We did not mean disrespect." "We have great professional relations with your force and regard it highly." "We did not have time to treat you with due respect, as you abruptly asked for our introductions." Five journalists representing reputed Delhi-based organizations were almost obsequiously trying to explain themselves. I remained silent. The explanations and mild arguments went on for half an hour. The officer mentioned that he belonged to a counterinsurgent unit, which we knew specialized in encounters. It seemed a veiled threat. The officer sank into the chair, spread his legs, and tossed his cap on the table. His surname helped me place him as being from Haryana. I asked if that was true. "How could you guess that?" he asked. "I lived in Delhi and had many friends from your caste," I answered.

The grip of the ancient Hindu caste system on northern India was evident in his first smile. He showed signs of relaxation and turned toward me. I talked about my friends from my Delhi University days. He had been at Delhi University, too. "I was in the law faculty, where were you?" I asked. He had been in a college next to mine. I talked about the university, about the college festivals, the hangouts, the rivalries, the girls' hostel nearby, and almost everything that one misses about university life. He seemed to have transformed into a Delhi University alumnus and forgotten he was an Indian paramilitary officer posted in Kashmir. His language changed as he spoke about the Jawahar book-store, where we bought cheap photocopies of texts and reference books;

of Kamala Nagar market, where students hung out after class; of Majnu Ka Tila, where Tibetan refugees sold cheap knockoff clothing and beer. "Give me a fag, man! And get me some tea," he said, smiling. We had tea and smoked. He apologized; the roomful of journalists apologized back. Peace was made. As he began to leave, he said, "I was a different man before I joined the force and came to Kashmir."

I thought about his instant switch upon being reminded of his civilian life. He didn't seem very different from my former militant friend Asif, who wanted to know about discotheques and girls in Delhi. Yet young men like them, on different sides of the military divide, had killed and died after they chose to become militants and soldiers. Those who had survived seemed to have cremated and buried the individuals they had once been.

I hoped that someday they could cease being part of processes that reduced individuals to suspects or military targets, shorn of all human complexity—processes that left them with bare nomenclatures such as militants, soldiers, paramilitaries. I hoped that someday they could return to their homes where they could sit on balconies or argue with their cousins about changing the television channel. I hoped that someday the war they were fighting and the reasons for its existence would disappear like footsteps on winter snow.

Epilogue

The car drove slowly toward the Srinagar airport. I was leaving again, carrying with me the furniture for a new life and a new room I had yet to find. We drove out of the city, past bunkers, soldiers, guns, loops of barbed wire, pedestrians raising hands and identity cards; honking cars and local buses; boys and girls in uniforms outside schools; competing posters of politicians making promises; shopkeepers yawning behind counters and unsold things; houses of friends and strangers; and then the heavily barricaded airport complex gate. After a few metal detectors and body searches, I walked into the decrepit waiting hall. I felt as if an iron hand had taken me in its grip and pulled me from my soil.

The journey was not over; it will never be. The sky has been red, the days fear-filled, and the nights curfewed since 1990. In that season, I was fourteen and enthralled by the heady slogans of freedom, by tales of dangerous treks through the border snows, by the naive hope of a new world about to be born. I left Kashmir, grew up, found and quit a job. I came back. I heard and remembered stories of brutality, courage, love, hatred, faith, loss, and even hope. Both Kashmir and I had changed. The heady, rebellious Kashmir I left as a teenager was now a land of brutalized, exhausted, and uncertain people. I was now in my late twenties, already old. The conflict might leave the streets, but it will not leave the soul.

Mini-tractors carried the luggage to the plane on the tarmac. Workers in blue overalls began loading the bags and briefcases. The certainty of departure pierced me. I knew I would return, leave, return, leave, and return again. The plane took off after a violent sprint on the runway. Houses grew smaller, paddies turned into neat green squares, metaled roads connecting villages shrank into black lines, and the coquettish clouds took new shapes. I turned away from the window. The poet had lied about paradise.

Delhi, too, hadn't changed much. The landlords still said, "You are like our own son. Give us a call on Sunday." And friends said, "Stay with us!" I began writing and rewriting in a rented room in a slumlike area populated by students, writers, and friends. I worked at a newsmagazine during the day and wrote and rewrote about Kashmir at night. Newspapers in Srinagar continued printing some headlines in red. And people were talking about the bus. India and Pakistan had agreed to open a bus service between Srinagar and Muzaffarabad. After fifty-eight years, a bus would cross the Line of Control and divided families would be allowed to visit each other. "Historic" and "hope" became oft-used words.

In the first week of April 2005, I returned home to report. Manmohan Singh and Pervez Musharaf shook hands on billboards in Srinagar. Kashmiris debated the difference the trans-LoC bus would make. Some equated it with the fall of the Berlin Wall. Some were more restrained and saw it as a step toward resolving the Kashmir dispute. Some militant groups saw it as a distraction from the real resolution of the dispute and threatened to attack the bus. Reporters looked for people who had families on the other side of the Line of Control, for people who had crossed the Line of Control, for people who had seen the Line of Control, for people who had thought about the Line of Control.

I was talking to some people in a coffeehouse near Lal Chowk when gunfire slashed the air. Militants opposing the bus had launched a suicide attack at the nearby Tourist Reception Center, adjacent to a cricket stadium where the bus service would be inaugurated the next day. Vans carrying television crews rushed toward the Tourist Center like wailing ambulances. Paramilitaries and police cordoned off the green-painted building that housed many offices. A gun battle followed, and in a few minutes, the wooden Tourist Center was burning.

I hid behind a police vehicle across the road from the burning building with a group of reporters. Bursts of gunfire made us duck to the ground, stay close together. A few minutes later, an elderly man in a brown suit jumped out of a first-floor window of the building and ran across the road. A reporter reached out and brought him to our group. He was Mohammed Ashraf, a manager for an airline, and had been working out of the Tourist Reception Center for years. He watched the dark smoke, the hellish flames, and the pieces of burned office files rise above the crumbling roof of his office. "I need to call my family," he said. "No! I need to call Atta first," he added almost immediately. His colleague Atta was trapped inside. An American correspondent gave him her phone. Ashraf dialed and dialed again, but the networks were jammed. He stayed with us for a long time, watching the building crumble and scared hordes of pigeons circle it from a distance.

The next morning, on my way to the cricket stadium to watch the inaugural ceremony, I passed the burned Tourist Reception Center. Piles of charcoal, ash, and rubble rested on its stony plinth. Leftovers of its charred columns were still smoldering. I walked ahead, past the stiff soldiers. In the cricket stadium, a police band played a Kashmiri folk song made famous by its Bollywood version. It was drizzling. Manmohan Singh made a speech and thanked Pervez Musharraf for making the bus service possible. Singh waved a blue flag, and the Srinagar Muzaffarabad bus drove out of the stadium amid applause from the modest crowd, strengthened by the presence of a few hundred recruits from the local police in civvies, whose regulation haircuts betrayed their true identity.

The bus drove toward the Line of Control, 140 kilometers north of Srinagar. A caravan of journalists followed it. We drove past hundreds of helmets and guns and climbed many mountains. We saw the Jhelum, a hundred feet wide, mighty and green, roaring through the mountains despite the two countries controlling its banks, announcing its freedom. And then, after all these years, I saw it: the Line of Control. A loopy razor-wire fence snaked through wild bushes and the greens of the rather barren mountain with a few mud houses. This razor wire, this mountain, was the Line of Control. Two girls playing outside a tiny mud house on the other bank waved at us. We waved back.

Passengers were to cross the LoC at Kaman Post, a military post where Indian and Pakistani soldiers faced each other from the two banks of a stream. The bridge over the stream at Kaman Post was destroyed in 1948 during the first India-Pakistan war. Now, with the peace process, the burned Kaman Bridge had been rebuilt. Indians had wanted to paint it in the colors of the Indian flag; Pakistanis had objected. They agreed on white, the color of peace, and rechristened it the Peace Bridge. On the Peace Bridge, too, control seemed to be the key word, despite the India-Pakistan bonhomie. An Indian army officer told me that two thirds of the Peace Bridge was Indian and the other third was Pakistani. This two-thirds Indian and one-third Pakistani bridge was the line of control; the shallow stream passing under it was the line of control. By evening thirty-nine Kashmiris from opposing sides of the border dividing Kashmir had walked across the bridge, the fifty-eight years of history of Indian and Pakistan, and the fifty-eight years of the division of Kashmir in 1947.

Sharif Hussein Bukhari was one of those men. In his early sixties, a beak-nosed man with soft eyes, wearing a light blue *salwar kameez*, he walked in a daze as he crossed the bridge from the Pakistani-controlled part into the Indian-controlled part, where he was born. He was returning home for the first time since 1950. Crossing the LoC had haunted him throughout the five decades he spent in Pakistan, as a student, a lawyer, a Lahore high-court judge, and now a professor of law. His two sisters and brother had stayed in his ancestral North Kashmir village when he trekked with his father across the LoC as a fifteen-year-old. For years he neither received nor sent any letters home. There were no phone calls, either. He communicated through his dreams. "I would dream of my school, of the apricot and the apple trees in our courtyard. I would dream of the house I was born in and of the journey back home," he said. The crossing had been unattainable even in his dreams. "In my dreams I would be arrested at the LoC and turned back," he said.

That failure of the subconscious was the border. The line of control did not run through 576 kilometers of militarized mountains. It ran through our souls, our hearts, and our minds. It ran through everything a Kashmiri, an Indian, and a Pakistani said, wrote, and did. It ran through the fingers of editors writing newspaper and magazine editorials, it ran through the eyes of reporters, it ran through the reels of Bollywood coming to life in dark theaters, it ran through conversations in coffee shops and on television screens showing cricket matches, it ran through families and dinner talk, it ran through whispers of lovers. And it ran through our grief, our anger, our tears, and our silence.

Hundreds of villagers had gathered at the Reception Center for the visitors from Pakistani-administered Kashmir at Salamabad village, half an hour from the Peace Bridge, as you drive back toward Srinagar. Schoolchildren dressed in traditional costumes, who had waited throughout the day for the bus to arrive, welcomed it by dancing to Bollywood songs. A young man rushed toward Bukhari. Bukhari didn't recognize the excited youth. "I am Showket, your sister's son," said the young man. "I am sorry, son. I didn't even get to see a picture of yours all these years," Bukhari said. Their moist eyes were the line of control.

The buses carrying the passengers from Muzaffarabad traveled under a drizzly gray sky to Srinagar. It was a road that had been deserted after dusk for a decade and a half. I watched thousands of women, men, and children stand along the soldier-laden road, welcoming the ones who had stepped across the line. There was no fear that evening. There were only hands reaching out of the bus windows, waving in the air, as if each wave would erase the lines of control.

⨋ Acknowledgments

I would love to thank the following for their support, friendship, and love. Foremost, Pankaj Mishra, Mary Mount, and Ananya Vajpeyi; Peter Straus at Rogers, Coleridge, and White in London and Rebecca Friedman at Sterling Lord in New York, superb readers and champions; and Alexis Gargagliano at Scribner, the best editor I could ever have.

In New York: Nicholas Lemann and Alexander Stille at the Journalism School, Columbia University; Keith Gessen, Marco Roth, Mark Grief, Ben Kunkel, and Allison Lorentzen at *N+1*; James Hoge Jr., Gideon Rose, Stephanie Giry, Daniel Kurtz-Phelan, and Sasha Polakow Suransky at *Foreign Affairs*; Siddhartha Deb; Mohamad Bazi; Alex Travelli; Sameer Mohammad; Matthew Power; Jessica Benko; Meera Subramanian; Christian Lorentzen; Adam Shatz; John Palatella; Anjali Mody; Rathin Roy; Nauman Naqvi; Madiha Tahir; Jessica Manners; Laura Wise; Tom Pitoniak; Ted Weesner; Raviet Riechman; Hungarian Pastry Shop; Butler Library; Labyrinth bookstore; and the 1, 6, and Q trains.

In London: Katharine Viner and Helen Oldfield at the *Guardian Weekend* magazine, Sue Matthias and Jason Cowley at *New Statesman*, Rebecca Gowers, Isabelle Onians, and Rowan Routh.

In Kashmir: Everyone who trusted me and told me his or her stories; Wajahat Ahmad, my brother and my most exacting critic; Tasleema, Fayaz, and their beautiful children, Madiha and Maleeha; Shahzada Salam; Masood Hussain; Waseem Yusuf; Hilal Bhat; Tariq Mir; Shahnawaz Khan; Malik Sajad; and Muzammil Jaleel.

In Delhi: Hartosh Singh Bal, Abdus Salam, Nadeem Shah, Praveen Dhonty, Asgar Qadri, Omair Ahmad, Vivek Narayanan, Feroz Rather, Chiki Sarkar, Rajni George, Rachel Tanzer, Chitra Padmanabhan, M. K. Venu, Ramesh Menon, Mahmood Farooqui, Anusha Rizvi and everyone at Sarai, Tarun Tejpal and others at Tehelka, and Nikhill Lakshman and others at Rediff.

⌒ About the Author

BASHARAT PEER was born in Kashmir in 1977. He studied journalism and politics at the Graduate School of Journalism, Columbia University. He has worked as an editor at *Foreign Affairs* and served as a correspondent at *Tehelka*, India's leading English-language newsweekly. His work has appeared in *The Guardian, New Statesman, The Nation, Financial Times Magazine, N+1,* and *Columbia Journalism Review,* among other publications. *Curfewed Night,* his first book, was published in India where it won one of the top literary awards, the Vodafone Crossword Book Award for English Nonfiction. Peer is a fellow at the Open Society Institute and lives in New York.